THE EVERYTHING
Celtic Wisdom
Book

Dear Reader,

My purpose in writing this book is to provide the book I would have liked to have read when I was learning about my ancestors and their beliefs: clear, accurate, and useful information on the history, mythology, and beliefs of the Celts through history. For the purposes of this book, the terms "Celt" and "Celtic" are applied to the ancient Gaulish tribes and their descendants in Britain, Ireland, and surrounding areas.

In this book, I refer to the Celts in the past tense; however, it is important to remember that the Celtic culture is very much alive and that the Celtic people currently reside in nearly every corner of the world. Although so many are so far from the place of their ancestors, the Celtic people are linked by the common thread of their spiritual heritage. Celtic spirituality is at its heart neither Christian nor pagan, but something greater and more transcendent than both. It is based on a deep connection to the natural world and one's ancestors and fellows, and very often even Celts who have never set foot in their ancestral lands feel a certain yearning for home and a special communion with the natural world.

This is not to say that only those of Celtic ancestry may appreciate and embrace the Celtic world view: from their first emergence into history, the Celtic peoples have been both great adventurers and determined hosts, traveling far in search of new experiences yet welcoming and embracing generations of outsiders.

Jennifer Emick

Welcome to the EVERYTHING® Series!

These handy, accessible books give you all you need to tackle a difficult project, gain a new hobby, comprehend a fascinating topic, prepare for an exam, or even brush up on something you learned back in school but have since forgotten.

You can choose to read an *Everything*® book from cover to cover or just pick out the information you want from our four useful boxes: e-questions, e-facts, e-alerts, and e-ssentials.

We give you everything you need to know on the subject, but throw in a lot of fun stuff along the way, too.

We now have more than 400 *Everything*® books in print, spanning such wide-ranging categories as weddings, pregnancy, cooking, music instruction, foreign language, crafts, pets, New Age, and so much more. When you're done reading them all, you can finally say you know *Everything*®!

QUESTIONS?
Answers to
common questions

FACTS
Important snippets
of information

ALERTS!
Urgent
warnings

ESSENTIALS
Quick
handy tips

PUBLISHER Karen Cooper

DIRECTOR OF ACQUISITIONS AND INNOVATION Paula Munier

MANAGING EDITOR, EVERYTHING SERIES Lisa Laing

COPY CHIEF Casey Ebert

ACQUISITIONS EDITOR Lisa Laing

DEVELOPMENT EDITOR Brett Palana-Shanahan

EDITORIAL ASSISTANT Hillary Thompson

Visit the entire Everything® series at *www.everything.com*

THE
EVERYTHING®
Celtic Wisdom Book

Find inspiration through ancient traditions,
rituals, and spirituality

Jennifer Emick

Avon, Massachusetts

An Everything® Series Book.
Everything® and everything.com® are registered trademarks of F+W Media, Inc.

Published by Adams Media, a division of F+W Media, Inc.
57 Littlefield Street, Avon, MA 02322 U.S.A.
www.adamsmedia.com

ISBN 10: 1-59869-540-1
ISBN 13: 978-1-59869-540-3

Printed in the United States of America.

J   I   H   G   F   E   D   C   B   A

Library of Congress Cataloging-in-Publication Data
available from the publisher.

This publication is designed to provide accurate and authoritative information with regard to the subject matter covered. It is sold with the understanding that the publisher is not engaged in rendering legal, accounting, or other professional advice. If legal advice or other expert assistance is required, the services of a competent professional person should be sought.

—From a *Declaration of Principles* jointly adopted by a Committee of the American Bar Association and a Committee of Publishers and Associations

Many of the designations used by manufacturers and sellers to distinguish their products are claimed as trademarks. Where those designations appear in this book and Adams Media was aware of a trademark claim, the designations have been printed with initial capital letters.

This book is available at quantity discounts for bulk purchases.
For information, please call 1-800-289-0963.

I would like to dedicate this book to my grandparents, Rose and Frank Emick, who have believed in me from the beginning, and to my husband and children for providing support and a welcome distraction from work.

Contents

Top Ten Things You'll Learn about Celtic Spirituality, History, and Culture

1. Celtic spirituality is greater than the sum of its parts—neither specifically pagan nor Christian.

2. The ancient Celts once occupied much of Western Europe before repeated invasions narrowed their sphere of influence to the British Isles.

3. Many of the common assumptions about the ancient druids are completely wrong, including the notion that they dressed in flowing white robes.

4. The Celtic people worshipped a variety of gods, and developed a rich, symbolic mythology.

5. The Celts embraced Christianity while maintaining many of their ancient beliefs and customs.

6. Druidic orders much resembling monasteries operated in Britain and Ireland long before.

7. Many pagan Celtic customs continue even to the present day in parts of Europe.

8. Many of the ancient pagan gods became saints of the Celtic Church.

9. Both the Celtic pagans and the Celtic Christians shared a reverence for the natural world.

10. The symbolism of Celtic spirituality is unique, and is often utilized across the pagan and Christian faiths.

Introduction

▶ I GREW UP IN a family that was tremendously proud of its European immigrant roots, which included a large proportion of Irish ancestors. As a child, I had a tremendous love of fantasy and fairy tales, especially when I discovered that my quite ordinary first name was in fact a variant of the name of a legendary queen—Guinevere, the wife of King Arthur. And although I was raised far away from ancestral haunts, I grew up convinced that the woods of upstate New York were as magical as those of Ireland. I believed that the fairy-folk had traveled with us, remaining just out of sight in the woods surrounding us. In a sense, I was sharing the same communion with the natural world that was a way of life to my distant ancestors.

Eventually, I discovered that my appreciation for nature and my love of fairy stories were more closely connected than I ever thought possible and that the characters in the stories I read were based on the exploits of the ancient Celtic gods and heroes, then real "fairy-folk."

The Celts emerged as a recognizable people thousands of years ago. They were brilliant poets, skilled artisans, adept farmers, and fierce warriors. But because of their reliance on oral tradition, they left no written record to tell of their accomplishments. Until recent times, this left the historical Celts with no voice with which to defend themselves from the history recorded by their political and religious enemies, who portrayed them as bloodthirsty, intemperate barbarians. Their Roman and Greek observers admired their skills in war but viewed Celts on the whole as largely violent, crass, and drunken. Likewise, the Christian missionaries who set out to convert druidic Celts were convinced that the whole of druid spirituality was violent sacrifice and superstitious omens.

Having little or no knowledge of the Celtic languages, these recorders were almost completely unaware of the complex and deeply spiritual oral traditions of the Celtic bards and druids. Archaeological evidence has gone a very long way toward establishment of an accurate depiction of the Celts, who represent one of Europe's greatest civilizations. Celtic artifacts, coupled with the very few firsthand accounts of Celtic life and religion, paint a picture of a rich culture of wealth, intelligence, and above all, spiritual accomplishment.

Celtic religion prized wisdom and study, but also focused on the liminal—Celtic belief focused on the threshold between man and the divine, using complex symbolism to express a doctrine of transformation, interconnectedness, and communion with the natural world. This spiritual wellspring runs so deeply in the hearts of the Celts that it has survived for thousands of years, creating a spirituality that is uniquely distinguished and crosses religious boundaries, inspiring both Christianity and paganism.

CHAPTER 1

The Celtic World

Warriors, poets, scholars, and visionaries—the ancient Celts were a people out of time. Celtic society was remarkably free, open, and democratic. Women were highly regarded, art and scholarship highly prized. Celts as warriors were fierce and fearless with a highly developed sense of justice, and an insult or injustice to one was generally regarded as an injury to all. The Celts were also renowned explorers, questing optimists ever seeking greener pastures. As a result, a majority of Americans and Europeans today have some Celtic ancestry, a testament to the tenacity of the Celtic spirit.

The Story of the Celts

The people we know today as Celts were already well established when their Greek neighbors began to refer to them as *Keltoi*, from which the word "Celt" was derived. The word was taken from a word used by a Celtic tribe to describe themselves, but its meaning is uncertain—some linguists believe it means "to strike or fight," others believe it means "hidden," referring to the intense secrecy surrounding Celtic spiritual knowledge.

There never was a unified body of people known collectively as "Celt." In historical terms, *Celt* or *Celtic* refers to any of the peoples who spoke one of the Celtic family of languages and shared common cultural influences.

Even today you hear the echoes of this ancient culture—the influence of artists thousands of years past can be seen nearly everywhere one looks, with ancient patterns appearing everywhere from tattoos to coffee cups. The mythic quest of Celtic mythology still excites the imagination of poets and writers, so that much of today's literature and cinema has roots in ancient Celtic tales of heroes, quests, and magical enchantment.

The words *Gael* or *Gaelic* today are often used interchangeably with *Celt* and *Celtic*. The word *Gael* comes from the Old Irish *Goídeleg* (from *Gaul*), and specifically refers to the people and languages of Ireland, Scotland, and the Isle of Man. British Celts and their languages are referred to as Brythonic, and the two groups together are referred to as *Insular*, differentiated from the Gallic or "continental" Celts.

Historically, the Celtic civilization did not so much emerge as erupt. Adventurous and technologically advanced tribes spread rapidly over European soil, absorbing and combining with the native cultures they encountered along the way.

It is not entirely certain when the magic moment occurred that set the Celtic people apart from the Indo-European peoples they are descended from, but we do know that some 7,000 years or so ago, the ancestors of the Celtic tribes began to migrate from the Caucasus Mountains region surrounding the Black Sea and began to settle in the areas of Europe now known as

France, Germany, Spain, and Italy—even as distant as Turkey. By the fourth century B.C.E., the Celtic tribes had established strongholds throughout Western Europe, where they were to remain the dominant power for hundreds of years.

Before the Celts: The Cosmic People

Little is known of the early Europeans who preceded the Celts; their day-to-day lives and customs can only be guessed at by the artifacts they left behind them. Long before the Celtic settlers began their westward sweep, these ancient people built astonishing monuments to the cosmos—their massive stone circles demonstrate a great knowledge of astronomy, and mysterious underground passage tombs reveal a belief in rebirth or resurrection. It is on these tombs that we find the earliest examples of the solar triple spiral, a symbol of eternity that is now nearly synonymous with Celtic spirituality.

As the Celts swept westward, they incorporated these ancient monuments and their symbols into their ceremonies and mythology. The stone circles became arenas of the gods, and the passage tombs became Sídhe, entrances to the Otherworld. Their people were viewed as the supernatural spiritual ancestors of the Celts, the Tuatha Dé Danann, or People of the Goddess Danu, who later passed into English folklore as the fairy-folk.

FACT

The word *banshee* (Ban sídhe) originally referred to a female of the Sídhe, but later came to refer to a type of mourning ghost in Celtic folklore whose appearance presaged death.

One of the best-known of these ancient monuments is the megalithic passage tomb at Newgrange, Ireland, a gigantic earthwork whose best-known feature is the annual illumination of its inner chamber by a shaft of sunlight at dawn during the winter solstice. Some theorize that the tomb was used to facilitate the passage of souls from death to new life, and the tomb is decorated with beautiful solar designs of spirals, lozenges, and circles carved into its gigantic stones. When the Gaels arrived in Ireland, they assumed that such an impressive structure must be the work of the Gods, and the tomb passed into lore as the home of Aenghus, the God of Love.

The Urnfield Culture

The archetypal early Celtic community began to take shape around 800 B.C.E., in what is now southwestern Germany, when a group of these early migrants met up with a local group and combined with them to form a new group. These people were called the Urnfield culture, after their practice of interring their cremated dead in decorated earthenware jars buried in the ground.

This combined culture had all the marks of a typical Celtic community. By all appearances, the Urnfielders loved life and attached great importance to simple acts of living—eating, drinking, and fighting with great gusto. They wore brightly colored clothing and elaborate jewelry, brewed mead and ale, raised cattle and crops, and skirmished endlessly amongst themselves.

The Urnfielders' burial practices clearly demonstrate a belief in the afterlife. Their dead were carefully cremated and interred in wood-lined earthen tombs known as barrows. Urnfield dead were well provided for, with stores of food, jewelry, and beautifully decorated pottery.

The Halstatt Culture

Following the Urnfield period was an even more recognizably Celtic community, the so-called Halstatt culture, named for the area of Austria where the rich remains of their communities have been uncovered. The Halstatt people were by all accounts a sophisticated Iron-Age aristocracy, wealthy traders whose power derived from their control over rich salt mines whose output provided much income through international trade.

The great wealth of Halstatt tribes was likely responsible for a change in burial custom. Abandoning the simple cremations of their forebears, the Halstatts opted for elaborate grave mounds, where their wealthy chieftains would be buried in high style. Instead of earthen jars, members of the Halstatt aristocracy were laid to rest in fancy wood and iron carts, in which they would travel to the afterlife with all of their earthly possessions arrayed about them. The typical wealth of a Halstatt chieftain included elaborate jewelry and ornaments of bronze, fine weapons and armor, pottery and utensils, and even provisions of meat and grain. Wealthier graves often contained elaborate metal cauldrons and even wagons or war chariots.

Warriors and Craftsmen

The most notable characteristic of the early Celts was their extraordinary artistic ability. Highly skilled metalworkers, they introduced all of Europe to the art of iron forging, and with it, brought advances in agriculture and warfare. From the forges of the Celtic smiths poured both farm implements and fearsome weapons, from swords and spears to great wheels for wagons and war chariots.

Celtic artisans were also adept at finer work. They produced exquisite adornments and jewelry in bronze and gold, extraordinarily intricate and detailed work that was also profoundly symbolic.

Decoration wasn't restricted to weapons and jewelry, either. The Celts were so fond of pattern that it covered every available surface—clothing, drinking vessels, even human skin were all treated as canvas by Celtic artisans.

La Tène Culture

Around 300 B.C.E., the center of Celtic power shifted, reflecting new trade routes with Etruscan settlements in Northern Italy. The primary feature of this shift in the culture is a change in artistic style, from a simple tribal symbolism to a more classical, recognizably Celtic style. The La Tène ("The Shallows") period is so called after the discovery of a large deposit of art and weaponry ritually disposed of in what is now Lake Neuchatel, Switzerland.

In La Tène art, the distinctive cosmic symbolism of earlier Celtic peoples is transformed through the addition of traditional techniques borrowed from Greek and Etruscan designs. The product of La Tène metalworkers is recognizably Celtic, full of undulating lines, spirals, and the first appearance of what we all instinctively recognize today as the Celtic knot, sinuous patterns of interlaced loops and curves.

Other aspects of La Tène culture are also recognizably Celtic. The La Tènes lived in large settlements, arrayed around large hill forts. They built log houses that might have made Abraham Lincoln proud.

One of the best-known examples of La Tène–period art is the Gundestrup cauldron, a richly detailed silver bowl decorated with images of Celtic deities and religious rituals. The cauldron was cut into pieces and deposited as a sacrificial offering in a peat bog in Denmark. It was left there undisturbed until the late nineteenth century, when it was rediscovered.

There is also much evidence of a rich spiritual life among the La Tènes. The cache of artifacts that define the La Tène culture are sacrificial in nature—the bounty of beautiful, expensive, and ornate weapons shows little or no sign of wear, indicating they were a sacrifice, most likely for success in battle.

The Celts and the Romans

To their neighbors in cultured Rome and Greece, the Celtic tribes were viewed largely as fierce, reckless barbarians—uncivilized, uncouth, boastful, and proud. But as much as their critics found fault, the criticism was tempered with a grudging admiration for the great strength and reckless abandon of the Celtic warriors, and many of the great armies of classical times counted bands of Celts among their elite fighters. Until this point, the Celts, although they continued to expand their territories, preferred not to provoke their powerful southern neighbors and trading partners.

Eventually, though, the boundaries chafed. Ever-growing populations and a restless nature led the Celts into the territories of their Etruscan neighbors. The tribes settled in and made friends with those neighbors that remained.

According to Roman accounts some of these neighbors, the Etruscan settlement of Clusium, underestimated the fierce nature of its neighbors and thought to involve them in a dispute with Roman aristocracy. Thinking the Celts simple barbarians, the Clusians enticed neighboring tribes with gifts of wine and promises of fertile land. They were quite unprepared for the arrival of heavily armed settlers who weren't exactly prepared to go marching back from whence they came when the dispute between Clusium and Rome ended. The Clusians issued panicky messages to Rome, which sent diplomatic envoys to prevent disaster.

FACT

The Celtic warriors were so renowned that they served as elite troops in many foreign armies, including those of Hannibal and even the Ptolemy pharaohs. Cleopatra kept a band of 300 Celtic warriors as her personal bodyguards.

Unfortunately, these would-be diplomats made the same mistake in assuming the Celts to be uncultured, and during a scuffle, they murdered an important Celtic chieftain. The Celts were appalled at the poor behavior of the Romans and went before the senate seeking reparations. The senate responded by rewarding the perpetrators with political powers, a move that disgusted the Celts and proved a very bad idea.

The Celtic warlords excelled at psychological warfare and were very effective at ensuring their enemies were thoroughly unnerved before battle even began. One of the most effective methods they used to terrorize the enemy was a form of martial theater—warriors entered battle naked but for tattoos and body paint, hair bleached with lime and arranged in spikes. Combatants reinforced their supernatural appearance with great athletic leaps and screaming cries, augmented by the use of specialized musical instruments such as wailing battle harps and the jarring carnyx, a long, harsh-sounding trumpet.

The Romans, as it turns out, were not prepared for barbarian invaders. After witnessing the spectacle of tall, painted, naked warriors with spiked hair singing, dancing, and blasting horns, they beat a terrified retreat all the way to the fortress on the Capitoline hill, where they remained barricaded until an epidemic of disease convinced the invaders to accept a cash bribe and vacate the city.

The Celts Under Roman Rule

From that point onward, the Celts were in near-constant conflict with the Romans. Despite the Celts' early success, they were no match for the organized war machine that was Rome, which responded to its humiliating defeat with a relentless forward push into Celtic territories. Within 200 years, the Romans were unquestionably in charge, and the era of the Celts gave way to Roman rule. The subsequent Romano-Celtic period was to last for hundreds of years.

The series of military campaigns that brought about the end of Celtic Europe is known collectively as the Gallic wars. It is through Julius Caesar's account of these wars that we know much of what we do about Celtic society and culture.

After the Roman conquest, Celtic society began to conform in many ways to Roman custom and societal norms. Religion began to follow Roman styles—worship moved from sacred groves to temples, and Celtic gods merged with their Roman counterparts and were more frequently depicted in human form, often with Roman-style written inscriptions. The ancient pastoral lifestyle gave way in many places to Roman-style cities, and the Celtic lifestyle gradually gave way until the only truly Celtic communities were those of Ireland and Scotland.

Celtic Society

Early Celtic society was divided into tribal groups called *tuatha*. A tuath (singular) was like a kingdom in miniature, a family group that usually claimed descent from a common ancestor. Most tuaths operated as independent entities, but many came together as part of larger kingdoms under a central ruler. This was the beginning of the succession of chieftains and high kings.

Each tuath was headed by a king (or, sometimes, a queen) who usually claimed descent from one or more tribal ancestral deities. In times of peace, the king was both ruler and an administrator of justice; in times of conflict, he was a warlord. The king was vested in his office through his symbolic marriage with the land, which was personified as a goddess. This rite of investiture ensured the fertility of the land and is echoed endlessly in mythological tales. The legendary Queen Medb of the Ulster Cycle is a personification of the sovereignty of the land, queen to nine kings who ruled only with her consent—a metaphor for the true source of a king's power and his true responsibilities.

ALERT!

A Celtic king was never above the law. A special judge called a *brithem rig* (literally, "judge of the king") oversaw cases and settled disputes involving the king and his rights. A king who angered his people could find himself removed from his throne.

The Celtic system of rulership was bound by a strict code of justice, given that the prosperity of a king's tribe depended upon his fairness and honesty. This was a practicality, as the king also acted as landlord to his people and provided them both protection and grazing land. In later times, these lesser kings themselves swore allegiance to an over-king, who traded military protection in return for tributes of food, supplies, or treasure. A Celtic king was often elected to his position, and if he did not fulfill the role as expected, he could be replaced.

Under the king were the nobles or *flaithi*—warriors, artisans, lawyers, poets, and other skilled citizens. Under the noble class were the freemen who kept the flocks, tilled the soil, and paid rent to the nobles. Each class contained subdivisions, each with its own rights and responsibilities.

Women in Celtic Society

Many of the most powerful deities of the Celtic pantheons were female, ranging from powerful, nurturing earth mothers to fierce goddesses of war.

The women of Celtic mythology are likewise portrayed as brave, resourceful, even crafty heroines. Unlike the wilting heroines and distressed damsels of the Greeks, these heroines did what they wanted, when they wanted, even when it meant disaster—and when matched with these larger-than-life women, the heroes of many Celtic tales are most often done in, whether by beauty, cleverness, or enchantment.

While customs varied according to region and circumstance, when compared to neighboring cultures like Rome or Greece, women enjoyed a very high status in Celtic society. Female aristocrats were afforded the same lavish burials as their male counterparts, with the same rich grave goods as the men. Women were often afforded positions of authority, often serving as leaders, chieftains, diplomats, and even warriors. Celtic women also served in religious life as seers, healers, poets, and even as druids.

Married women had unparalleled rights of property and divorce. A married woman with greater wealth than her husband would control all of their combined property, unlike the Roman women, who left their fathers' homes only to become the property of their husbands. Divorce was available to both men and women, and women who divorced retained their property.

Celtic wives often accompanied their husbands to battle and were not always content to keep to the sidelines; there are numerous accounts of Celtic warrior women and their achievements in battle. Some of these warrior women were so notable in their achievements that they became teachers of the art of war, owners of their own martial academies. Many became legendary.

The Greek historian Marcellinus, writing of Celtic warriors, marveled:

> *In a fight, any one of them can resist several strangers at once, with no other help than his wife, who is even more formidable.*

The Story of Boudicca

Perhaps the most famous Celtic heroine of history is Boudicca, the legendary warrior queen of the Iceni. The Iceni were a tribe of eastern Briton, a somewhat independent ally of the Roman Empire—that is, until the Iceni King Prasutagus died. The king had hoped to maintain some independence for his tribe upon his death by leaving half of his kingdom to his daughters and bequeathing the rest to the Emperor Nero, but this proved a mistake. The Romans moved in almost immediately, and had no interest in royal daughters. When Boudicca protested the Roman takeover along with her daughters, she was publicly flogged, and her daughters were raped by Roman soldiers. Iceni chieftains were deprived of their position and property, many of Boudicca's relatives were sold as slaves, and the kingdom was reduced almost overnight to the status of province.

Boudicca was understandably outraged at this great humiliation. When Roman Governor Paulinius Suetonius left on a campaign against a stronghold of rebel druids on the Isle of Mona, Boudicca easily convinced the oppressed Celts to take on the hated Romans, and 80,000 Iceni warriors rallied behind her.

The queen and her all-female guard made quite an impression on the enemy. Roman historian Cassius Dio described her appearance:

> *In stature she was very tall. In appearance most terrifying, in the glance of her eye most fierce, and her voice was harsh; a great mass of the tawniest hair fell to her hips; around her neck was a large golden necklace; and she wore a tunic of diverse colors over which a thick mantle was fastened with a brooch. This was her invariable attire.*

The Iceni queen's armies initially swept the Romans and laid waste to three Roman cities and an entire Roman legion in a very short time. Boudicca, having no soft spot for her own sex, slaughtered her enemies to the last woman.

Boudicca's story ended in defeat. Suetonius and his men, fresh from victory over the druids at Mona, gained a tactical advantage over Boudicca's forces and decimated her army in one devastating battle. The queen's warriors were destroyed, and she is reported to have ended her life by poison.

The Celtic Cosmos

Unlike the Greeks and Romans, whose gods lived far from human reach, the deities of the Celts were ever-present, embodied in the natural world around them. The visible, everyday world was interpenetrated by the Otherworld, the abode of the gods, elemental spirits, and the souls of the dead.

The abode of the gods was delineated by three elemental domains, those of earth, sea (water), and sky. These domains of spirit were not distinct but instead operated in a continual state of flux and overlap.

The elements were both physical and spiritual—the domain of water, for instance, encompassed not only the oceans, wells, and streams, but was also the source of wisdom and inspiration. The lords of the sky provided not only sunlight for crops but also strength and vigor to warriors and heroes. The woodland creatures gave not only their flesh to those who consumed them but their qualities as well—the boar gave strength, the salmon wisdom, and rabbits, cleverness.

The elements were both the home and the substance of the gods. Goddesses of earth brought forth and nurtured the crops; gods of the sky brought rain and lightning, and so on.

The ubiquitous motif of the triskele, with its three interlocking and flowing spirals, originated as a solar symbol, an emblem of birth, death, regeneration. However, it also illustrates the interplay of the three worlds, as well as the labyrinthine path to the Otherworld.

Gods and goddesses all over Celtic lands appear in triplicate form. Two of the best-known are the Morrigan, a goddess of the battlefield who also had command of birth and death, and Brigid, the patron of artisans and a goddess of healing. Three-headed gods made their first appearance in prehistoric rock-carvings and persisted into Roman occupation, eventually associated with the god Mercury.

Celtic stories, poems, and even riddles are likewise divided into threes, a tradition that carried over in Christian times. It is widely believed that it was the Celts' threefold view of divinity that aided the ready acceptance of Christianity in Ireland.

Rebirth and Reincarnation

The body of Celtic mythology gives much evidence of Celtic beliefs in reincarnation and life after death. The Celts had an underworld similar in some ways to the beliefs of the Romans and Greeks, but all indications are that it was a place much like the everyday world. It is most commonly referred to as the Otherworld, for although its entrances are usually under the earth, it is believed to exist commingled with the world of men and can even be reached by sea. At certain times of the year, and in certain geographical locations, the veils or mists that conceal one world from the next could be broached, and both men and spirits could travel between them.

ALERT!

The Welsh Otherworld was called Annwn, the Isle of Apples, which came to be known later as Avalon and figures heavily in Arthurian legend. Although Arthur is portrayed as a Christian king, it is to Avalon where he is taken to die after being mortally wounded by his nephew Mordred.

There is also much evidence that Celts believed in reincarnation. Mythological stories abound with episodes of rebirth and reincarnation, especially in relation to water. A repeating feature of battle stories is the cauldron or spring of rebirth, by which slain warriors return to life.

Another kind of transmigration is hinted at in stories of gods and heroes who take the form of animals, often in succession. Many are reborn as humans after being consumed by women or goddesses, which gives some insight into the reverence the Celts had for animals.

The Head

For the Celts, the head was regarded as the seat of the human soul, the container of the life force. The head, therefore, had enormous talismanic properties. Severed heads were placed for protection at the entrances of homes and temples and buried at the base of bridges and at crossroads. Celtic warriors took great pains to collect the heads of fallen enemies. Heads, especially of the battle-slain, were among offerings made to the gods and are found in ritual deposits alongside offerings of animals and wares. The heads of friends and military leaders were also kept sacred, a practice that remained a frequent theme in hero's tales.

Celtic warriors were known to enthusiastically collect the heads of slain enemies, preserving them in oil in earthen jars and even nailing them over the lintels of doorways. Many a startled visitor to Celtic lands expressed shock when enthusiastic hosts showed off their treasured collections of captured heads. Historian Diodorus Siculus writes:

> *When the enemies fall, the Gauls cut off their heads and fasten them to the necks of their horses. They nail up the heads in their houses. They embalm in cedar-oil the heads of the most distinguished of their enemies and keep them carefully in a chest; they display them with pride to strangers.*

The head in ancient Celtic art is also emphasized, sometimes exaggerated out of all sense of proportion. When the Celts depicted the deities as humans, they very often pictured them as gigantic, solitary heads—bodies were perfunctory, and often ignored.

FACT

The most famous Celtic talisman is the head of Bran the Blessed, a legendary god-king of Britain. Upon his death, the head of Bran was buried under the Tower of London to ward off foreign invasion. According to legend, it remained in place until the time of Arthur, who turned the head inward, as Arthur claimed to be Britain's sole protector.

Gods and Goddesses of the Celts

The Gallic Celts had no supreme or all-pervasive deities. Gods and goddesses were usually particular to geography, tribe, and place, although they shared many characteristics. Most Celtic gods had an amorphous character. Later, the Romans recognized many Celtic gods as their own in character, and under Roman rule many Celtic gods became strongly associated with Celtic deities.

Scholars typically sort Celtic deities into three main classes. The first group of deities comprises the ancient Gaulish deities. What little that is known about them comes from the writings of the Romans, from inscriptions and from images on ritual artifacts, and from their assimilation into the Irish pantheon.

The second group of deities is the Sidhe, or Tuatha Dé Danann, the Irish pantheon of legend whose myth tales are the best-known in Celtic lore. They are often referred to as the chthonic gods because they are believed to reside underground, in caves and Sidhe-mounds.

While the three main groups of Celtic deities once belonged to separate pantheons, they are often muddled together in late mythological stories. Lugh, for example, is of the older, Gaulish deities, but appears in many tales of the Irish Tuatha Dé Danann.

The third group is known as the rebirth or resurrection gods because of their close association with healing waters. The origin of the rebirth gods is unclear, but later tales give their descent from the sea. These sea-gods have largely passed out of memory, but they exist in vestigial form as mythical creatures such as mermaids, selkies, and kelpies. Of the few who transitioned into the Irish pantheon are Mannanan mac Lir, the sea-god, and Etain, a goddess who lives and is continuously reborn as her own daughter. There are also numerous local deities of wells, streams, and rivers, whose names are mostly lost to history.

The Gallic Gods

Little is known about these ancient, pre-Irish Celtic gods. They were similar in many ways to the Northern gods; when the Romans encountered the Celts, they found that the Celtic gods closely resembled their own. The Gallic gods are also referred to as *continental deities,* referring to the area of

Britain and Western Europe, excluding Ireland, Scotland, and Wales, whose deities are detailed separately.

Some of the better known of the ancient Gallic gods are the following:

- Teutates, a war god closely related to the Norse god Tyr or Tiw
- An unnamed father god called by the Romans Dis Pater, (Latin for "Great Father")
- Ogmios, likened to the Greek Hercules
- A stag-horned god of the hunt, called Cernunnos ("Horned One") by the Romans
- Epona, a goddess of horses and patroness of cavalrymen
- Lugos, the sun god, called the Celtic Apollo, who would become Lugh or the Dé Dananns and Lleu to the Welsh
- Succellos, "The Good Striker," a hammer-wielding god of good fortune
- Esus, the spirit of the oak, closely identified with the Norse Odin
- Taranis, god of thunder, associated with the Norse Thor and the Roman Jupiter
- The Matronae ("Mothers"), a triplicity of earth goddesses who symbolize nurture, fertility, and abundance
- Belenos, the personification of the sun; the annual Beltaine festival was held in his honor

CHAPTER 2

The Myth Cycles

The ancient Celts had a noted abhorrence of written records. They kept no scriptures, history, or genealogy and preferred to preserve their religious teachings through the sacred oral traditions of the druids. Unfortunately, the majority of this ancient wisdom was lost forever with the coming of Christianity to the Celtic Isles. Druidry gave way to the persuasive proselytizing of westward-sweeping Christians, and with none to take on the bardic task, the old ways gradually fell away. Ironically, the task of recording the remnants of Celtic mythology fell to the Christian monasteries; thus, the remnant of Celtic wisdom was preserved by those who destroyed it.

Sources of Celtic Mythology

In the time of the druids, the ancient oral myths and stories were maintained in strict secrecy. Ironically, it was only in the death of the druidic tradition that they were maintained. The Irish Church undertook to preserve Celtic mythology in the seventh century, when its monasteries began to set pagan tales to paper. These scribes of the Church rewrote the ancient gods as human beings, heroes, and magicians whose tales they regarded as the history of the Celts. Because these tales are presented as histories, they neglect any intentional exploration of Celtic theological ideas, resulting in a pitiful lack of stories of the creation of earth or mankind. If the Celts had origin stories, they are forever lost. The myth cycles do, however, give a very good idea of ancient Celtic customs and lifestyles, and they reveal much about the character of the ancient gods and goddesses.

The greatest wealth of Celtic mythology is contained in three major collections of texts known as the Mythological Cycle, the Ulster Cycle, and the Fenian or Fionn Cycle. A looser, less-regarded collection is known as the Historical or Kings Cycle, a record of the lives and adventures of the legendary kings of Ireland. Another popular source of mythological tales is The Mabinogion, a series of four cycles of Welsh mythological tales with early Arthurian elements.

The Book of Invasions

The chief work of the Mythological Cycle is known as the Book of Invasions, compiled in the twelfth century by monks of the Irish Church. The Book of Invasions purports to be a chronological history of successive waves of invading tribes said to have occupied ancient Ireland, but most of the stories it contains are bowdlerized versions of ancient tales of Celtic gods and goddesses.

The Son of Noah

The Book of Invasions does away with Celtic mythological tales of origin and begins with the biblical account of the great flood. Unlike the canonical story of the flood, however, the monks gave their version a twist. A Celtic son of Noah, Bith (meaning "life"), is excluded from his father's ark and therefore constructs his own ships. Bith and his ships sail into the unknown, and all but his own vessel are lost. Bith's solitary ship with its passengers wanders lost for many months, finally arriving in Ireland, where they await the deluge. The floods eventually arrive and wipe out all but a single man called Finntan, who survives for many thousands of years by shape-shifting into the forms of various animals.

It was Finntan, claimed the monks, who returned after so many years with the countenance of an ancient druid and prophesied to the Gaels the coming of St. Patrick, whom he describes as a "druid of an unknown faith." Patrick, according to this prophecy, would cleanse Finntan his sins and allow him to cease his endless wanderings.

FACT

Finntan is also credited with the traditional division of Ireland into five parts: Ulster, Leinster, Connaught, and Munster all ringed about Meath, the location of the Hill of Tara, the legendary seat of Irish kings.

After the time of Bith, the islands remained devoid of human life until the coming of Partholon, another descendant of Noah, who sets foot on Irish shores with Ireland's next wave of colonists. Partholon is more successful at colonization than Bith; he goes about the business of settlement, building houses, planting crops, and battling monstrous, mutated invaders called Fomorians.

Tuan the Shapeshifter

It is not the Fomorians who doom Partholon's settlers, but a fatal disease. All but one man, a nephew of Partholon named Tuan, are destroyed. In an odd echo of Finntan's story, this lone survivor again must make his way through successive shape-shifting. Tuan becomes a stag that leads herds of deer; a boar that roots in the woods; and an eagle that takes to the skies. At last he becomes a salmon, and swims in the sacred pools until humans return to Ireland.

The salmon Tuan is caught and eaten by an Irish queen, who in turn becomes his mother. The newly reborn Tuan is born with all of his wisdom intact and recounts to his mother's people the history of Ireland, continuing the tale where it left off: with Partholon's successors Nemed and his people, who are driven out of Ireland by the Fomorians and who return as the noble Tuatha Dé Danann and the wicked and clumsy Fir Bolg.

Nemed is recounted as a Scythian Greek, who comes to Ireland with his four sons. Nemed and his followers are enslaved and oppressed by the Fomorians, who finally drive them away. Some move to the far shores to be left in peace and become the ancestors of the Fir Bolg. The remainder travel to the west, where they are schooled in the magical arts. The descendents of Nemed return many years later as the Tuatha Dé Danann to drive the Fomorians away and retake Ireland.

The Tuatha Dé Danann

The Fir Bolg tribes are also vanquished by the Tuatha Dé Danann, the "People of Danu," who are but the gods of the pagan Celts in disguise. The stories of the Tuatha Dé Danann provide the best record of Celtic mythological tales—the gods are stripped of their divinity but retain most of their magical powers and abilities. The gods of the Irish are recounted in the Book of Invasions as yet another conquering tribe, albeit one with fantastic occult powers. The Danann hero Lugh finally defeats the Fomorians by driving them into the sea.

The works of fantasy fiction author J. R. R. Tolkien are heavily based in ancient Norse and Irish mythological tales. The inspiration for the races of elves who "sail into the West" in Tolkien's ring trilogy is the story of the Tuatha Dé Danann, who recede into the underworld at the coming of the Gaels.

The Coming of the Milesians

The Tuatha Dé Danann continue to rule Ireland in peace until the arrival of the last invaders, the Gaulish Milesians. The Milesians are named for their chieftain, Míl. The Milesians sail to Ireland on the advice of druid seers, and among their party is Míl's son, the legendary bard Amergin. The Milesians are not welcomed by the Dé Dananns, and a series of fierce battles ensues, in which the kings of both tribes are killed. Eventually, the warring parties reach a compromise. The Milesians will rule the upper, daylight world, and the People of Danu will take the Otherworld and pass into legend. Ever after, they are known as the Sídhe, the people of the fairy mounds.

The Ulster Cycle

The Ulster Cycle was told in two places: the eleventh century Book of the Dun Cow, and the fourteenth century Yellow Book of Lecan. The Ulster Cycle chronicles the adventures of a succession of great heroes, most notably Cuchulainn, a warrior of tremendous stature and ferocity. The cycle begins with the tale of Fergus, an impossibly gigantic king of Ulster. Fergus wishes to marry Nessa, his brother's widow, who will only consent if Fergus will make her young son king. Fergus, all too glad to be rid of the responsibility, readily agrees, and seven-year-old Connor becomes king of Ulster.

FACT

Macha, one of the older Celtic goddesses, was often portrayed as a horse. She is sometimes seen as an attribute of the Morrigan, a triplicate goddess of fertility, war, and death. It was to Macha that the heads of the battle-dead belonged.

Despite King Connor's youth, all goes well under his reign until one terrible incident. A wealthy cattleman by the name of Cruinniuc boasts that his wife Macha, a swift runner, can outrace the king's chariots. Despite her protests, the king forces the heavily pregnant Macha to compete. She wins the race, but the exertion proves too much. After giving birth to twin babies, she expires at the finish line, cursing the insensitive men of Ulster to suffer a woman's labor pains whenever the kingdom is under threat. Macha's curse carries down nine generations of Ulster men, until the birth of the semi-divine hero Cuchulainn.

The Cattle Raid of Cooley

The central tale of the Ulster Cycle is known as the Cattle Raid of Cooley, which tells the tales of two magical bulls. These are Donn Cuailnge, the brown bull of Cooley, and Finnbennach, the white-horned bull of Ai. The white-horned bull belongs to the wealthy, powerful, and exceedingly avaricious Queen Medb (Maeve), whose enormous greed cannot be satisfied. Medb wishes to humiliate her ineffectual husband and desires to add the brown bull to her already prodigious wealth. Upon hearing of the mysterious affliction of the Ulster men, she sets off with her armies to seize the great bull.

Medb's armies are not aware of the existence of Cuchulainn, however, and soon meet with furious resistance. Clever Cuchulainn invokes the ancient right of single combat and staves off Medb's army for months, slaying every champion the queen sends to meet him.

ALERT!

The brown and white bulls of the Cooley saga are no ordinary bulls, of course, but the result of a magical battle between two enchanted shape-changers, a pair of foolish magicians whose end comes in a most fitting way.

Cuchulainn's distractions are successful, and the men of Ulster, recovered from their labor pains, are able to easily defeat Medb's depleted forces.

But Queen Medb is clever. She succeeds in stealing the bull anyway, while the men are distracted by the battles. In the end, all the fighting is to no avail. The two bulls, having picked up an old disagreement, soon commence battling between themselves over which is superior. The battle between the bulls rages all night and ranges the breadth of Ireland, until at last the white-horned bull Finnbennach lies dead. The brown bull, now bored, breaks free and returns to his home in Ulster, where he too expires from his exertions.

Medb, of course, is not finished with Cuchulainn, and seeks her revenge on him through more trickery. Cuchulainn, like most Celtic heroes, is under a *geas*, a magical proscription which becomes a curse if broken. Cuchulainn's geas is that he must accept any meal offered him but he must never eat dog's meat. When the geas is discovered, Medb's simple solution is to offer the hero a meal of dog's meat. Spiritually broken, Cuchulainn is easily defeated, felled by the spear of Lugaid.

Fionn and the Fianna

The Fenian Cycle concerns the hero Fionn mac Cumhaill (Finn MacCool) and his followers, the Fianna, whose adventures were the inspiration for many of the tales of King Arthur. Fionn is believed to be a form of the ubiquitous Celtic antlered god Cernunnos, a forest deity who eventually acquired human characteristics over time. Most of the naming conventions used in stories of Fionn, from his youthful alias to the name of his wife, are related to deer.

As Fionn's legend begins, he is Demne ("Deer"), a young man apprenticed to a druid poet, Finnegas. Fionn's heroic career begins when he is entrusted by the druid to cook a magical salmon. Fionn is sternly warned not to eat even a morsel, as the fish's magic is reserved for Finnegas—but while the young man is minding the fire, a heat blister rises on the side of the fish. Finn unthinkingly pops the hot blister with his thumb. When he sucks on the burnt finger, the salmon's wisdom is transferred to him, and Finn receives the power of prophecy.

QUESTION?

Does Fionn's tale exist in other mythologies?
The story of Fionn has a parallel in Welsh mythology. This time, it is Gwion who tends to the goddess Cerridwen's cauldron of knowledge. When he accidentally receives the gift of prophecy, the goddess is angered. Gwion transforms himself into a grain of wheat, and Cerridwen becomes a hen and devours him. When she becomes a woman again, she finds herself pregnant with him, and soon gives birth. Cerridwen binds the infant into a sack and throws him into a river. He is discovered by a king, who calls him Taliesin, "Radiant Brow."

The Fianna

After many adventures, Fionn finds himself back in Tara, at the court of the Irish High King, Cormac mac Art, near the time of Samhain. Instead of the holiday preparations he expects, Fionn finds the kingdom in an uproar of panic. During Fionn's absence, Cormac's kingdom has been plagued by a rogue specter, a wandering fairy of the Tuatha Dé Danann. This is Aillen mac Midna, a musician who appears every year at Samhain. Aillen always approachs as a musician—at first by invoking the king's hospitality, but later by charming his way through the doors. He then plays a melody of enchantment, putting all of the court to sleep, after which he roams the countryside all night, breathing fire and laying waste to the kingdom.

Fionn offers his services to King Cormac, offering to guard the land against their supernatural enemy in return for a request granted. Like Cuchulainn, Fionn is possessed of a magical spear created in the Otherworld. At the fairy's approach, Fionn uses the spear to prod himself awake, avoiding the sleep-spell. When Aillen opens his mouth to loose his flames, Fionn lets fly his infallible spear and dispatchs the murderous fairy with a blow to the back. His quest fulfilled, Fionn returns to King Cormac for his boon: He requests the leadership of the Fianna, a force of 20,000 men.

The Fianna are an elite force of warriors, highly skilled in poetry as well as in the arts of war. The members of this small army are skilled bards as well as accomplished fighters. Additionally, the warriors are subjected to extraordinary tests of strength and skill—a man wishing to join the Fianna must be able to leap over a stave of his own height, dive under one the height of his knee, and pluck a thorn from his foot—all while running paces. Another test involves burying the candidate up to his waist in sand, where he must defend himself from spear-wielding warriors using only a staff and a wooden shield.

The Red Deer

Fionn and his warriors have many adventures and win many battles. When Fionn is not with the Fianna, however, he prefers the company of his magical hounds, Bran and Sceolan. His hounds, like himself, are the product of magical marriage, their mother being a fairy-woman.

One of Fionn's most famous adventures occurs during a hunting expedition with Bran and Sceolan, during which he encounters a beautiful red fawn. As much as Fionn desires this deer, however, his enchanted hounds balk and refuse to attack it. He watches, amazed, as his hounds joyfully cavort about the meadow with his would-be prey.

A disappointed Fionn finally gives up and heads for home, but the deer follows. As the hunting party enters the gate of Fionn's estate, the red deer suddenly transforms into a beautiful woman. The woman is Sadbh ("Doe"), who has labored under a curse for refusing the advances of a love-struck druid. Because Fionn's hounds recognized her predicament, the curse is lifted. Fionn and Sadbh fall in love and marry, and Sadbh soon becomes pregnant.

Unfortunately, because Sadbh is innocent and trusting, she is lured away once more by the wicked enchanter and forced to return to the forest with him. Fionn searches endlessly for his missing bride, but he is never able to recover her from the wily druid. One day, seven years after Sadbh's disappearance, Fionn is once again on a hunting expedition, when his party encounters a strange boy who cannot speak. Fionn's hounds once again intervene, and the boy is taken into Fionn's care. As he learns to speak, it is revealed that the boy is the son of Fionn and Sadbh, cared for over the years by his mother, the red deer. Fionn names his son Oisin, "Small Deer," and the boy grows up to become an accomplished bard and a distinguished member of the Fianna.

According to legend, Fionn sleeps in a cave, where he will awaken once more to defend Ireland in the time of its greatest need.

The Cycle of the Kings

The Kings Cycle, also known as the Historical Cycle, refers not to a discrete work but to a loose collection of more than a hundred stories. As its name implies, the Kings Cycle is a quasi-historical account of the deeds of the high kings of Ireland. Unlike the previous cycles, most of the characters and central events described in the Kings Cycle can be traced to actual historical persons and places, although the tales are heavily embroidered with mythological elements.

One of the better known tales of the Kings Cycle is the story of Suidhne (Sweeney), a pagan king. Suidhne is awakened one morning by a bell. Seeking out the source of his irritation, he finds a newly built church. Suidhne breaks the church bell, enraging the bishop, who lays a curse on him. He becomes mad and spends the remainder of his life flitting from place to place like a bird, naked, hungry, and frightened. He dies a broken man— ironically, while under the care of a loving bishop. Suidhne's misadventure is probably the inspiration for the madness of Lancelot in the Arthurian tales.

The Mabinogion

Lady Charlotte Guest, the folklorist who first translated a collection of Welsh prose tales drawn from the fourteenth century Red Book of Hergest and the White Book of Rhydderch, called those stories The Mabinogion. The stories are mostly drawn from earlier literary sources and concern the family of the goddess Don, a Welsh variation of the tales of the Tuatha Dé Danann. In four branches, they recount legends of the Welsh gods, all revolving around the hero Pryderi (Peredur), son of the goddess Rhiannon. The remainder of the tales associated with The Mabinogion are largely made up of Arthurian tales and romances.

FACT

The Welsh family of gods were also descended from a goddess, Don. Don is no doubt related to Danu, the mother of the Tuatha Dé Danann, but there is little mention of either goddess in the entire remaining body of Celtic mythology.

One of the most popular stories from The Mabinogion concerns the Welsh god Lleu, the Welsh equivalent of Lugh of the Tuatha Dé Danann. Lleu is the son of the goddess Arianrhod, who has cursed Lleu with a tynged (geas) that he may take no wife from any human race. Lleu turns to the sorcerer Math for help, and Math uses a magic wand to create Lleu a bride made entirely of flowers. Lleu's floral bride is named Blodeuedd, which means "Bride of Flowers."

Unfortunately, although Blodeuedd is beautiful, she has her own will and isn't pleased to become Lleu's wife. One day, while her husband is away visiting, Lleu's bride meets a handsome young hunter named Goronwy, and they soon fall in love. Desperate for a way to be together, the young lovers plot to be rid of Lleu so they will be free to marry.

It is not easy to kill a god, so it takes much conniving to get Lleu to reveal the means by which he can be killed. Through seduction, Blodeuedd learns that Lleu can only be killed by a spear of an entire year's making, and only while keeping one foot in a cauldron of water and another on a goat's back. Lleu's treacherous bride and her lover immediately set to work on the spear, and upon its completion, Blodeuedd convinces her husband to take a bath on a riverbank. She arranges to have a goat set at the base of the tub, and as Lleu steps out, Goronwy hurls his spear.

Lleu is too fast for Goronwy, however, and he escapes death by transforming himself into an eagle. His bride and her lover take his kingdom and rule in his place, but Lleu's friends are quick to discover his fate and are able to restore Lleu to human form. Lleu dispatches his wife's lover with his spear, but Blodeuedd's punishment is more fitting. It is decided that the woman of flowers will be transformed into a bird, but not just any bird. Because she has rejected the lord of light, she will be forced to remain in darkness for the remainder of her days, and so the lady of flowers becomes an owl, mourning forever her wicked deeds.

CHAPTER 3

The Tuatha Dé Danann

The Tuatha Dé Danann is a mythological race unlike any other. They are the mysterious pre-Celtic inhabitants of Ireland, the gods of the Celtic myth cycles, and the fairies of Celtic folklore. Masters of magic, craftsmanship, and secret knowledge, they carried the four legendary hallows, or Treasures of Ireland—the magical Sword of Nuada, the Spear of Lugh, the Cauldron of Bounty (belonging to Dagda), and the Lia Fail or "Stone of Destiny," which would foretell the succession of Irish kings. The Dé Dananns inhabited the same land as the Celts, shrouded from sight in the mystical Otherworld, and eventually became known as the fey, or fairies.

Old Gods to Fairy-folk

Tuatha Dé Danann means the "People of the Goddess Danu." They are a primarily Irish pantheon descended from a great mother goddess, about whom very little is recorded. According to legend, these divine ancestors of the Celts built the Sídhe-mounds, stone circles, and ancient tombs that dot the Irish landscape. When the Celts first arrived in Ireland, they immediately assigned these mysterious, abandoned places to their ancient ancestral gods, imagining these locations as doorways to the Otherworld.

ALERT!

An old superstition about fairies is that they fear iron, which may be used to ward them off. This may stem from early Iron Age settlers' attempts to explain discoveries of stone weapons and implements left behind by these early Stone Age residents.

The oldest of the Tuatha Dé Danann was the goddess Danu, also called Anu or Anand, or Don by the Welsh. Very little is recorded about the goddess. Near Tara, the mythical home of the gods, are two raised earthworks resembling breasts, called the "paps of Anu," likely symbolizing the goddess as the embodiment of the land. Even from ancient times, the goddess was closely linked to horses and husbandry, and she is also closely associated with other mother goddesses—Epona, Macha, and the Morrigan.

Gods of the Dé Danann

The ranks of the Dé Danann are seemingly unlimited in number. Originally, different localities had their own tribal deities, who were often very closely related; over time, many of these blended together, and some took on the aspects of others. The best-known gods of the Dé Danann are these:

- Im Dagda, "The Good God," the son of Danu
- Nuada of the Silver Arm, god of war and divine justice

- Lugh of the Long Arms, "son of the sun" and "Lugh the many-skilled," a pre-Irish Celtic god
- Ogmios, Oghma, or Ogma, god of poetry and eloquence, of Gaulish origin
- Manannan mac Lir, god of the sea and weather
- Angus mac Oc, the son of Lir and a god of love, sometime guardian of Mag Mell or the Blessed Isles

Triple Goddesses

A number of triple goddesses are associated with the Dé Danann. They are triple in the sense that they are usually portrayed with three aspects or personalities, sometimes portrayed as sisters in later literature. The triple goddesses are related to the Matronae of the European Celts. They are closely linked to the land, and many at one time or another were goddesses of sovereignty, personifications of the earth and the symbolic spouses of its rulers. Triple goddesses of the Dé Danann include these:

- Epona, a goddess of horses and cavalry
- The Morrigan, goddess of fertility, war, and death
- Brigid, goddess of metalworking, poetry, and fire

In the tales of the Invasion Cycle, the Tuatha Dé Danann are recast as the ancient race who lived in Ireland before the coming of the Milesian Celts. They are described as a race of mystical sorcerers of great skill, whose druids could raise the dead and even conceal the entirety of their people in mist. With these skills, they wrest the island from the grasp of the clumsy and poorly equipped Fir Bolg ("bag men") in the first of two legendary battles at Mag Tuireadh. In the second great battle, they defeat the fearsome Fomorian giants and drive them into the sea. They do not fare as well with the next invaders, who call themselves the "Sons of Míl" and bring their own magic with them.

Into the Mists

Historians gives the name Milesians to the "Sons of Míl," a semi-mythical invasion force of Spanish Celts. The Milesians were followers of the Gaulish (some say Scythian) leader Golam, known by his title Míl Espáine, the "Soldier of Hispania." Míl's legend tells that he dreamed his descendents would someday rule Ireland, and he fights his way westward with an army, intending to take it by force. Míl is killed in battle before reaching the island, but his wife and sons carry on his quest.

The Tuatha Dé Danann are a powerful race, but the Milesians, with the aid of their powerful bard, Amergin, eventually defeat them. The Milesians then settle on the land they call Eire, after the wife of a defeated Danann king. The Milesians are the last of the invaders and the ancestors of the modern Irish.

After their loss at the hands of the Milesians, the Tuatha Dé Danann retreat fully into the Otherworld. Upon reaching a truce with the Milesians, they agree to divide the land between them, with the Milesians taking the visible world and the Dé Danann choosing the Otherworld, which is mysteriously located both to the West and under the earth. The Tuatha Dé Danann are led into the Sídhe-mounds by the Dagda and remain hidden from human view. They occasionally appear in the human world to aid in battles, engage in mischief, or entice mortals into their realm.

People of the Sídhe

Over time, the old religion faded away, but the Celtic sense of the Otherworld did not. Even long after Christianity flowed through every acre of Celtic land, the denizens of the Sídhe remained. In many cases they took on a sinister cast and were viewed with great superstition. Sometimes, they were called fey, after the Roman *fata*, or "fates," because to see a fairy was an omen of an impending death—a sign that the veil was thinning, and a journey to the Otherworld was imminent.

Playwright William Shakespeare's Mab, Queen of the Fairies, is likely none other than Madb, the Dé Danann queen of the Ulster Cycle who contends with Fionn for possession of the Brown Bull of Cooley. Over time, most of the Irish gods became relegated to the Land of Faerie.

Once a divine race of warriors, the people of the Sidhe were now regarded as supernatural, tricksy folk who often worked mischief on mortals, which ranged from pranks like souring the milk of cows to stealing children or causing disease. They were superstitiously referred to as the "fair folk" or "good people," in hopes that such an utterance of respect would deflect mischief.

Nuada of the Silver Hand

Nuada was the first king of the Tuatha Dé Danann, who brought his tribe to Ireland and contended with its inhabitants for possession of the island. At the first battle at Mag Tuireadh, Nuada's warriors clash with the Fir Bolg. The battle is carried out as a series of single combats, one warrior against another, until Nuada is matched with a Fir Bolg champion, Streng. Nuada fights fiercely, but he suffers a great loss—the enemy warrior slices off his left hand at the wrist. Even so, the Fir Bolg are eventually driven back, and they retreat to the western province of Connacht.

Because sacred law decrees that a king of the Dé Danann must be whole in body and mind, the maimed Nuada is forced to step down as ruler of the gods. A council is convened, and a new king is appointed by vote, a half-Fomorian named Bres the Beautiful. Bres, despite his dashing figure, proves a very unpopular king. He identifies with his Fomorian side and treats the Dé Dananns terribly, levying large taxes and forgoing the usual hospitality and entertainments a king is expected to provide. A solution is sought, and finally, the Dé Danann physician Dian Cecht uses his healing skill to fashion for Nuada a fantastic silver hand, which functions as well as a human hand. Restored to wholeness, Nuada seeks to regain his position.

Bres, however, is having none of it. He enjoys being king and naturally refuses to step aside. All seems hopeless until a bard, Cairpre, seeks the hospitality of Bres' court and, like so many before him, is refused. The offended Cairpre composes the first bardic satire of legend, a scathing indictment of Bres's stinginess:

No meat on the plates;
No milk of the cows;
No shelter after sunset;
No money for minstrels:
May Bres's cheer be what he gives others!

The poem embarrasses Bres so greatly that his face breaks out in gigantic boils, a disfiguration great enough to force Bres to abdicate the throne according to the ancient rules. In short order, Nuada is once again king of the Tuatha Dé Danann.

The dethroned Bres has no intention of going quietly. He complains of his humiliation to his Fomorian relatives, and the Tuatha Dé Danann soon face a wave of invaders. Unlike the rather conventional Fir Bolgs, the Fomorians are, like the Dé Dananns, a magical race, described as misshapen one-eyed giants who live under the waves.

Lugh the Long-Armed

As the Dé Dananns prepare to meet the Fomorians on the battlefield at Mag Tuireadh, a stranger comes to the court, an arrogant man who dresses like a king and declares himself to be Lugh, a master of all arts. King Nuada invites the man to come to court and display his many skills. After witnessing Lugh's abilities as a warrior, a smith, a hunter, and a bard, Nuada is so impressed that he declares that Lugh should be king in his place, and that he should lead the warriors to battle against the Fomorians.

The second battle of Mag Tuireadh begins with the usual custom of single combat, with Fomorian champions paired against the best Dé Danann warriors. The Fomorian paired with Nuada is Lugh's own grandfather, one-eyed Balor, whose gaze is fatal to all it falls upon. Nuada cannot escape Balor's glare and is killed, but Lugh possesses a magical spear which never fails to hit its target. He kills the giant with one blow to his terrible eye. The eye is pushed clear through the giant's head, killing the Fomorian forces arrayed behind him.

FACT

In Irish folk belief, the "eye of Balor" was the term given for a curse received from a baleful look, akin to the "evil eye" in Italy and Greece.

As the Fomorians are driven back, Lugh pursues Bres and corners him. The deposed leader begs for his life, offering in return any secret Lugh wishes to possess. Lugh agrees to the terms and asks Bres to tell him the correct days for plowing, sowing, and reaping crops. Bres obliges, and the Tuatha Dé Danann become masters of agriculture.

The Four Hallows

The Tuatha Dé Danann possessed four magical talismanic weapons, or hallows, which are probably the most famous mystical objects of all time. Although many other magical items occur in Celtic legends, these four receive the most attention and notoriety.

All four symbols were of obvious importance to the Celts, and long before they appeared in literature, they were depicted on a variety of ritual artifacts. Although later mythological accounts of the sacred weapons appear on the surface to be little more than imaginative tales, they hint at much deeper meanings.

These are the four hallows:

- The Sword of Light, attributed to the god Nuada, which cannot be escaped
- The Invincible Spear, attributed to the sun-god Lugh, which never misses
- The Cauldron of Bounty, belonging to the Dagda, a source of endless sustenance
- The Stone of Destiny, or Lia Fail, which cries out when walked over by a true king of Tara

Each of the four legendary weapons was said to have originated in a different city of the Otherworld, each ruled by one of the powerful druids who had taught the secrets of magick and poetry to the Tuatha Dé Danann. The four hallows are also obviously chosen because they are associated with the elements of the cosmos—air, fire, water, and earth.

The Sword of Light

The most famous account of the hallows is found in the Book of Invasions. The first of these was the magical sword of the Dé Danann king Nuada, the Celtic god of divine justice and truth. The sword is called the Sword of Light or the Sword of Truth. Nuada's weapon was otherworldly, forged in the city of Findias in the land of Tir Na Nog. Nuada's sword was irresistible. When pulled from its scabbard, no enemy could flee from it, and its blow was always fatal.

The Sword of Nuada is the prototypical magical sword that inspired many literary magical swords, among them Arthur's Excalibur and Narsil from J. R. R. Tolkien's *Lord of the Rings*.

Swords were a very important part of Celtic culture, and, along with the spear, they were the ever-present symbol of the warrior class. The weapons of the warrior were not simply tools but deeply important spiritual symbols that stood for the ideal qualities of the warrior. The makers of weapons were highly regarded artisans, metalworkers whose skills were literally perceived as a gift of the gods. As a consequence, a sword was not simply an implement but an emblem of a higher spiritual truth, an emulation of the attributes of the gods.

Sword of Illumination

A sword is a slicing instrument, one that dissects, divides, and cuts away. Symbolically, Nuada's sword is a sword of illumination, and it can be viewed as an attribute of wisdom. It represents the quality of discernment, the ability to cut away the irrelevant and make judgments and correct divisions—to get to the heart of a matter. Thus, the sword symbolizes justice, truth, and the application of the law, concepts dear to the Celtic heart.

ALERT!

The story of Nuada has a curious parallel to the story of the Egyptian god Osirus. Both are gods of the underworld and judges of the dead. Like Nuada, Osirus was maimed and restored, losing his left eye in battle with his brother Seth.

A clue to the meaning of the sword can be found in the story of Nuada, who loses his ability to rule when he loses his hand. The loss of the hand symbolizes imbalance, and without balance, a Celtic king cannot justly rule. With the creation of his silver hand, balance is restored, and Nuada is once again fit to rule. Clues to the cause of Nuada's imbalance are also given, as it is his left hand that is severed, and its replacement is a hand of silver. Both the left hand and silver are attributes of the moon, a symbol of femininity and intuition. The implication is that Nuada's martial male side has overcome his feminine, lunar side, and the new hand represents the restoration of the two forces to their proper balance.

Nuada's sword is the embodiment of justice, from which no one, not even a king or a god, can escape. Celtic mythology is filled with tales of divine justice catching up to those who thought they could avoid it; this tale illustrates that even a god needs balance.

The Invincible Spear

The Spear of Lugh, also called the Spear of Victory or the Invincible Spear, had properties similar to the Sword of Nuada—when thrown, it unerringly hit its target. The spear was blazingly hot, and it became hotter the longer it was used. It was stored in a vat of water at night to keep it from catching fire and scorching the earth.

Lugh of the Long Arms (sometimes, "Long Hands" or even "Artful Hands") was the Celtic sun god, who predates even the Tuatha Dé Danann. The name *Lugh* means "light" or "bright," and both the spear and the epithet "long armed" are symbolic, representing the penetrating qualities of sunlight.

Balor

The Spear of Lugh makes its appearance in the myth cycle at the second battle of Mag Tuiread, when Lugh uses it to pierce the eye of the giant Balor and prevents his magic from wiping out the Dé Dananns. Lugh and Balor in this story could be seen as two opposite aspects of the sun. Lugh is the beneficial solar energy, the source of fertility, nourishment, and illumination. Balor, on the other side, represents the harmful solar aspect as the scorching glare that withers crops, dries up lakes and streams, and causes drought and famine. Lugh's precise aim, which destroys Balor's withering gaze, is the application of knowledge. Another clue comes from the traditional ending of the story—it is the knowledge of planting and sowing that harnesses the sun's energy for human benefit, so radiant Lugh with his spear replaces the death-dealing giant.

The Cauldron of Rebirth

Cauldrons figure heavily in Celtic art, ritual, and mythology. Cauldrons were an ever-present ritual item in Celtic religious practices. Many beautifully worked examples have been found intentionally deposited in the bottoms of lakes, springs, and wells as offerings to the gods of water.

In Celtic daily life, the cauldron was the most important item a household possessed. It was used for cooking and brewing, for dyeing, and for working leather. The cauldron's usual place was in the center of the home, and so it was associated with the *axis mundi*, a symbolic representation of the center of the cosmos. The cauldron itself was a microcosm of water, a miniature representation of the abundant well at the base of the world tree.

Cauldrons were also an essential accoutrement of the druid, and there is much evidence of their ritual use in temples, where the cauldron would have been used for divinatory purposes, for collecting the blood of a sacrifice, or for holding sacramental meals.

The cauldron found at Gundestrup is the most famous example of the druids' ritual cauldrons. It is worked with pictorial narratives of mythological tales, including the Spear of Lugh and the Cauldron of Rebirth.

The Dagda's Cauldron of Plenty

The Cauldron of Bounty belonged to the Dagda, or "Good God." The Dagda was the son of the goddess Danu, one of the eldest of the Dé Danann. The Dagda was a god of excess and abundance, and also of music and inspiration. He was especially associated with the craft of the bards and is often depicted in statuary with a harp in his hands.

According to the later legends of Dagda's Cauldron of Plenty, it contained an endless supply of sustenance and could never be emptied. Symbolically, it is the sea, with its endless supply of fish, water for the rains, and the source of healing springs and pools.

Rebirth and Regeneration

Many stories revolve around the Cauldron of Rebirth, which is another form of the Dagda's cauldron. In innumerable mythological stories, the cauldron is used to resurrect warriors slain on the battlefield. Indeed, many early examples of Celtic ritual art depict lines of warriors patiently standing in line as the god dips them, one by one, into the cauldron.

In this aspect, the cauldron is closely related to Celtic ideas of the afterlife and rebirth. The gods of water were themselves continuously reborn, and the waters of the cauldron have obvious parallels to the watery environment of the womb, the passageway to new life.

A related Welsh myth tale tells of the cauldron of Bran, in which slain fighters are placed during a battle. The warriors emerge overnight from the cauldron unharmed, save for the loss of their powers of speech, a probable reference to the reborn soul as an infant incapable of speaking.

FACT

The importance to druid ritual of ritual immersion in cauldrons may be one of the reasons the Celts readily accepted Christianity. Resurrected gods and rebirth by watery immersion were already an integral part of Celtic spirituality when Christian missionaries arrived in Ireland with their own ideas about baptism.

The womb analogy carries over in the role of the cauldron as a source of inspiration. Artistic and poetic inspiration arose from the depths of water, and the bards and poets attributed their ideas to the guardian of the waters.

The Stone of Destiny

The Stone of Destiny, or Lia Fail, is the most famous of the four hallows and the only one believed to exist outside the Otherworld. The stone was used for untold years in the inaugurations of Irish kings at the hill of Tara, the legendary seat of the kings of the Tuatha Dé Danann. According to Irish legend, the Lia Fail was "borrowed" by the Scottish king Fergus and never returned. The stone was moved to England in 1300 and now resides in Westminster, where it has been an integral part of the coronation of British kings and queens. It is now called the "Stone of Scone" after its one-time home in the Scottish city of Scone.

Stones were long associated with the Tuatha Dé Danann, who the Celts believed were responsible for the multitude of stone monuments scattered about Europe. The Celts also believed these monuments to be the doorways the Tuatha Dé Danann used to travel to and from the Otherworld. The Celts themselves used stones for altars and as markers of boundaries, roads, and areas sacred to the gods. In the story related in the Book of Invasions, the Stone of Destiny served a singular oracular purpose, which was to identify a destined king of Tara. Before the election of a king, the candidates would step on the stone, which let out a great cry when the true, destined king set his foot upon it.

A Christian version of the stone's history posits that the Lia Fail was once the pillow of the Old Testament patriarch Jacob, who laid his head on it before dreaming of a stairway to heaven. Joseph of Arimathea, a follower of Jesus, was believed to have sailed to Ireland using the stone as a boat.

Stones and Sovereignty

The Stone of Destiny is not the only one that could identify kings. Arthur, the legendary High King of Britain, learns of his destiny when he pulls a sword from a stone. The Arthurian stone is, of course, an echo of the ancient Celtic ritual of kingship.

Symbolically, the stone represents the earth, and its significance harks back to the ancient tradition of Celtic kings, whereby a ruler was not vested in his power until he had performed a symbolic marriage with the goddess of the earth. This ritual ensured the fertility of the land and the prosperity of his people.

King Stones

The legends of king-making stones have some origin in actual practice; several outside observers of Celtic culture noted the druids' use of stones as sacrificial altars and divinatory tools. Rites of kingship among the Celtic tribes often involved sacrifice and divinatory rites. In one account, a horse, the animal sacred to the goddess, was slaughtered on a stone altar. Wrapped in the horse's skin, the diviner then spent the night on the stone altar in order that the identity of the new king might come to him in his dreams.

CHAPTER 4

The Druids

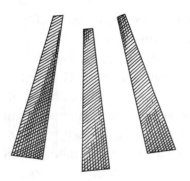

Druids held a high place in Celtic society. While Celtic kings held secular power, druids ruled all functions of religious life, acting as priests, judges, and seers. The druids were the repository of sacred lore and the intermediaries between the gods and man. Besides presiding over religious ceremonies and sacrifices, the druids were the guardians of genealogies, complex legal codes, healing lore, and mythology. The druids also acted as astronomers, keeping the calendars by which the timing of festivals and auspicious days were determined. Upon the death of a king, druid seers conducted ritual divination to determine the next ruler.

Who Were the Druids?

The exact origin of the druid class is unknown although it is sometimes supposed that, at least in some form, they pre-existed the Celts in Europe. The Irish historical record isn't very clear on the matter. Every tribe of people that figures in it are said to have had their own druids, from the Fir Bolgs to the Gallic Milesians; even the mythical northern homeland of the Tuatha Dé Danann was reputedly ruled by powerful druids. In reality, the druids are probably in some way descended from the Neolithic tribal shaman-priests recorded in ancient cave drawings.

Adding to the aura of mystery around the ancient druids was the Celts' seeming abhorrence of the written word. The Celts were neither ignorant or unlearned, prizing wisdom and learning above all things. While writing was eventually used for lesser purposes such as marking roads or keeping monetary records or contracts, Celtic history, law, and religion were instead preserved through an elaborate system of memorization and oral transmission. The priestly classes charged with the keeping of this great body of knowledge and lore were the druids, who commanded tremendous respect among the Celts and constituted a societal class equal in stature to the nobility. The druid ability to mediate between worlds afforded them a great deal of secular power as well; having the ear of the gods gave them influence over nearly every aspect of Celtic society.

Druids Through Foreign Eyes

Most of what is known about the Gallic druids is drawn from the writings of Roman and Greek observers; most notably from the pen of Julius Caesar, who gave a detailed (if flawed) account of Celtic culture in his history of the Roman incursion on Celtic territory. Other important biographies of the druids come from the Roman author Pliny and Greek historians Diodorus Siculus and Strabo. While the Roman account tends to be hostile, the Greek writers tended to be more sympathetic to the druids, praising them for their wisdom and intellect. Diodorus praised their preference for austere living conditions, and Strabo referred to druids as "the most just of men."

While all of these are valuable sources, Caesar created the best record of the druids, outlining their rank in society, their inner hierarchies, their methods of training, and the manner of their rituals and sacrifice. Although

Caesar regarded the Celts as barbarians, he too affords the druids some admiration for their intellectual pursuits, even if he recounts with horror their sacrificial practices. It is of course important to remember that Caesar is writing about a culture he has been at war with, and that he never personally witnessed any of the events he describes.

Becoming a Druid

The ranks of druidry were not closed. Any who managed to complete the rigorous training required could become a druid and thus a privileged member of society, exempt from paying taxes or going to war.

The druids also undertook the role of educators, and druid schools enjoyed a fine reputation. Classical writers often praised druid schools, where sons of the noble classes were taught alongside aspiring druids.

Caesar notes that the druids were heavily organized, with a chief "archdruid" above all the others. When the leader died, a successor was elected by committee. Each tribe had its own complement of druids, with some acting as advisers to the king while others might have held roles as physicians or musicians. Likewise, each sacred shrine or grove had its priests and attendants. Again according to Caesar, the druids held annual meetings in the "land of the Carnutes," a tribe that lived near what is now Chartres, France.

Immortality

Druid theology centered on the doctrine of metempsychosis, the transmigration of souls. Unlike many other groups who believed in reincarnation doctrines, the druids did not appear to believe there was any hierarchy of souls. Rather, one could move from man to animal and vice versa, in an endless cycle of rebirth. One could be a king, a peasant, a warrior, or even, it appears, an animal or bird.

The Roman poet Lucan, in a diatribe against the druids, remarked sourly:

> It is you [druids] who say that the shades of the dead seek not the silent land of Erebus and the pale halls of Pluto; rather, you tell us that the same spirit has a body again elsewhere, and that death, if what you sing is true, is but the midpoint of a long life.

Caesar surmises, with some disgust, that the druid doctrine of reincarnation was largely responsible for the fearlessness of the Celtic warriors. The Celts' general attitude of "eat, drink, and be merry" may also be attributed to this easygoing attitude toward death.

The Keepers of Wisdom

The true origin of the word *druid* is somewhat mysterious. The common explanation is that it is a combination of two roots, *deru*, meaning "oak," and *weid*, meaning "wise." This oversimplification is almost universally rejected by Celtic scholars. *Deru* more properly translates as "firm" or "solid," and relates to concepts of truth and steadfastness, while *weid* means "to see." The word *druid* therefore denotes one who sees well or truly: a seer or prophet.

Training a Druid

Becoming a druid was a huge undertaking; some observers claimed the process took up to twenty years of intense study and memorization. The number of years of training one underwent to join the ranks of the druids varies from one early historian's accounts to the next. However, most agree it was somewhere between twelve and twenty years.

Druid was both an institution and a title. The druids, along with the bards and the filidh, together made up the druid class. The Gallic druids held to a similar categorization of druid, bard, and vate, with the latter holding a position equivalent to the later Irish filidh.

The early chroniclers of the druids generally agree that the druidic class was divided into the three categories of druid, vates, and bards. The Irish referred to these as drui, faithi or filidh, and baird. These three groups had overlapping responsibilities. The druids were priests, magicians, and adjudicators who shared the role of seer with the filidh. The filidh were diviners and poets who specialized in magical singing and satire. The bards were poets also charged with the much larger responsibility of keeping the records of the tribe. Within these three divisions were further specializations, encompassing numerous types of song and poetry, musical instruments, and so on.

The Druid Class

Priests were by far the most powerful members of the druid class and the highest in rank. They oversaw the annual festivals of the gods and presided over the sacrificial ceremonies that were the main rite of worship in Celtic society. As keepers of the sacred calendar, priests were also charged with determining auspicious days for planting and harvesting, for going to war, and for the coronation of kings.

ALERT!

One of the powers the druids had over kings was the *geas*, or sacred taboo. The geas was a magical obligation or injunction that the recipient was bound to honor. Failure to honor a geas could bring dishonor, misfortune, or death.

In addition to their religious duties, the druids were the chief administrators of the Celtic legal system. They were called upon to arbitrate all kinds of disputes, presiding over civil matters such as boundary disputes or the division of estates, as well as negotiating treaties and agreements between groups, tribes, and even kings. Their intense training gave them immense authority in legal matters, and they were always on hand to advise their rulers on matters of law. They also acted as ambassadors, often traveling great distances to enact treaties and trade agreements among tribes.

Wise Judges

The Celtic legal system over which the druids presided was complicated, arranged around an intricate system of balances. Punishments for crimes varied according to the severity of the offense, the relationship between the parties involved, and the class of both the offender and the victim. Both civil and criminal offenses usually involved fines, which were paid either by the offender or his kin.

FACT

The common depiction of a Celtic druid is as a somber, white-robed priest. In reality, the druids were known to dress rather flamboyantly, in brightly colored cloaks and headdresses decorated with feathers.

Druids were also responsible for deciding the fate of criminals and for carrying out whatever punishment the gods decreed. Some crimes carried the penalty of death, and executions were carried out as an offering to the gods. The discovered remains of such killings show various methods of execution, all highly ritualistic.

Druid Specialties

There were many further divisions of responsibility among the druids of the priestly class. These included the *gutuater*, or "father of voice," the chief ceremonial chanter who gave the invocation of the gods in ritual, and the *cainte* ("chanter") who was a master of religious chants. The *liaig* ("leech") acted as physician and was trained in surgery and the use of healing plants and medicines. The *deogbaire* ("cup bearer") was a sort of wine-steward who was also trained in the use of psychotropic drugs.

Filidh: Seers and Poets

A special class among the Celtic druids was the filidh, the poet-seers, who also acted as composers, councilors, diviners, and healers. Where the druids functioned as high priests and judges, the filidh were more accessible to the people.

There is also evidence of further specialties within the ranks of the filidh. In addition to their duties as repositories of sacred songs and stories, they composed, divined the future, and even entertained with riddles and political satire.

The filidh kept their high status in Celtic society, even as their ancient religion faded away. The filidh continued to command respect after Christianity was firmly established in Ireland, even into the Renaissance.

A fili made his (or her—female filidh were not unheard of) living composing heroic songs or satires or performing divination for his patrons; patrons who neglected to pay might even be satirized themselves. The satire of the filidh was not looked upon as simple social commentary—it was potent magic that could cause all sorts of misfortune for the recipient of the fili's withering songs.

According to ancient sources, divination was one of the most important roles of a druid. They give many examples of divination styles, especially augury, interpreting the flight of birds or the movement of animals. Some writers also mention a form of divination involving reading omens into the entrails of freshly sacrificed animal—and, occasionally, human—victims.

Bards: The Wisdom Keepers

To the Celt, words were potent magic, and no words were more potent than those of the bard. The duty of the bard was also that of a poet, but the bard's specialty was the heroic eulogy. One of the ways a Celtic warrior achieved immortality was through valorous acts on the battlefield. Without the bard to memorialize his heroism, the warrior would be forgotten by his people.

In later times, the lines between bard and fili became somewhat blurred, and the terms were sometimes used almost interchangeably.

The training of a bard was lengthy and required the memorization of a vast amount of material. In addition to memorizing hundreds of songs, bards learned complicated genealogies, ancestral stories, and histories by heart.

Another specialty of the bard was genealogy, the history of the people of the tribe and their deeds. As such, the bard was the guardian of his tribe's identity. Without their bard, the people would have no sense of who they were or where they had been.

Female Druids

There are numerous written references to female druids, who appear to have filled a variety of roles in Celtic religious life. There are many mentions of *Ban-drui* ("female druid") and *Ban-fili* ("woman poet") in the historical records, and Celtic myth stories are of course filled with references to female magicians, seers, and wise women. The great hero Cuchulainn is trained by Scathach ("Shadowy"), a legendary warrior in her own right who teaches Cuchulainn his legendary battle-leap and, in her capacity as seer, predicts his eventual misfortune.

FACT

Women with political power were often described as priestesses of religion. One of the most famous of the purported female druids is Queen Boudicca, who was a priestess of the war goddess Andraste. Records of her victories include the brutal sacrifice of hundreds of female Roman captives.

The Roman historian Tacitus makes note of female druids attending meetings at the druid sanctuary at Mona, where they reportedly encouraged the Britons to rebel against the Roman armies.

Another Roman story claims that the ascent of the emperor Diocletian was predicted by a druid seeress. It seems the young emperor, while still a soldier in the Roman army, was quite rude to his druid hostess, failing to pay adequately for food and board. She upbraided him for his stinginess, to which he joked that he would be more liberal with his money when he was emperor. At this, the druidess drew herself up and warned Diocletian not to makes jokes, for he would indeed be emperor, after slaying "the boar." True to her prediction, Diocletian did rise to throne after slaying the Roman prefect Arius, whose surname was Aper, meaning boar.

Tacitus also gives an account of the Veleda, a powerful oracle of the Germanic Bructeri tribe, who ruled over a large portion of Germany and was considered semi-divine. The Veleda was involved in political negotiations and was known to have successfully arbitrated several conflicts between tribes. She was eventually captured by the Romans around the year 77 C.E. for her involvement in rebellion against the Empire.

Sacrifice

The druid religion was closely tied to the natural world, which was the domain of both humans and the gods. All of nature not only flowed from the gods, but made up their substance as well. The creatures and growing things of the earth had communion with the gods; they functioned as messengers between man and the Otherworld, even embodying the gods themselves. Animals provided meat, milk, and clothing; the trees of the forest offered shelter and nourishment; and plants provided not only food but medicine for the healers—all gifts of the gods requiring gratitude and repayment.

The Celts thus had great respect for both animals and plants. That which was sustenance for the body was also the body of the gods and therefore deserving of propitiation and respect. Sacrifice in return for what was received kept the cycle of life continuous, and ensured fertility and abundance.

Thanks to the Gods

Because the Celts viewed animals and plants as the embodiment of the gods, they sought to maintain balance between the worlds. As the living creatures gave of their substance for the nourishment of the people, the people gave of theirs for the sustenance of the gods. Sacrifice was an integral part of the spiritual lives of the Celtic tribes. Gifts of weaponry and art, trophies of war, even the blood of animals and humans were given in return for what the gods gave. As in many other early cultures, the form of these sacrifices could appear quite brutal. The Celts may have felt close connections to the earth, but they were hardly sentimental.

Caesar remarks on the practice of sacrifice, "when they have determined on a decisive battle, they dedicate as a rule whatever spoil they may take. After a victory they sacrifice such living things as they have taken, and all the other effects they gather into one place."

Offerings of wealth were also common. Large deposits of unused, high-quality weapons, adornments, and implements have been discovered buried deep in earthen shafts, peat bogs, and in sacred wells and waterways. The spoils of war also belonged to the gods—captured weapons, treasures, and even livestock were offered en masse as sacrifice for a victory.

Human Sacrifice

The issue of human sacrifice is the dark shadow that haunts the legacy of the druids. Many outsiders' accounts of druid ritual describe the brutal, bloody sacrifice of criminals and prisoners of war, and bodies of many apparent victims have been uncovered preserved in peat bogs and earthen shafts.

Historical accounts of human sacrifice among the Celts are of course not unbiased, and they tend to be secondhand accounts filled with exaggeration. Most accounts of druid sacrificial custom come from the pens of Roman chroniclers who made little attempt to conceal their contempt for their subjects.

FACT

The Romans made much of what they deemed druidic savagery, but the customs they deride are not so different from Roman treatment of criminals, and they are probably far less brutal than the customs of the gladiatorial arena, for example, or the feeding of Christians to lions.

In any case, it is well known that to the Celts, matters of justice were paramount. As the gods were the source of the legal system, it naturally follows that the dispensation of criminals would be a matter of religion as well. Druid law was based on the Celts' deeply held belief in the balance of forces and the necessity of maintaining that balance. Where breaches of the sacred law created imbalance in the natural order, punishment restored that balance. It is also important to keep in mind the religious beliefs of the Celts that death was not the end of life, but was, in fact, a birth into the next world.

A criminal was likely sacrificed to the god he had offended, in repayment for what was upset. Adding to this view is archaeological evidence that the method of sacrifice varied according to the deity receiving the sacrifice. Those sacrificed to Esus (called "Lord," a deity who was similar in many ways to the Norse Odin) were reportedly strangled or hung from trees, while those sacrificed to Teutates (a god of war and healing comparable to the Norse Tyr or the Roman Mars), were drowned in a cauldron or body of water, a ritual closely linked with regeneration in mythical tales of war.

Some remains of sacrificial victims of the druids show signs of highly ritualized death, wherein the victim is killed three ways—usually by blows, strangulation, and drowning. One such victim is called the Lindow Man, a mummified Celt uncovered in the remains of an English peat bog. Lindow Man's perfectly preserved body shows every sign of ritual execution—he had been struck, his throat was cut, and he had been strangled.

Voluntary Sacrifice?

One theory of druidic sacrifice claims that in addition to convicted criminals and prisoners of war, some sacrifices consisted of special emissaries to the Otherworld. These would be members of the priestly class, either volunteers or victims chosen by a special lottery. Some researchers have speculated that the victim would not be an offering per se, but a messenger who was chosen to communicate directly with the gods of the Otherworld.

One such sacrifice has been deduced from circumstantial evidence uncovered from the bodies of victims such as the Lindow Man, and related customs still practiced in rural Celtic communities. The evidence suggests the use of a lottery system, whereby a bannock cake (a cake of wheat, barley, oats, hazel nuts, and mistletoe) would be deliberately scorched in one corner, and then broken into bits and passed blindly among the candidates. The recipient of the burned portion would be ritually dispatched to the

Otherworld. Forensic testing of the contents of Lindow Man's stomach contents—burned bannock and mistletoe—bear out these theories. Because Lindow Man died during the time of the Roman invasion, some speculate he may have been chosen as a special emissary to the gods, in a desperate attempt to stave off destruction.

The Decline of the Druids

From about the first century, under heavy Roman influence, the institution of druidry began to fade away, and with the establishment of European Christianity, it disappeared almost entirely. The influence of religion, however, was not responsible for this decline, which instead was largely an issue of language, law, and, ironically, religious tolerance.

What contributed the most to the druids' disappearance was language. Romans were generally religiously neutral. They were not terribly interested in eradicating Celtic religion, except where druid power influenced uprisings and disturbed their carefully planned social order. Further, the Romans identified the Celtic gods as simply foreign versions of their own deities. They encouraged syncretism between the pantheons, which of course benefited the Roman rulers more than the druids.

The Celts under Roman rule were Roman citizens, and they were encouraged (sometimes by force) to make use of the Roman legal system, whose operative language was, of course, Latin. Latin eventually supplanted the Gallic languages, which the druid oral tradition relied on. Druid schools crumbled, and the hierarchical structure of druidry failed. What remained of druidry was pushed into Ireland and Scotland, outside the reaches of the Roman Empire.

The Druids and the Christians

With the coming of the Christians, the use of Latin became a matter of religion as well. The old languages were relegated to the pagans and derided as the tongue of uneducated peasants, and so whatever remained of the druidic intellectual structure declined rapidly.

There are still reports of druids operating all the way into the twelfth century. But because the ancient institutional structures were gone, the initiatory teachings of druidry passed from one individual to the next. Eventually, druids were viewed as little more than solitary healers, wizards, or even common fortune tellers.

The Christians in Ireland were of a different sort than those who had earlier conquered other parts of Europe. They were primarily scholarly monks. Although they were largely disdainful of the pagan religions, they retained enough respect for the institution of druidry that many elements of Celtic theology became intertwined with Celtic Christianity.

Transition

In their histories, the Christian monks painted an often contradictory view of druidry. Druids portrayed in the monks' accounts of Ireland's ancient heroic past are stern, powerful, and dignified. Many are even portrayed as wise prophets, foretelling the coming of Christianity to the island. Later, reflecting real-life political power struggles, druids were depicted more as devious wizards or scheming, superstitious pagans. This strange dichotomy persisted into medieval times—Irish ancestral pride perhaps at odds with proper Christian sentiment.

ALERT!

Not all of the recorded predictions of the coming of Christianity were positive. The druids of the court of Loeghaire, Lochru, and Lucat-Mael made a dark prediction that a "shaven-headed foreigner" would appear and seduce the people and that this stranger's new doctrine would forever supplant the religion of the druids. This stranger of course was St. Patrick. Patrick is credited with the conversion of Ireland to Christianity.

Not everything was peaceful, however. The conversion of the Celts, whose spirituality already gave them a unique understanding of Christian ideas of trinities, baptisms, prophets, and resurrected gods, were not too resistant to the new faith. Many of Ireland's druids, on the other hand, faced a loss of power, prestige, and property under the new regime, and conflicts between local druids and Rome's bishops were inevitable. This was not helped any by the animosity that St. Patrick exhibited toward the druids.

CHAPTER 5

Celtic Christianity

There are no clear boundaries between Celtic paganism and the beginning of Christianity in Ireland. The process of transition from pagan to Christian was a gradual one, and many elements of the pagan religion were absorbed, making Celtic Christianity quite unique from that practiced in the rest of Europe, which had long been under Roman rule. The Celtic monasteries established in Ireland were not considered very different from the schools of druidry, and for a long time the people looked on these monks as more or less a new class of druids.

The Coming of Christianity

Christianity was introduced to Ireland around 440 c.e., only a few decades after the Romans began recalling their troops from Britain. The faith was brought by a bishop named Patrick, who established his domain at the ancient fortress of Emain Macha (Armagh), a city reputedly founded by the ancient Celtic Queen Macha.

FACT

The ubiquitous tonsure haircut of the Catholic monk, in which the hair is cut to leave a portion of the head bald, with a fringe around or in the back, is a custom that originated in druidry. It was later adopted by early monastic groups in Ireland. To the druids, baldness was a sign of wisdom, and the haircut symbolized the adoption of the path of wisdom.

Christianity in Ireland followed a different path of development than in most other European countries. Where European Christianity followed powerful bishops who had immense power over local governments, Christianity came to Ireland at a time when Roman military control over Europe was fading, making for a unique set of circumstances for the newborn Irish church.

Irish Christianity flowered in the form of independent monasteries, which operated in many respects outside the authority of the Roman Church. These monasteries absorbed not only pagan clerics, but pagan customs, superstitions, and even gods. Because of the autonomy enjoyed by these early churches, they were able to incorporate many elements of the local religion into their doctrines.

Because of their isolation from both church and government, the Celtic Church avoided many of the eruptions, conflicts, and doctrinal wars that plagued Rome, and the result was a church heavily concerned with the mystical, spiritual side. To the Celtic Church, God was not a distant concept, but a continual presence, manifest in the wholeness of nature. It was not uncommon for the Irish monk to seek the life of a forest hermit, finding God imminent in his natural surroundings.

The similarity between Irish pagan symbolism and Christian symbolism is striking. Along with a tripartite god, the newcomers brought with them a god who was sacrificed and reborn, and the practice of baptism by immersion in water for the purpose of attaining eternal life—both concepts already well understood by the druids and their devotees.

It has long been taught that St. Patrick, when explaining his religion to the pagan Irish, picked up a three-lobed shamrock and used it to expound on the nature of the trinity. The story is unlikely, but it probably has a grain of truth in it, as the compatibility of druid symbolism would have made many aspects of Christianity easier to assimilate.

Because of the relative ease with which the two faiths mingled, Celtic Christianity also absorbed elements of pagan belief. Celtic gods were slowly transformed into Celtic saints, and in turn, Celtic saints took on the characteristics of the Celtic gods—tales of Ireland's first Christians are as fanciful and filled with magic as the tales of the Tuatha Dé Danann. Early Irish images of Jesus on the cross show not the sorrowful Latin corpus christi but a resplendent, smiling god with wide-open eyes who looks not the least bit concerned about his crucifixion, and if not for the presence of the cross, might be mistaken for the visage of Lugh.

Patrick: Patron of Ireland

Tales of the Irish saints are filled with as much fantastic embellishment as those of the ancient Celtic gods. They are attributed miraculous powers that rival those of the ancient druids, and their biographies detail all sorts of fantastic adventures, from flying to battling dragons. The reality of their lives is more difficult to pin down.

Accounts of the life of Patrick are no exception, filled with fanciful details and miraculous feats. Patrick's biographies are muddled, complicated by the fact that written records were not introduced to Ireland until well after the introduction of Christianity. Further complicating matters, no connection can be made between Patrick and any of Ireland's early churches, although the general consensus is that he was active in Ireland at the end of the fifth century C.E.

The earliest record of the life of Patrick is contained in two letters that are generally recognized as his own. One of these is a letter condemning Roman raiders who have carried off some of his congregants, but the more important document is his confessio, or confession, which contains a brief account of his early life along with his defense against barbs from unknown accusers. While St. Patrick's confessio is filled with self-deprecation, it is also filled with boasts about the many people he has converted and baptized. He seems especially proud to have converted a number of wealthy members of the nobility.

The Confessio

Patrick relates in his confessio that he was born to a wealthy Roman family in Britain, the son of a deacon, although he claims he himself was not a Christian. He enjoyed a life of privilege until, at the age of sixteen, he was kidnapped along with many of his countrymen by Irish raiders. He was taken to Ireland, where he lived the next six years under the servitude of Milchu, a chieftain and a druid priest, working as a shepherd and suffering from cold and deprivation.

By Patrick's account, Milchu was a cruel and intolerant master, and Patrick grew to hate the druid religion. The young slave sought solace through daily prayer, and he tells that after six years of fervent supplication, a voice appeared and commanded him to seek "his ship," as his captivity was at an end. Patrick fled his master and sought out the nearest port, where he found a waiting ship. He credited God for his deliverance from slavery, and when he returned to his family, he made the decision to devote his life to God.

Patrick traveled to France and entered the religious life, eventually becoming ordained. He spent twenty years rising through the ranks of the church, until, twenty years after leaving Ireland, he was consecrated a bishop. Patrick then made the decision to return to the place of his captivity, and to Christianize pagan Ireland. His family implored him not to leave, but a vision convinced him that he had to return. He writes:

> *And after a few years I was again in Britain with my parents, and they welcomed me as a son, and asked me, in faith, that after the great tribulations I had endured I should not go anywhere else away from them. And, of course, there, in a vision of the night, I saw a man whose name was Victoricus coming as it from Ireland with innumerable letters, and he gave me one of them, and I read the beginning of the letter: "The Voice of the Irish," and as I was reading the beginning of the letter I seemed at that moment to hear the voice of those who were beside the forest of Foclut which is near the western sea, and they were crying as if with one voice: "We beg you, holy youth, that you shall come and shall walk again among us." And I was stung intensely in my heart so that I could read no more, and thus I awoke. Thanks be to God, because after so many ears the Lord bestowed on them according to their cry.*

Patrick records in his confessio his many successes in baptizing thousands, ordaining priests, and convincing many women to become nuns. Patrick remained in Ireland until he died, a few years before the end of the fifth century.

Patrick of Legend

Later tales of St. Patrick have none of the humility of Patrick's own writing. They rival the tales of the druids in their fantastic accounts of wizard's battles, although Patrick accomplishes his miracles through prayer rather than magic. Many stories of Patrick's exploits involve triumphs over the druids. In a version of the story of Loeghaire, his druid councilors stand against Patrick in his attempt to light an Easter fire, an opposition to pagan custom. Patrick prays for the death of the pagan priests, and the ground opens up to swallow them. There are numerous variations on this theme—Patrick prays, and God smites the pagans.

Not all of Patrick's magic came about by prayer. Irish tradition claims that Patrick possessed many of the same spells credited to the druids, including the ability to make himself invisible, through the use of the *faeth fiada* ("cry of the wild beasts").

Patrick and the Snakes

One of the most famous tales of St. Patrick is his driving of the serpents from Ireland. This certainly mythical tale purports to explain the lack of snakes in Ireland, but it also carries overtones of Christian/pagan conflict. If the snakes are viewed as the emblems of the druids (who revered the serpent as one of their holy symbols), the tale takes on another level of meaning; namely, that the serpents are not animals, but the pagan way of life.

This interpretation is borne out by many other references to battles with dragons or serpents undertaken by the saints, which invariably occur on sites formerly sacred to the druids. This is not to say such battles necessarily took place at all. Instead, these stories may use poetic license to deal with the embarrassing reality of many a church sited on former pagan holy grounds, which may have mattered much more as the centuries passed.

Oddly, the tale of the snakes echoes the ancient story of the Fomorians, described as sea-serpents, who are driven into the sea by the Tuatha Dé Danann.

St. Brigid: Mary of the Gaels

There is much speculation over the life of Ireland's second patron saint, so-called Brigid of Kildare. Brigid is the name of both a saint and a great Celtic goddess. The ancient Celtic Brigid was the daughter of the Dagda and the patroness of poetry and seership. Brigid was especially revered by the filidh as their special goddess. Brigid was one of the triple goddesses, with two sister aspects, also called Brigid, goddesses of healing and of the forge. Additionally, the legendary Brigid was guardian over livestock, and her feast day was celebrated on the first of February, which marked the first day of spring and the lactation of the ewes.

Whether or not the Christian St. Brigid existed is a mystery lost to time. It is, however, indisputable that the saint took on many of the attributes of the Brigid who had gone before, and many of the legends of the goddess became legends of the saint.

Life of Brigid

According to Irish tradition, Brigid was born in Faughart, in Northern Ireland. She was the daughter of a powerful druid, Dubthach, a king of Leinster, and his Pictish slave, Brocca, reputedly one of St. Patrick's converts. The young Brigid was reportedly entranced by the preaching of St. Patrick, and she opted to enter religious life as a nun over much opposition from her father. She became a nun and quickly progressed to a position of leadership, eventually founding a combination monastery/convent at Cill Dara (Kildare), over which she presided as abbess. Brigid wielded considerable power in the Irish Church, and her abbey became renowned throughout Europe.

FACT

One of the curious legends of St. Brigid concerns her consecration as abbess, which was carried out by another well-known Irish saint, St. Mel. The story tells that Mel inadvertently read the rite to ordain a bishop, an irrevocable act that is meant to explain the great authority held by the abbess, who was said to have had the power to appoint bishops in Ireland.

Alongside the abbey, Brigid was said to have founded a thriving community of artisans. Most notable of these were the scriptorium, which produced illuminated manuscripts, including the beautifully decorated Book of Kildare, and a legendary forge, which specialized in fine metalwork.

Miracles of Plenty

A great many of Brigid's miracles have to do with milk and the fertility of cows, an echo of the great goddess for whom she is named. Among the miracles attributed to Brigid are turning water into milk or beer. She is also credited with many miracles of increase—creating large quantities of beer with a little malt, or causing a single cow to produce the milk of ten. On one occasion, she touched an altar post at communion and caused it to burst into flower. Another legend of Brigid concerns her acting as midwife to the Virgin Mary to deliver the infant Jesus, an impossible act that earns her the moniker "Mary of the Gaels."

The name Brigid is derived from the Gaelic *breo-saigit*, or "fire-arrow." Both the goddess and the saint are heavily associated with fire and the forge. On Brigid's death, an eternal flame was kindled in her honor, which burned continuously for hundreds of years. It is widely believed that this flame may have been a pre-existing sanctuary of the goddess Brighid.

Brigid reportedly died in 525 at the age of seventy and was entombed near the altar of her church. She inspired widespread devotion, and her feast day was not so coincidentally fixed at February 1, the feast day of the goddess. Her emblem as a saint is the flame, and she is often depicted in the act of milking. Brigid is the patron saint of brewers, blacksmiths, poets, midwives, and newborn.

Today, there are dozens of churches dedicated to Brigid throughout Europe, and hundreds of place names in Ireland reflect her influence. Variations on the name Brigid (Bridget, Bride, Bree) remain some of the most popular for Irish girls. Brigid's sacred flame was extinguished during the Reformation, but it was rekindled at Kildare in 1993 and is tended there by the sisters of Solas Bhríde.

Columba: Christ Is My Druid

The life of Columcille, popularly known as St. Columba ("The Dove"), is one of the most interesting of the saints. Columba was a contemporary of Patrick's, although his journey began under very different circumstances. Columba was born as Creimthne ("Fox") into an Irish royal family, the

Nialls, which put him in line for the throne. He was the nephew of one king, and the uncle of another. As a child, Columcille reportedly studied under both a priest and a druid, learning writing from the former and poetry from the latter. As an adult, Columcille was described as a tall, imposing man with a booming voice and many talents—he is an accomplished navigator, poet, and a scholar. Even though he could have chosen a career in politics, Columba became a Christian and forsook his privileged life, opting to become a simple monk. He was ordained in Glasnevin, on the eastern coast.

A line from a poem attributed to Columba reads:

> *I do not hold to the voice of birds, or any luck on the earthly world, or chance or a son or a woman. Christ the Son of God is my druid; Christ the Son of Mary, the great Abbot; the Father the Son and the Holy Spirit. My estates are with the King of Kings; my order is at Cenacles and Moen.*

Columba's love of learning was legendary. One story tells of an episode early in his career which set his destiny. It appears Columba desired a psalter, or prayer book, but the only one he had access to was the single precious copy owned by Finnian, abbot of the local church, which could not be removed. Columba undertook to copy the psalter, and sealed himself inside the church with the precious book, copying it painstakingly by hand. Unfortunately, he was discovered in the act, and the abbot demanded his copy, claiming it was too precious to allow outside the confines of the church. Columba refused to surrender his book, and the matter was referred to the king, Diarmaid, who decided in favor of Finnian.

FACT

Columba's dispute over his copy of Finnian's book is sometimes referred to as the first recorded copyright dispute. Although Columba labored hard over his surreptitious copy, King Diarmaid ruled that because his book was but a copy, it belonged to the owner of the original, "To every cow her calf, and to every book its son-book. Therefore the copy you made belongs to Finnian."

The Monastery at Iona

The dispute carried over when Columba offered sanctuary to the son of the king of Connacht, who had killed the son of Diarmaid's steward in the course of a dispute. The shelter of the church was supposed to be sacrosanct, but Diarmaid had the boy dragged from Columba's sheltering arms and slaughtered. Columba, outraged at this great injustice, sought help from his powerful family. He returned at the head of an army, which deposed the king in a long and bloody conflict, resulting in tremendous bloodshed.

The result of the battle was condemnation of Columba by his closest friends and his peers in the church. Accounts differ whether Columba's next action was of his own accord, out of sorrow for what he had caused, or ordered by the church. Filled with remorse, Columba exiled himself to the land of the Picts, on a mission to convert as many of the Scottish pagans as possible. With twelve companions, he traveled to the tiny isle of Iona, off the west coast of Scotland, which was at that time a wilderness.

Columba and his companions set to work immediately. He chose a high spot on the western side of the island and commenced work on a monastery. Despite its remote location, Columba's monastery grew and thrived, eventually becoming one of the largest and most active seminaries in Britain. One of the most important activities of Columba's monastery was the creation and preservation of books and scripture. The best-known achievement of Columba's order was the creation of the fabulously decorated Book of Kells, arguably the most famous work of art ever produced in Ireland.

ALERT!

Many miracles are ascribed to Columba, too. Columba's talent, fitting for a member of the filidh, was prophecy. Columba made many prophecies regarding the future of Ireland, the reign of kings, and the victors of battles. On one occasion, he predicted his own impending death.

One of the strangest episodes in Columba's biography concerns the poets of Ireland, the druid filidh. It seems the poets, while exceedingly popular among the people, were not much appreciated by the lords and kings they satirized so the poet class was threatened with banishment. Columba, himself raised as a filidh and still a poet, interceded on their behalf. Columba pleaded the bards' case to the chieftains, asking the king to consider who would keep their histories if they did away with them. This is not Columba's only friendly encounter with druidry, and accounts of his encounters with druid priests indicate that they held him in some esteem.

Columba went on to found dozens (some say hundreds) of churches and monasteries throughout Scotland. He lived to the age of seventy-seven, a fantastic age in a time when one was considered fortunate to live beyond forty.

A favorite story tells that the aged Columba was out walking one afternoon when he grew weary and sat down by the roadside to rest. As he sat there, the old white horse who carried milk for the monastery came to him and laid his head upon the saint's breast, to give farewell to the master he knew was dying.

The Cross of Life

The unique symbol of Celtic Christianity is the so-called Celtic cross, also known as the Cross of Iona, after the belief that Columba erected one at his monastery on the island. The connection with Columba, who represents the union of pagan and Christian spirituality in Ireland, is apt. The Celtic cross is said to be derived from the ancient Roman monogram of Christ, made from the combination of the Greek letters *chi* and *rho*, but this seems unlikely. The form of the cross, with its scooped-out arms and enclosing circle, is derived from an ancient form dating thousands of years before Christianity, an ancient symbol of the sun. The placement of the crosses at crossroads and marketplaces also echoes ancient custom, and some suppose this was done in conscious imitation of pagan monuments.

The Solar Calendar

The ancient Celtic solar calendar consisted of two solstices, two equinoxes, and four cross-quarter days marking the seasons. The four solar festivals, marked on a round representing the path of the year, form a solar cross, the basis of the Celtic cross.

As a spiritual symbol, the Ionic cross represents the coming together of earth and heaven—the crossroad of life and death joined with the eternal circle of heaven. From the pagan viewpoint, it can be seen as the joining of male and female symbolism. The four arms can also be seen to represent the zodiacal calendar important to early Christians—four cardinal directions, and the four fixed signs of the zodiac as represented by the evangelists Matthew (and his emblem, the angel), Mark (the lion), Luke (the ox), and John (the eagle), with Christ represented by the center solar disk.

Celtic Christian Art

The founding monastic communities of Ireland and Scotland, free of the political and religious strife of the mainland, developed into hubs of intellectual and artistic activity, which reached a peak in the sixth to eighth centuries. The ability of the monastic communities to draw membership from a variety of backgrounds led to a harmonious blending of artistic styles known as the Celtic Insular period. Some of the most fantastic art produced by the Celtic religious groups includes fine metalwork, intricate stone carving, and vivid illuminated manuscripts.

Fine metalworking of the period encompasses shrines and reliquaries, liturgical implements such as chalices and patens, ornamental covers for books, and personal ornamentation. Some of the finest examples include these works:

- The Ardagh chalice is a fantastic liturgical chalice of gold, silver, and bronze that was created using numerous techniques, including casting, engraving, filigree, and enameling.
- The Monymusk reliquary, housing the bones of Columcille, is covered in copper and silver and decorated with leaping beasts and intricate knotwork.
- The so-called "Tara Brooch," a decorative clasp of gold, silver, copper, and glass, is decorated with enamel, filigree, and gilt. At just

under seven inches long, the brooch contains more than twenty tiny dragons in its decorations.

Illuminated Beauty

The great illuminated manuscripts produced during this period are some of the finest ever created in Europe. The designs woven into and around the text of these brilliant illuminated books draw from both classical and ancient Celtic art. The texts are rich with intricate spirals and interlaced knots, loops, and whorls, as well as detailed portraits of angels, saints, and biblical figures alongside images drawn from nature. Typically, every free space not taken up by text is filled in with geometric designs, curling vines, mythological creatures, intertwined people and animals, and ornamented letters. Some of the finer examples of the art are the seventh century Book of Durrow and the Lindisfarne Gospel.

These books were so elaborate, detailed, and magical in appearance that Christians of later periods believed them to have curative powers. A twelfth century commentator remarked after viewing one such book:

> *If you take the trouble to look very closely, and penetrate with your eyes to the secrets of the artistry, you will notice such intricacies, so delicate and subtle, so close together and well-knitted, so involved and bound together, and so fresh still in their colorings that you will not hesitate to declare that all these things must have been the result of the work, not of men, but angels.*

The most precious and beautiful of all the Celtic illuminated books is the gospel manuscript attributed to the monks of St. Columba, the Book of Kells. The book contains the elaborately hand-copied text of the four synoptic gospels—Matthew, Mark, Luke, and John. Each gospel is preceded by richly colored illustrated portraits of each evangelist. The book also abounds with Christian symbolism, including crosses, monograms of Christ, and images of the four tetramorphs representing the eponymous authors of the gospels.

The Viking Invasions

Sadly, the small renaissance of Celtic art came to an abrupt end with the arrival of Viking raiders in the late eighth century. Precious artworks were stolen, manuscripts destroyed, and reliquaries emptied of their remains. The Viking onslaught began with raids of monasteries in Lindisfarne and Dublin, and a new era of foreign invasions began.

Anam Cara: The Soul Friend

A custom unique to Celtic Christianity is the tradition of the anam cara. Anam cara is Gaelic for "soul friend," referring to a tradition that arose in the convents and monasteries of Ireland and Scotland. The anam cara was a lifelong platonic friend and spiritual guide who acted as a counselor and confessor and usually read the last rites of the deceased. As time went on, the idea became popular with the laity, who would have such a relationship with a member of the clergy.

The anam cara became indispensable to Celtic Christians; the anam cara was not simply a friend, but a soulmate who was one's connection to God. A ninth century story of St. Brigid of Kildare, recounted in the Martyrology of Oengus, illustrates the importance of the soul friend:

> *A young cleric of the community of Ferns, a foster son of Brigid's, used to come to her with wishes. He was with her in the refectory, to partake of food. Once after coming to communion she struck a clapper. "Well, young cleric there," said Brigid, "hast thou a soul friend?" "I have," replied the young cleric. "Let us sing his requiem," said Brigid, "for he has died. I saw when half thy portion had gone, that thy quota was put into thy trunk, and thou without any head on thee, for thy soulfriend died, and anyone without a soul friend is a body without a head; and eat no more till thou gettest a soul friend."*

This story shows that the spirit companion is so vital, one is considered imperiled without one. The anam cara's function wasn't just as a close friend, but as someone entrusted with the well-being of one's soul. The anam cara was vital to a healthy soul.

Nobody is quite certain where the concept of the soul friend originated. There is some speculation that the practice developed from traditions of the monasteries of the Eastern Church, where monks typically paired up to support one another's spiritual progress. Still others suggest the concept is a carryover from earlier pagan tradition, an adaptation of druid mentorship to fit the Christian demand for confession. Though this idea would have been unfamiliar to the Celts, it would have naturally been likened to the druid traditions of spiritual mentorship.

CHAPTER 6

The Divine Female

The most ancient and best-known deity of the Celts was the great mother goddess, who embodied the earth and represented fertility, abundance, and regeneration. She was the mother of the gods and the first ancestor of the people. The Celts were deeply concerned with the command of the female powers in both their aspects—the Celtic goddess could be a loving nurturer and provider, but she was also a violent warrior and a cruel enchantress.

The Three Mothers

The Celts had special reverence for the number three, and many of their important goddesses appeared in groups of three. One of the earliest groups of "triple" goddesses was the goddesses of motherhood known in Roman Britain as the deaes matres or matronae, the "mother goddesses." Icons of the matres have been found all over northwestern Europe. They invariably appear together, almost always seated in a row, often with breasts bared. The three are usually depicted as a younger woman flanked by older matrons, and they hold in their lap various symbols of nurture: breads, fruits, and meats, or cornucopias. They are also sometimes shown with nursing infants and accoutrements of motherhood such as diapers or bathing sponges.

FACT

The mothers are not the only deities to appear in threes in early Celtic iconography. The god Lugh was often portrayed as having three faces or even three heads, and the water goddess Coventina is often depicted in triple form.

There is some speculation the three mothers represent the three seasons and their fruits—spring, summer, and winter—or perhaps each is a seasonal aspect of a single goddess. The three mothers appear to have been tutelary deities, viewed as guardians of homes and communities.

Danu and the People of Danu

Little is known about the goddess Danu, the progenitor of the Irish gods. The gods are the Tuatha Dé Danann, the "People of Danu," yet very little is recorded about her other than her name. There is possibly some connection between the lack of mention of Danu and the conspicuous absence of Irish pagan creation stories. Danu might have had little function other than as an ancestress or creatrix, and her story may thus have been discarded by the Christian monks who recorded the myths of the Tuatha, as they preferred to portray them as ancestral humans rather than as deities in their own right.

Danu is related to the Welsh goddess Don, and possibly Anu/Ainu. There is some speculation that the river Danube is named for her. The roots of the names *Dana* and *Don* have connotations of wealth, abundance, and flowing water.

The Horse-Mothers

The horse was of incalculable value to the Celts. For 3,000 years, the horse served as a domestic animal in Western Europe and was hunted as a major source of sustenance for thousands of years before that. Horses provided meat, milk, transportation, and labor, and they were necessary to the survival of Celtic culture. Thus the horse was closely connected with divinity and was often venerated as a god on its own.

The mother-goddesses had many curious connections with horses, often appearing in iconography astride or alongside horses. This may have a connection with the idea of the goddess as consort to the ancient father-god, who was often depicted as a horse. Eventually, however, the goddess herself became more important, and the horse lessened in importance.

Epona: The Divine Mare

Though a number of Celtic goddesses were connected with horses, the most popular of these was Epona, whose name means "divine mare." Epona is almost invariably depicted with horses—often astride as a rider, sometimes enthroned like the Roman goddess Cybele, and occasionally as a mare and accompanying foal.

While most Celtic goddesses were connected to a specific locality, Epona's worship was widespread. In fact, Epona had the singular honor of being the only Celtic deity to be venerated within the borders of Rome itself. She is connected with fertility and prosperity, but above all, she is a protector of horses, donkeys, and other transport animals. Her image is found in stables everywhere, even in Rome and Greece. Epona was especially popular with the Roman cavalry.

Epona makes no appearances by that name in Ireland, but she is similar enough to the goddess Macha that is the two are sometimes assumed to be the same goddess. Macha is best-known from the tales of the Tuatha Dé Danann recounted in the Ulster Cycle, but even here she is closely associated with horses. Macha's win in a race against the king's horses precipitates her labor and death and begins the curse of the Ulstermen. Later, it is Macha's own horse who carries the hero Cuchulainn to his death on the battlefield and who mourns him afterward. Macha's name itself means "plain" or "pasture," a grazing spot.

ALERT!

Epona may have had early connections to the ancient Greek earth-goddess Demeter. There is evidence that in some early forms, Demeter was worshipped in the form of a mare.

The Morrigan

These Celtic earth goddesses were not sweet earth mothers by any means. While they represented the fertility of the land and the nurture of its people, they were often portrayed as harsh or even cruel, much like nature itself. A number of goddesses were associated with the sovereignty of the land, and most of these were also goddesses of war and death. They embodied the earth itself in both its positive and negative aspects.

The most famous of the goddesses of sovereignty was the Morrigan, whose name means "great queen" or "phantom queen." The Morrigan was of fearsome aspect, often appearing in the form of a carrion crow. She was primarily a goddess of war, ruler of the battlefield and the taker of fallen warriors. Despite the seeming contradiction, the Morrigan was also the goddess of fertility, cattle, and crops.

While it may seem a contradiction that a goddess of life and fertility would also be a goddess of war and death, it is actually an insight into the worldview of the Celts, who correctly observed that death was necessary for the generation of life. The Celts were most aware of natural cycles, and they ascribed mystical importance to the necessity of blood and decay as the sustenance of new life.

The rulership of kings was only by proxy, by authority of the goddess. Kings were symbolically wed to the goddess, and their mandate to rule depended on the whim of the earth—if the fertility of the land failed, or natural disasters struck, this could be seen as the goddess herself expressing displeasure with her earthly husband.

There is some debate over whether or not the Morrigan was one goddess with several aspects, or whether the name was a title applied to many goddesses. In any case, she is generally regarded as a triple goddess, most commonly as a trinity with Badb Catha, ("Battle Crow") and Macha ("Fury," also sometimes called Nemain, "Frenzied").

The Morrigan's earliest written appearance is in the stories of the Ulster Cycle. She first appears to the hero Cuchulainn, who catches her attempting to steal one of his cows. The hero does not recognize her, and in his attempt to prevent her taking the cow, he incites her to anger. She makes a prophecy of his death in battle, which comes to pass.

In the Tain bo Cuilainge, or Cattle Raid of Cooley, she first appears in the form of a crow to warn away the brown bull. Later, the Morrigan appears to Cuchulainn as a beautiful girl and attempts to seduce him, but he rejects her advances. This time, it is the scorned goddess herself who attempts to kill him, by first transforming into an eel, then a wolf, then a red heifer.

She is wounded each time by the hero, and finally she reappears in the form of a wounded elderly woman. Cuchulainn shows sudden compassion, and offers milk to the old woman, which heals her wounds. In gratitude, she makes a prophecy of the coming battle. In all versions of the story, the goddess appears as women in different stages of life, from maiden to old woman.

The Morrigan's guises of age appear connected with her various functions. As maiden, she appears as sovereignty, the ruling principle, and Cuchulainn's rejection can be seen as a rejection of sovereignty itself—his refusal to couple with the goddess may be directly responsible for his death in battle. As the crone, she is a seer, and a harbinger of death.

In direct contrast to Cuchulainn's encounter with sovereignty is Dagda's similar meeting. On the eve of the battle of Mag Tuireadh, the god encounters the goddess as a beautiful maiden washing in the river. He mates with her, and she predicts he will triumph over the Fomorians. The goddess even aids in that victory, appearing in the battlefield with an incantation that rallies the troops to victory: "Kings, arise to the battle!"

FACT

It is to Andraste, another form of the war-goddess, that the Celtic warrior queen Boudicca sacrificed hundreds of captive Roman women after her defeat of Roman troops.

In another telling, as Cuchulainn makes his way to the battlefield, he passes the Morrigan, who in the guise of an old woman is washing bloody garments in the river. When he asks what she is doing, she replies that she is washing the funeral clothes of the hero. In this guise, the Morrigan was called the "washer at the ford," and her appearance presaged death.

The Morrigan and her related goddesses are heavily associated with crows, birds of death and decay. In most versions of the death of Cuchulainn, his death on the battlefield is only recognized when a crow lands upon the hero's upright body. The Morrigan was ruler over the battlefield, and the heads of the slain were euphemistically referred to as "Morrigan's acorn crop," a likely reference to the ravens' habit of pecking out the eyes of the dead.

Morgan le Fay

A most curious figure in Arthurian legends is Morgan le Fay, or "Morgan of the Fairies," portrayed in the stories as the often evil half-sister of King Arthur. While the names of the two women do not appear to be linguistically related, their similarities are remarkable. Like the goddess, Morgan is filled with contradictions—she is Arthur's healer and protector, yet tries to kill him on a number of occasions. Both Morgan and the Morrigan are associated with crows, and Morgan takes on many of the initiatory aspects of the Morrigan.

Morgan has another connection to the Great Goddess through the Welsh Modron, "Mother." Modron was also married to a Urien and, like Morgan, had a son named Owain. Curiously, a tale of Modron repeats an old legend about the washer at the stream, wherein the lady is said to be under a curse until she bears a Christian son.

In her appearances in the Arthurian cycles, in a parallel of the older myth tales, Morgan assumes the role of sovereignty and mates with the young Arthur. It is Morgan who heals a wounded Arthur and gives him the magical protective scabbard that enables him to succeed in battle, and when scorned, she rescinds the gift, allowing him to become fatally wounded. In the end, Morgan receives the dying King and ferries him to Avalon.

The Cailleach

Another of the goddesses of sovereignty was Cailleach. Cailleach in Gaelic means "veiled," a reference to the habitual garb of an old woman. There are numerous appellations to the name Cailleach, such as Cailleach Bheara (Cailleach of Bheare, Scotland). This suggests that the name "Cailleach" may have been a nickname of sorts applied to local sovereignty goddesses.

The Cailleach is similar to goddesses like the Morrigan in many ways. She is connected with lakes and streams, and appears to have also been a goddess of sovereignty. Like the Morrigan, she appears in many stories attempting to seduce the hero, only the scenario is reversed, and Cailleach retains her haglike appearance. Like the other goddesses of sovereignty, Cailleachs are strongly associated with waterways, and she is said to be the source of many rivers and streams, as well as the guardian of wells.

The Loathly Lady

There are many instances in myth tales wherein the hero is challenged to kiss or even marry a hideous old hag, who is but a goddess in disguise. The courageous man is rewarded when she suddenly transforms into a beautiful maiden. Such is the story of Niall, son of Eochaid, who is named the rightful high king after daring to embrace the hag who taunts him from her well. This story, too, is carried over into Arthurian lore. In the tale of Peredur and other Arthurian romances, the knight Gawain, in order to save the life of the king, must marry a foul hag. Gawain, however, accepts his fate with good cheer, only to find his acceptance has broken a spell and his hideous wife is transformed into a beauty without parallel. In these tales, the "loathly lady" represents the goddess as sovereignty and all the responsibilities it entails.

Cerridwen

Another goddess who varied in aspect from maiden to crone was the Welsh Cerridwen, an enchantress who lived under a lake. Cerridwen's name is from roots meaning "fair poetry," and Cerridwen is a patron of poets and poetry. Cerridwen is also mother to the renowned bard Taliesin. Cerridwen was a trickster of sorts who took the appearance of a hag or a maiden, depending on her purpose, and who also had the power to shapeshift. She was the keeper of the cauldron of poetic inspiration, but guarded it jealously.

Brighid

One of the most widely worshipped of the Celtic goddesses was Brighid, a goddess of poetry, fire, healing waters, and inspiration. Brighid was the patron goddess of artisans of all kinds, including poets, smiths, and metalworkers. The name *Brighid* comes from a root with connotations of fire and heat, and may mean "fire arrow" or even "exalted one."

FACT

Brighid has a double connection to poets and their art. She is not only the goddess of poetry, but the mother of Oghma, the god of eloquence. Originally, she was Brigantia, the sovereignty goddess of the Brigantes, a powerful tribe of British Celts. It was in this form she was related to Minerva, both as a goddess of craftsmanship and of war.

The Irish Brighid was a triple goddess, the name belonging to not one but three daughters of the Dagda, each of whom had a separate specialty. As goddess of poetry, Brighid is sovereign over magic and is also associated with spoken enchantment, seership, and prophecy. Brighid as the goddess of fire ruled over the smith's fire as well as the hearth fire, and her temples contained a sacred flame watched over by a company of virgin priestesses, much like those of the temples of Vesta in Rome. This tradition was imitated by the nuns at Kildare, who kept a perpetual flame lit in honor of St. Brigid.

The Brighid of water was sovereign over healing baths and wells. In this form, she often appears as a hideous hag and may be related to Cailleach, who is also mentioned in the context of sacred wells. According to some sources, Brighid and the Cailleach are two sides of the same goddess, a young Brighid ruling over the summer months beginning with the festival of Imbolc, and Cailleach ruling the months of winter, from Samhuinn onward.

FACT

The name Kildare is from the Irish Cill-Dara, meaning "church of the oak." According to Irish Christian legend, the Abbess Brigid chose a location containing a gigantic oak tree as a site on which to found her abbey.

The ancient town of Kildare, Ireland, was once home to an ancient temple of Brighid. In later times, the site was home to the abbey of Brigid, who may have been a Catholic abbess or simply a Christianized remolding of the goddess. Evidence points to the latter, as the site is home to both a sacred well and an eternal flame, and is sited on the former location of a temple dedicated to the goddess.

Giraldus Cambrensis gives an account of his visit to Kildare in 1185, in which he describes the perpetual fires kept there in Brighid's honor:

At Kildare, in Leinster, celebrated for the glorious Brigid, many miracles have been wrought worthy of memory. Among these, the first that occurs is the fire of St. Brigid, which is reported never to go out. Not that it cannot be extinguished, but the nuns and holy women tend and feed it, adding fuel with such watchful and diligent care, that from the time of the Virgin, it has continued burning through a long course of years; and although such heaps of wood have been consumed during this long period, there has been no accumulation of ash.

At the time of St. Brigid, twenty nuns were engaged in the Lord's warfare, she herself being the twentieth; after her glorious departure, nineteen have always formed the society, the number having never increased. Each of them has the care of the fire for a single night, the last nun, having heaped wood upon the fire, says: "Brigid take charge of your own fire; for this night belongs to you." She then leaves the fire, and in the morning it is found that the fire has not gone out, and that the usual quantity of fuel has been used.

The fire is surrounded by a hedge, made of stakes and brushwood, and forming a circle, within which no male can enter; and if any one should presume to enter, which has been sometimes attempted by rash men, he will not escape the divine vengeance. Moreover, it is only lawful for women to blow the fire, fanning it or using bellows only, and not with their breath.

It seems quite certain that the practice which Cambrensis describes is a very ancient one, and almost certainly initiated by the priestesses of the Great Goddess. Especially telling is the prohibition against men near the sacred fires, and the promise of divine vengeance that Cambrensis so innocently attributes to the Christian God.

CHAPTER 7

The Divine Male

The Celts had numerous male deities, so many that only the names and attributes of a fraction of their number are known. The gods of the Gauls were various. Although many were bound to localities or tribes, a number were probably viewed as universal and were popular throughout the Celtic territories. The Romans recognized these gods as identical to their own (although the Gauls may not have felt that way). Some of these early Gaulish gods remain mysterious, with little more known than their names. A few remained popular and became part of the Gaelic and Brythonic pantheons.

Dagda: The Good God

Dagda, or "The Good God" was the preeminent Irish god, the father and ruler of the Tuatha Dé Danann, although due to archaeological evidence, he is assumed to be an older, assimilated deity. The Dagda was also called Eochaid Ollathair, "Great Father Horse," and In Ruad Rofhessa, "The Red One of Great Knowledge," with *red* most likely referring to the Dagda's sunburned complexion. The Dagda is not called "good" in reference to his benevolence but in regard to his many skills in fighting, singing, games, and sport.

The Dagda possessed three magical accoutrements. The best-known was his gigantic, phallic club, which had the power to kill with one blow—although when reversed, a strike with the handle could return the dead to life. The club was reportedly so large that it needed to be dragged about on a wheeled cart.

He also owned an equally large cauldron called Coire Ansic, "Undry," which was always filled with whatever one desired to eat and which could never be emptied. This cauldron housed the invincible Spear of Lugh when it was not in use.

The Dagda's third and most prized possession was Daurdabla, his magical harp, which had the power to bring great joy, great sorrow, or profound prophetic sleep.

The appetites of the Dagda were large. When it came to food or women, he was insatiable. During the wars with the Fomorians, the Dagda sought audience with them in order to stall their war-making plans while the Tuatha Dé Danann rallied to arms. The Fomorians were no fools, and hearing of his great love of porridge, arranged to have a gigantic bowl filled with porridge, into which they threw many animals—hundreds of sheep, pigs, and cows. A guest was expected to eat all he was offered or risk a grave insult to his host—which the Fomorians were hoping for. The Dagda had the last laugh, however; he pulled out his gigantic spoon and set to work, devouring every last drop in very little time.

The Dagda liked women as much as he liked food, and he went to great lengths to be with women he desired, even those who belonged to others. One of his great risks was going after the goddess Boann, the wife of Elcmar.

To accomplish this, he simply stopped time. Their tryst had an unintended consequence, however, and Boann became pregnant. To avoid being caught by an angry husband, the Dagda had to keep time at a standstill until nine months were up and his son was born. This child was Aenghus, the god of love, who due to the circumstance of his birth was called "forever young."

Aenghus, the God of Love

The Celtic god of love and health was known by various names. He was Aenghus mac Og, "Son of Youth," to the Irish, and Mabon ap Modron, "Youth, Son of the Mother" to the Welsh.

Aenghus and his equivalents were very different from the average Celtic god. While the typical Celtic deity, even a poet, was invariably portrayed as a brawny, mustached warrior, the god of eternal youth was depicted as a beardless young man or a small child.

The Welsh equivalent of Aenghus is the youth-god Mabon ap Modron, also the son of a water goddess and also associated with love and healing. Mabon was a favorite in medieval Welsh romances and appears as a character in many early Arthurian tales. There is some evidence that medieval Welsh poets identified the youthful deity with the infant Jesus.

Aenghus was the ruler over the Neolithic tomb at Newgrange, viewed by the Irish as the home of the god and an entrance to the Otherworld. The nearby river Boyne is named for the rover goddess Boann, his mother. The circumstances of Aenghus's birth are quite peculiar—he is the product of an affair between Boann, a river goddess, and Dagda. In order to keep the pregnancy secret, the Dagda halted the sun for the term of the goddess's pregnancy, and so Aenghus was born out of time. He was fostered either by Midir or by Manannan mac Lir, depending on the source.

Aenghus is closely associated with water birds, and both he and his bride Caer had the ability to take on the form of swans.

Gods of Light and Art

Of the Gaulish gods who enjoyed wide recognition, only a few remained popular by the time the Celts had receded to the British Isles. These were Lugos, who became Lugh, god of arts and craftsmanship, and Ogmios, who remained throughout the god of eloquence and poetic skill, called Oghma by the Irish.

Belenos

Belenos (sometimes Belenus) was an early Gallic sun god, about whom very little is known. To the Welsh, he was Beli Mawr. The festival of Belenos was Beltaine, held on the first of May to mark the beginning of summer.

Belenos was identified with the Greek Apollo, as the driver of a vast horse-drawn sunwagon. The emblems of Belenos were the lightning bolt, the wagon, and the solar wheel. Like many of the early Celtic father-gods, Belenos was closely associated with horses. Belenos represented the light and heat of the sun, and in later times, he was associated with healing hot springs and baths.

ALERT!

It can often get confusing trying to keep straight which Celtic deities ruled what and to which classical gods they corresponded. It is important to keep in mind that the gods did not always have the same aspects in every area they were worshipped, and that different cultures within the Celtic milieu stressed some over others.

Lugh

Irish mythology often revolves around the forces of light and darkness and their constant struggle for control. Unlike other such worldviews, however, the Irish appear to have embraced both the light and the darkness. One deity who embodies this dualistic view was the Gallic god Lugos, eventually known to the Irish as Lugh and to the Welsh as Lleu.

The god Lugos was very popular with the Gauls, and several ancient cities were named for him. Lugos was a god of light and had affinities with both Mercury and Apollo. Lugos could be considered a sun god, but he was also a god of industry and art. Lugos above all the Celtic gods was most often associated with Mercury, to the extent that in some areas, the two gods became completely identified. Lugo's icons were ravens and dogs.

Lugos may have had a triple aspect, as some older images depict him with three heads or faces. Some scholars have even suggested that Lugos was not a single god, but a trinity of sorts—the god Esus, Taranis, and Teutates as one triune deity. There is also a possible connection between an epithet of the Irish Lugh ("Fierce Striker") and the ancient nameless hammer god.

FACT

With the coming of Christianity, Lugos was associated with the archangel Michael, who was also considered to have solar affinities. Many of the sacred places once dedicated to Lugos were rededicated to the angel.

In a commentary on the Celtic reverence for a deity he referred to as Mercury, but who was certainly Lugos, Caesar remarked:

> . . . of all the gods they most worship is Mercury. He has the largest number of images, and they regard him as the inventor of all the arts, as their guide on the roads and in travel, and as chiefly influential in making money and in trade.

Lugos was one of the few Gaulish gods to transition into the Irish and British pantheons—as Lugh, he became one of the Tuatha Dé Danann. His feast day, Lughnasadh, was held on the first of August. Lugh was a god of intellect, a patron of craftsmanship and skill. In mythological stories he wins many battles of wit and makes many displays of cleverness. The legend of Lugh's entry into the Tuatha Dé Danann tells that he was refused admittance unless he could demonstrate a unique skill. He demonstrated his abilities as a smith, a warrior, a poet, a magician, and a harpist, but each time was told the tribe had someone with each of these skills. Clever Lugh asked if they had one who can do all of these at once, and stumped, the gods had to allow him to join them. Lugh quickly earned their respect, however, and even became their chief.

In Welsh mythology, Lugos became Lleu, the brother of Dylan and the son of the goddess Arianrhod. Lleu's aspects are essentially the same as Lugh's, and both are connected to agriculture and the calendar, but their personal mythologies and relationships differ.

Ogmios

Ogmios is a bit odd even in the unusual Celtic pantheon. He was one of the ancient Celtic gods, known as Ogmios to the Gauls and Oghma to the Irish. In ancient times, Ogmios was depicted with the bald-front tonsure of a druid and a grinning countenance, often carrying aloft a gigantic club. In many appearances, he appears with a train of men following behind him, attached to him (often, to his tongue) by chains. He is sometimes called Ogmios sun-face and appears wizened or sunburned.

There are further records of the god in medieval Ireland, where he is referred to as the Oghma, a heroic member of the Tuatha Dé Danann and the son of Brigid, the goddess of poetry and fire. Oghma, like his predecessor, was a god of language and a patron of bards. Ogmios's words weren't just useful for leading men, however. Gaulish artifacts invoking the god are often in the form of appeals asking the god to curse enemies and bind lovers. Oghma is credited with the creation of the Ogham alphabet, an Irish alphabet used mainly for inscriptions that began appearing around the fifth century. The medieval Book of Ballymote contains a tract on the letters and their mytholical origin.

> *The father of Ogham was Oghma;*
> *The mother of Ogham was the hand or knife of Oghma.*

The excerpt implies that Oghma was a god not only of words but of artistry. It connects the act of speaking with the creative impetus behind craftmanship and the relationship between word and action. It also calls to mind several instances in mythological tales about the god, where the ogham are used magically to locate or bind, abilities ascribed to the eloquence of Oghma. In Celtic mythology, magic, artisanship, and eloquence are always linked.

Gods of Blood and War

Several Gaulish gods are generally considered to have been universally worshipped throughout Celtic territories. Caesar also briefly mentions many of them, but instead of calling them by their Celtic names he falls back on the Roman habit of calling foreign gods by Roman names. Caesar refers to six of these gods, three of which he identifies as Jupiter, Mars, and Mercury.

Of the six, three are mentioned in the poet Lucan's epic *Pharsalia*, which describes Caesar's campaigns in Gaul. These are Taranis, Teutates, and Esus, whom Lucan describes as savage and cruel deities whose altars are soaked with blood. Lucan was probably using more than a little poetic license, but the gist of it was true.

Taranis

Taranis is in all likelihood the Gaulish god whom Caesar equated with the Roman Jupiter in his writings on the Gallic Wars. The sole mention of Taranis by name in this context is by Lucan, who mentions him as one of three gods to whom human sacrifices were given. Lucan claims that victims were given to each god, killed in a manner appropriate for that god. Victims sacrificed to Taranis were reportedly burned, as would befit a god of lightning and fire. It is often speculated that the Wicker Man sacrifices described by Caesar might have been carried out under the auspices of Taranis.

Taranis is unmistakably a sky god. While he is often pictured riding across the heavens in a great chariot, he is less a god of the sun than a god of thunder. The main emblems of Taranis are his wheel, which he often holds aloft, and a thunderbolt. The name Taranis comes from a root meaning "thunder," and he is closely related to the Norse god Thor. It was to Taranis that the collected heads of the slain were dedicated.

Esus, The Lord

The second of the bloodthirsty gods mentioned by Lucan was Esus or Hesus, whose name literally means "lord." Little is known about this god, but the few remaining images of Esus depict him dressed as a woodsman, usually in the act of cutting down a willow tree. Sometimes, he appears to be emerging from the tree itself. Another emblem associated with Esus is the Tarvos Trigaranus, a bull accompanied by three cranes riding on its back, who appears to be a sacrificial figure associated with the willow tree.

Esus was closely connected to trees, and according to the same source, his victims were hung from trees and bled, with the direction of the runoff reportedly interpreted as an omen. This is evocative of rites to the Norse Odin, who may have originated as a Gaulish god. In the Norse Havamal, or sayings of Odin, a similar rite of sacrifice is mentioned, only with a twist—in order to gain the magical rune alphabet, Odin is sacrificed to himself.

Esus may also be connected to the legend of the Green Man, or forest spirit, the ever-present personification of the wildlands, or, in later tales, to the mysterious character called the "Man in the Tree," or Derg Corra. Some have also speculated that there is a connection between Esus and Cuchulainn, the hero of the Tuatha Dé Danann. An episode wherein Cuchulainn fells a tree is often cited as evidence of a connection.

Strangely, Esus's appellation "Lord," his self-sacrifice, and his iconic relation to trees caused both druids and Christians alike to associate him with Jesus, a rather strange comparison that continued to be made hundreds of years later. Even more strangely, images of Esus are often littered with nautical symbols—anchors, sea birds, and so on—and one of the best-preserved monuments in his honor was erected by ancient sailors in France, called the Pilier des Nautes, "Pillar of the Sailors." Commenters on the Pharsalia have equated Esus with both Mercury and Mars.

Tuetates

The third god Lucan mentions is Teutates, a god of war. Teutates (also Teutatis and Teutanos) was often associated with the Roman Mars. Lucan records that those victims sacrificed to Teutates were drowned in cauldrons, bringing to mind the ancient tales of the resurrection of warriors through the waters of the cauldron of life. Teutates is referred to in some accounts in the plural, which has led to speculation that there were multiple instances of the god who may have been tribal patrons or protectors.

Cernunnos and the Forest Gods

The most mysterious of the Celtic deities are the mostly nameless lords of the hunt. Foremost of these is the antlered deity dubbed Cernunnos, a Romanized Gaulish appellation taken from a small handful of inscriptions, only one of which is associated with an image. Cernunnos simply means "The Horned One"; his Celtic name or names are unknown, although there are some clues to his identity.

Cernunnos was likely not one but many deities who shared similar attributes. He appears in art almost invariably as a stag-antlered man, seated in a cross-legged pose among the animals and plants of the forest. He is associated with animals of the forest, symbols of the Otherworld. Both snakes and stags are emblems of renewal and rebirth—as the snake sheds its skin and is reborn, so too does the stag throw off its antlers, only to form new ones in the spring. The Horned One then could be viewed as not only a god of resurrection, but also of death, and could be looked upon as a guardian of the Otherworld.

The snake which accompanies Cernunnos and other Celtic deities is something of a mystery. Snakes in general are associated with fertility, death, and regeneration or healing. Cernunnos' serpent is no ordinary snake but a particular oddity known as a horned or ram-head serpent, sporting a pair of curved horns. Horned snakes (in Celtic iconography) are often associated with healing, especially healing springs.

Cernunnos was a god of fertility and hunting. He appears to have been the most widely worshipped of the Celtic deities, if not a supreme deity—

although strangely enough, the body of Celtic mythology that remains is entirely silent on the antlered god. Cernunnos may have been carried over into Irish mythology as Fionn, a deity who is very closely associated with deer and hunting.

QUESTION?

Is Cernunnos a representation of the devil?
The depiction of the Christian devil as a horned figure is no coincidence. As Christianity swept westward over the former domains of the Celtic gods, many monuments and temples were abandoned to the elements. In medieval times, these images of a serpent-entwined deity took on a sinister significance and were looked upon as images of Satan.

One of the most famous depictions of Cernunnos is among the mythological scenes depicted on the Gundestrup cauldron, where he sits cross-legged among birds, deer, and other animals. He wears a torque, a circular choker with open, decorated ends that is an emblem of sovereignty, and holds another in his right hand. In his left, he grasps a horned serpent, an emblem of fertility. The torque suggests a connection with sovereignty.

The worship of Cernunnos may be ancient, as Neolithic burial sites have revealed the burials of tribal priests buried in antlered costumes, often in the same cross-legged pose in which Cernunnos appears in later stone carvings. Images of antlered men and gods also appear in very early stone pictographs, and some are presumed to represent the deity. Figures of (presumed) shamanic figures wearing antlered garb appear in ecstatic poses on cave paintings from as far back as 10,000 B.C.E.

In later Roman period carvings, Cernunnos appears to be associated with material wealth and prosperity, perhaps a god of commerce. He is pictured as an enthroned character whose lap overflows with acorns, nuts, and even gold coins, or surrounded by overflowing cornucopias. He is often flanked by images of the Roman gods Apollo and Mercury, whose attributes he probably shared.

The Green Man/Derg Corra

A mysterious character who appears in tales connected with the god Fionn is Derg Corra, ("Man in the Tree"). He is a symbol of wisdom, closely connected, like Fionn, with the stag. He is described as a curious character who sometimes goes about "on the shanks of a deer," but is described in the tale of Fionn as seated in a tree, with a raven on his shoulder and a deer at his feet. He carries a bronze cup with a salmon and shares among his companions various fruits of wisdom. Derg Corra is an obvious personification of the forest and its creatures, perhaps an embodiment of the tree of life itself. His creatures represent all of the domains of earth—a bird for the sky, a stag for the land, and a salmon to represent the waters.

There is every reason to believe that this ancient forest deity is directly related to the phenomenon known as the Green Man. Scarcely a medieval building anywhere of any note is without one or more representations of the Green Man in its decorations—in some cases, dozens may be found worked in stone, carved into the woodwork, and hidden amongst more ordinary decorations. The most common appearance of the Green Man is found carved in wood or stone. He is a great foliate creature, with a face made entirely of leaves and vines, often with wild tendrils sprouting from his mouth. His look is often wild and staring, and he appears to be the absolute embodiment of unfettered natural force.

Manannan mac Lir

Manannan mac Lir, or "Manannan, son of sea" was the Irish god of the sea, and especially connected with the Isle of Man, which is named for him. He was peripherally a member of the Tuatha Dé Danann but most likely predates the majority of the Irish pantheon. Manannan seems to have been a psychopomp, and at one point was counted as a ruler of the Otherworld Mag Mell or Emain Afallach.

FACT

Manannan was a bit of a trickster, often visiting disaster on unsuspecting victims. Most of the stories in which he is a central character revolve around plots of trickery; in one instance, he tricks King Cormac out of his own children. In the end, though, when the lesson is learned, the god returns everything to order.

Manannan's accoutrements include a goblet of truth, which breaks if three lies are told over it and is magically restored when the truth is spoken over it three times. He also owns a magical ship that sails without sails, and a magical cloak of invisibility that can draw down a covering mist. Manannan, like most rulers of the Otherworlds, owns a cauldron of never-ending plenty and a magical white horse that can travel as easily over water as over land.

CHAPTER 8

The Otherworld

The Celtic Otherworld was unlike most others of the ancient world. The Celtic Otherworld was at the same time the abode of the gods and the land of the dead. It was a contradictory place, existing both in the world and far from it. It was a place of happiness and eternal youth, yet it was sometimes perceived as transitory, a temporary abode between mortal lives. It was a place of joy and plenty to the dead who dwelt there, yet it was a curse to mortals who chanced to stray beyond its borders because they would find themselves enchanted, while the outside world passed them by.

Beyond the Visible

In earlier times, the Otherworld was described as a land of origin, the magical homeland of the divine ancestors of the Irish people. The Irish Otherworld was Tir Na Nog, the "Land of Youth," which was originally located on an island far to the west, and from which the Tuatha Dé Danann came when they migrated to Ireland. It was a land of powerful magic, inhabited by powerful druids who were the source of the gods' tremendous skill and learning.

FACT

The entrances to the Otherworld were said to be hidden throughout the landscape, an idea that persisted long after the coming of Christianity and even lingers today. One could stay too long in the forest, or slumber too long beneath a particular tree, and find oneself in the realm of the fairy—yet the Otherworld was remarkably resistant to intentional attempts at trespass.

In later accounts, the Otherworld was said to exist concurrently alongside the mortal realm, inaccessible to most by virtue of the powerful magic that made it invisible to mortal eyes. A veil of invisibility kept all but the most determined from finding its entrances, although some occasionally found their way in by happenstance. Many a tale tells of the hero who penetrates the veil, only to return to discover friends and family long dead and the world unrecognizable.

Annwn

To the Welsh, the Otherworld was Annwn, also a land of youth and plenty. Annwn was ruled by Arawn or Gwynn ap Nudd, equivalent to the Irish Nuada. Annwn was said to be accessible only through death or through a single door accessible one day a year, located at Glastonbury Tor.

The door to Annwn may of course be an allusion to the feast of Samhain, the solar feast day on which the doorway to the underworld was believed to lay open. The name Annwn means "deep" or "under earth."

The chief treasure of Annwn was its cauldron, which overflowed with an abundance of plenty, an object similar to the Irish Cauldron of Plenty. One of the earliest Arthurian tales, "The Spoils of Annwn," concerns a fateful quest for the cauldron, from which only seven men return.

The Welsh story of Annwn was probably the genesis of the Arthurian legend of Avalon, and the cauldron appears to be an early pagan version of the tale of the Holy Grail. Christians seem to have some difficulty with the concepts of the Otherworld, as many tales attempt to reconcile belief in the old pagan concepts of the afterlife. In one Christianized tale of Annwn, Gwyn ap Nudd is given dominion over the demons in order to prevent them from overtaking the earth.

Annwn came to be called Avalon, the name by which the Otherworld is most commonly known today. The name Avalon is believed to derive from the Welsh Ynys Afallach, "Isle of Apples," a reference to the abundant fruit of the Otherworld. According to Arthurian legends, Avalon was both a place of healing and the final resting place of the king. Strangely, Arthur is accompanied to his final rest by his treacherous sister Morgan le Fey—who may be a version of the Morrigan, the Celtic goddess of death—a fitting escort for a king who ends his life in battle. Arthur was first connected to Avalon by twelfth century chronicler Geoffrey of Monmouth, who also identified it as the birthplace of Arthur's magical sword Excalibur.

FACT

Another tradition claims Arthur's burial to be at Glastonbury, an idea not as contradictory as it seems. Avalon was, after all, conceived to be an island, and Glastonbury at one time had the appearance of an island, with its great Tor arising from a wetland. Also notable is the continued presence of ancient apple orchards at the site.

The Sidhe-Mounds

When the Iron Age Celts came upon remnants of their Stone Age predecessors, they imagined their imposing monuments and tombs as doorways to the underworld. These tombs and earth mounds were referred to as Sidhe, and eventually, the name for these ancient sites became synonymous with the gods who inhabited them. These were the Tuatha Dé Danann, the race of gods led underground by the Dagda upon the arrival of the conquering Milesian Celts.

ALERT!

Nobody is certain whether the Irish gods were associated with the underground from the beginning or if the existence of the Sidhe inspired the idea, but the places are considered the abode of the gods in most accounts thereafter.

With the ascendancy of Christianity, the Otherworld gods passed into legend. They metamorphosed into the fairy-folk, and their domain became a place of enchantment and even trickery, where mortals were enticed to neglect their responsibilities for idylls from which some never returned. Eventually, the land of eternal youth came to be viewed as a pitfall, a danger to be avoided, inhabited by malicious spirits and even demons.

Tir Na Nog

The chief Irish Otherworld was called Tir na Nog, "Land of the Always Young." Tir na Nog was difficult to reach, at least for humans—animals could seemingly cross over at will. Tir Na Nog is described variously as a distant land, far over the western seas, and as one that was also located in the same place as the ordinary world, but magically hidden so that it was only accessible through magic, chance, or by invitation from one of its residents. In Tir na Nog, there is no illness, no aging, and no death. Everyone is eternally young and beautiful, and there is an endless supply of food and drink.

Mag Mell

Another variation of the land of the dead in Ireland was Mag Mell, the "Plain of Joy," an underwater realm ruled by the sea god, Manannan mac Lir. Like Tir Na Nog, Mag Mell was inhabited by the spirits of the dead and visited by the living, even an occasional Christian monk. Mag Mell features in tales of the hero Bran and in the adventures of St. Brendan.

Hy-Brasil

A later name for the Irish Otherworld was Breasil, or Hy-Brasil, "Princely Isle," or "the Isle of the Blessed." According to Irish myth, the island belonged to the sea god, Manannan mac Lir. Like the Greek Elysium, Breasil was a place of rest and eternal youth.

FACT

According to legend, Breasil spent most of its existence underwater. It appeared above the surface only once every seven years although it could be fixed in place by fire. A typical tale recounts that the island was forced to remain in place for a time after being pinned by a fiery arrow.

During the Middle Ages, it was generally accepted that Breasil was a real island to the west of Ireland, and it was even added to a number of maps. There were numerous accounts of visits there, all filled with fanciful detail. Belief in the mythical island was so strong it influenced the naming of a country on the other side of the world. When explorer Pedro Alvares spotted South America for the first time, he named it Brasil for the mythical island he may have believed he had discovered.

Oisin and Niamh

Oisin, or "Little Deer," was the son of the hero Fionn and the doe Sabd, a legendary hero and poet in his own right. Oisin played a peculiar role in Irish mythology, a reconciler of pagan and Christian wisdom. It is Oisin who recounts to St. Patrick the glories of the Otherworld and the heroics of the Fianna, long after they have passed. He tells Patrick of his journey to the Otherworld, where he has lived 300 years while time has passed him by.

Oisin's journey begins while he is on a hunting trip with his father, Fionn. The hunting party spies a strange, beautiful queen astride a white horse. She announces that she is Niamh, the daughter of the king of Tir na Nog, and has traveled a long distance, all to declare her love for Oisin. Oisin, struck by her beauty, is instantly smitten. He agrees to follow her anywhere she might go, even before she describes her home as a place of beauty, abundance, and eternal youth and wellness:

Delightful is the land beyond all dreams,
Fairer than anything your eyes have ever seen.
There all the year the fruit is on the tree,
And all the year the bloom is on the flower.
There with wild honey drip the forest trees;
The stores of wine and mead shall never fail.
Nor pain nor sickness knows the dweller there,
Death and decay come near him never more.

Oisin accompanies his fairy bride on her magical horse to the Otherworld, which is reached by sea. The Otherworld is just as she has described, a place of eternal merrymaking and pleasures, but after three years, Oisin grows weary of the place. Homesick, he tells his bride he desires to return home. She acquiesces, telling him that time has passed much more quickly in the mortal realm. She gives him her horse to ride and warns him never to dismount. He returns to find his father's estates a ruin and the Fianna no more than a legend. Saddened, he makes ready to return to Niamh, when he spies some men struggling to move a great stone from their cropland. He stoops to assist, but his saddle breaks, and he is thrown to the ground, whereupon he instantly ages 300 years. Niamh's horse returns to Tir na Nog without him, and the astonished farmers bring the now feeble old man to

St. Patrick, who shelters him. Oisin is not easily won over, either. When Patrick observes him pining, Oisin snappishly remarks that he will convert if Patrick's heaven is half as good as his own Otherworld.

St. Patrick's Purgatory/The Journey to Purgatory

The pagan faith of the Irish may have faded fairly quickly, but belief in the Otherworld remained strong. A popular pilgrimage for Irish Catholics through the Middle Ages and even today is to a tiny island on Lough Derg ("Red Lake") in the northwest of Ireland, where pilgrims flock to visit "St. Patrick's Purgatory," the place where St. Patrick reputedly experienced visions of heaven and hell. The usual legend of Lough Derg and the saint claims that Patrick received a vision of purgatory while sleeping in the island's cave. The story is probably apocryphal, as there were no known connections to the island until long after the saint's death.

FACT

Originally, the tale of the purgatory cave, right down to the details of the epic struggle with the sea monster, was attributed to St. Brendan. The protagonist of the story was later switched to St. Patrick, as it probably made the then-lucrative pilgrimage more attractive.

Every year, pilgrims visit the lake's tiny Station Island, site of an ancient monastery, where they fast and pray while walking circuits around the ruins of the ancient hermits' cells. The actual site of Patrick's alleged vision, however, is believed to be a cave on nearby Saints' Island.

The earliest known reference to St. Patrick's purgatory is in *The Treatise on St. Patrick's Purgatory*, the late twelfth century work of Gilbert, a Cistercian monk who recounts the tale as told to him by a fellow monk named Owain who visited the Otherworld on the site and survived to tell of it.

According to Gilbert's tale, Owain was once a knight of ill repute who lived a life of greed, violence, and immorality. He journeys to the island to repent of his sins. After many days of rites and preparation, he enters the cave, where he stumbles around in the dark until he eventually spies a glimmer of light. He follows the light as it brightens, and passes through to what is described as purgatory but is more reminiscent of the Otherworld. There he encounters two men in white robes and shaved heads—it is unclear if they are monks or even druids—who tell him how to prepare for an onslaught of evil spirits to come. Most importantly, they warn, he must not turn back before the journey is complete.

Owain continues onward and encounters a nightmare landscape filled with devils, demons, and anguished souls in torment. Owain follows the instructions of his mysterious teachers, using prayer to save himself from one peril after another, as the demons torment him and continually urge him to return home. Eventually, Owain encounters the gates of paradise, and his experiences there leave him wishing to be a new man. He not only repents of his former life but abandons it wholly to enter the monastery.

Amongst the Christian imagery are more hints of the story's ancient pagan origins. Patrick's purgatory is accessed not through death but via a mysterious mode of travel. The most telling detail is the appearance of paradise. It is a fortress of glass, an idea with no parallel in Christian mythology but with plenty in Celtic paganism. The traditional entrance to the Otherworld in Welsh mythology was Caer Wydr, the Tower of Glass.

The story of Owain's journey is followed by many others, most of which follow the same basic formula. A penitent would enter an underground cave or chamber on the island, and in the dark he would be overcome by sleep, during which he would have visions of purgatory and its inhabitants. Many of these followed the formula of *Dante's Inferno*, with successive levels of punishments for different degrees of sinfulness.

In later times, the tale of purgatory was conflated with the legend of St. Patrick, and Owain was all but forgotten as the island became a hugely popular destination for pilgrims wishing to recreate the visionary experience.

Purgatory is not the island's only connection to the Otherworld. According to local legend, it was in this lake that St. Patrick fought and defeated a water monster placed there by Fionn mac Cumhaill himself. The blood of the monster supposedly gives the lake its red coloration. By some accounts, Patrick was said to have driven the infamous snakes of Ireland to this lake— at the same time, it was also supposedly the last colony of Ireland's druids.

These stories, very odd for Christian tales, are almost certainly reworked from older legends. Even if the loch was the site of a showdown between Christians and druids, the connotation of the place as otherworldly has remained. Lough Derg is also where the children of Lir were said to have ended their enchantment, and some Celtic scholars speculate that rites in honor of the god Aenghus were conducted on the island in ancient times. The spot crops up in a number of Arthurian stories as well, where it is conflated with the pagan Otherworld.

Near the end of the fifteenth century, the cave was sealed, on the order of the pope, after a Dutch monk complained he had visited the site and found it to be an ordinary cave. Ironically, the cave was closed on St. Patrick's Day, 1497. Pilgrimages continue to a neighboring island, but the current location of the cave is unknown. Curiously, visitors today are not permitted to bring cameras or recording equipment on the lake.

The Wild Hunt

A particularly persistent Otherworld legend that survived into Christian times was the theme of the wild hunt, or "fairy raid," a myth that appeared in numerous European cultures. The Wild Hunt was led by a hunter whose identity varied from one region to the next—sometimes it was Nudd, sometimes a goddess, sometimes even King Arthur. The hunt is a wild stampede of horses, dogs, and riders who tumble out of the Otherworld in a wild procession, followed by animals of the forest, fairies, and spirits of the dead. The procession is spectral and fierce, with its participants often described as red-eyed, flaming, even flesh devouring.

One particularly detailed account of a local legend comes from twelfth-century historian Walter Mapp, who recounts the appearance of the ghostly host under the command of a former king:

> The nocturnal companies and squadrons, too, which were called of Herlethingus, were sufficiently well-known appearances in England down to the time of Henry II, our present lord. They were troops engaged in endless wandering, in an aimless round, keeping an awe-struck silence, and in them many persons were seen alive who were known to have died. This household of Herlethingus was last seen in the marches of Wales and Hereford in the first year of the reign of Henry II, about noonday: they traveled as we do, with carts and sumpter horses, pack-saddles and panniers, hawks and hounds, and a concourse of men and women. Those who saw them first raised the whole country against them with horns and shouts, and . . . because they were unable to wring a word from them by addressing them, made ready to extort an answer with their weapons. They, however, rose up into the air and vanished on a sudden.

The wild hunt is sometimes called "the fairy raid," but the basic elements are pretty much universal. A seated rider, be it goddess, wild man, ghost, or fairy, leads a wild procession of animals and specters that kills, destroys, or devours everything in its path.

The hunt retained its appeal through Christian times, and later versions of the hunt include cursed or damned characters from Christian legends, from biblical villains to kings or priests who made poor choices in life. One such tale describes the misfortune of Hans von Hackelnberg, a huntsman for the Duke of Brunswick, who is condemned to lead the wild ride until Judgment Day as punishment for hunting on Sundays.

FACT

One leader of the hunt was the British wild man called Herne the Hunter. Herne was a forest spirit, strongly associated with deer. He was almost certainly related to the ancient fertility gods of the forest, perhaps even Cernunnos himself. Herne is portrayed as a male rider with the antlers (and sometimes even the head) of a deer.

The leaders of the hunt can be viewed as fertility spirits, representations of unrestrained sexuality. In earlier times, the wild hunt was associated with fertility cults, but in Christian times it became a symbol of the devil at work, which perhaps highlights the differing sexual attitudes of pagans and Christians. To the former, the sexual urge is wild, chaotic, and celebrated, while to the Christians it is fearsome, demonic, and strange.

CHAPTER 9

Celtic Art and Symbols

There are very few written records of Celtic mythology. The little that can be surmised about the Celts and their religious beliefs and practices must be pieced together from the surviving mythology and from the abundance of icons and symbols they so generously left behind for us to decipher. Celtic iconography abounds with symbols of spirit, emblems of gods and goddesses, and images from mythological tales. The task is to gather these scattered threads in an attempt to reconstruct the rich tapestry of Celtic spirituality.

Knotwork (Celtic Interlace)

The winding, interlaced design motifs known today as Celtic knotwork are some of the most recognizable Celtic symbols. The complex, winding designs, in a variety of abstract, human, and animal shapes, are found in ancient stone carvings, tattoos, and in the illuminated manuscripts of the Celtic monasteries. Today, the ancient designs continue to resonate, and they are equally likely to be found on bumper stickers, key chains, and coffee cups. A cottage industry has sprung up around knotwork symbols that stand for any number of modern concepts.

ALERT!

A great number of gift shops, books, and websites purport to offer a Celtic knot for just about any meaning or purpose one could imagine, mostly for the purpose of selling trinkets or symbolic tattoos. It is important to remember that to the ancients, the symbolism was ritualized and religious. Consequently, they did not create symbols for concepts of eternal love, sisterhood, faith, or any of the other myriad modern meanings assigned by modern folks.

While the ancient interlace designs had an obvious connection with religious belief, their exact meanings have been lost. The contiguous looping and twining of the designs suggest eternal continuity. Motifs of entangled people, animals, and foliage most likely represented the interconnectedness, rebirth, and interdependency of the natural elements, reflecting the Celtic worldview that life was in a constant state of flux and renewal. Recurring themes in knotwork include hunters

A typical Celtic knot.

entangled with their prey, animals with their natural enemies, and lovers entwined—the fates of all eternally bound together.

In the Christian era, there is evidence the symbols may have been used for talismanic purposes, protecting against evil forces. Designs used in scriptures and on Christian monuments carried over some of this symbolism, although in many cases the designs were simply used for ornamentation.

Triquetra

The most recognizable knot design adopted for Christian use is the triquetra (from the Latin meaning "three cornered"), an ancient emblem of three interlocked *vesica pisces* symbols, marking where three circles intersect. The triquetra is a very ancient symbol, associated with Neolithic and early Celtic mother goddesses, most likely an emblem of the intertwined domains of earth, ocean, and sky. Later, it was adapted to Christian use,

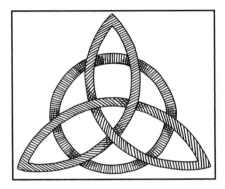

One variation of the triquetra.

as a representation of the trinity of Father, Son, and Holy Spirit. The triquetra became emblematic of the Protestant church under James Stuart of England, and it was also used as the logo of the 1611 King James Bible.

The triqueta is also popular among Wiccans and neopagans, for whom it represents a variety of ideas—most notably, the triple goddess ideal of maiden, mother, and crone.

Animal Symbolism

To the Celts, animals were not considered separate from humanity but part of the same continuum of existence. Animal existence was considered part of the human cycle of life, death, and rebirth. Animals by their natures symbolized human and divine traits, both desirable and undesirable, and embodied also the domains they inhabited. (For more on sacred animals, see Chapter 13.)

Salmon of Wisdom

Fish, especially salmon, were symbols of wisdom. Bards and other wise heroes of Celtic mythology are closely associated with fish and the sacred waters they inhabited. As an infant, Taliesin, the legendary Welsh bard, was found by a hapless prince among the fish, and the discovery changed the prince's fortunes. In the story of Cuchulainn, a salmon run is used as an entrance to the Otherworld abode of Scáthach.

The salmon is tied to many stories, most notably that of Fionn, who eats the salmon that has grazed on the sacred hazelnuts in the pool of wisdom and gains the power of foresight. Salmon spawn in Ireland around the winter solstice, the time of the birth of the sun, which may have contributed to their reputation as the wisest of creatures.

Boar: Savage Strength

The boar was a frequent meal of the Irish Celts, and it was also symbol of masculinity, strength, and fertility. The boar makes regular appearances in mythological tales of plenty. The Dagda is said to possess a pair of magical boars, whose meat is endless—while one is eaten, the other returns to life to await

A Celtic boar.

the spit. The boar is also a symbol of winter, an emblem of the Cailleach; the ritual killing of winter's boar represents hope and the return of spring.

The boar is also an emblem of royalty and of the warrior, as well as an omen of death. An Otherworld creature, the boar's appearance often precedes extreme mischief or the death of a hero. The boar is a traditional symbol of the hero's eternal adversary, the wild animal nature that must be overcome in order for wisdom to triumph. Sometimes, the boar is a king or warrior enchanted, a sign that things are not what they seem.

The Horse: Sovereign Sun

The horse is the emblem of the goddess, the earth, and sovereignty. The goddesses upon whose authority kings ruled were all strongly associated with horses. Druid rituals to divine the identity of the goddess's chosen rulers involved the sacrifice of a horse, and the ceremony of investiture for a new king involved a symbolic mating with a mare. Horses were not only associated with the divine female; the Gauls associated them with the sun, and the Irish deity Im Dagda was sometimes called Eochaid Rofhessa, "Father Horse."

FACT

A white horse is an emblem of the Otherworld, and it is upon such a horse that the rulers of the Otherworld ride. Gwyn ap Nudd, Rhiannon, and Oisin all employ magical white horses to travel to and from the land of youth. The Otherworld horse can travel over land and sea at supernatural speeds.

The Hound: Loyalty and Determination

The hound was of inestimable value to the Celts, being the constant companion of the hunter. A number of gods were anthropomorphized as dogs. The god Cuchulainn's name translates literally as "Hound of Culann," and the magical hounds who accompany the god Fionn are actually transformed humans. Overall, the hound is a symbol of loyalty, discernment, and determination.

Birds: Divine Messengers

Birds of all kinds were sacred to the Celts, especially the raven, the swan, and the crane. The raven was the messenger of the goddess of war, often the embodiment of the goddess herself or fallen warriors in her keep. The raven was also sacred to the druids and was a favored bird in augury.

The swan was the symbol of Aenghus, the god of love, and there is evidence of an early swan god venerated by the Urnfielders. The swan features in many tales of magical transformation and is often viewed as a human in bird form. The swan is an emblem of love but also of enchantment—its song can inspire love or prophetic sleep. In a tragic turn, the children of Lir are transformed into swans by their jealous stepmother.

A Celtic raven.

The crane was venerated by early Celts, but it takes on a much lesser importance in later mythology. The crane appears in several stories of the Tuatha Dé Danann, usually in malevolent context. The god Midir possesses three cranes that run off any would-be guests who approach his home, and to see three cranes is a portent of a violent death.

The crane is also a symbol of jealousy, and Irish legend is filled with tales of women magically transformed into cranes by love rivals or for various transgressions. The crane also features in a number of Christian tales, where it is especially connected with Columcille, who transforms two women into cranes for their refusal to show him respect.

The Sacred Spiral

The spiritual significance of the ancient Neolithic spiral can only be guessed at. It appears mainly on tombs and is connected with the sun and with rebirth. At the Neolithic passage tomb of Newgrange, believed by the Celts to be the home of Aenghus, a series of spirals are carved into the structure's stonework. Many of these spirals occur in triplicate form, following the path of the sun in the sky.

Triple spiral.

Many of these Neolithic spirals are triple spirals, drawn unicursally to form one continuous design. Because of this, they are probably symbolic of the sun, which traces a spiral in the sky every three months. As each triple spiral represents a period of nine months, it has been proposed that the emblems at Newgrange represent pregnancy and resurrection, an idea reinforced by the womblike nature of the ancient structure. As the rays of the morning sun at the winter solstice entered the sacred chamber and illuminated one such spiral carving, it may have represented a passageway to rebirth.

The Labyrinth

Labyrinths appear most often in conjunction with spirals, and they are commonly found etched in the entrances and chambers of the ancient Neolithic tombs. On the surface, a labyrinth may resemble a maze, but in fact they are quite different. A labyrinth is continuous and always ends where it begins. While a maze has many turns and blind alleys, a labyrinth traces a single path. Labyrinths are associated with rebirth and the afterlife.

The Power of Three: The Female Power

While the god was the embodiment of the sun, the Celts revered the earth as a goddess, whose domains were the earth, the sea, and the sky. Thus, goddesses were often portrayed in triplicities: The Morrigan, a goddess of sovereignty, was portrayed in three persons, Morrigan, Badb, and Nemain. These goddesses were associated with war, bloodshed, and death but also with fertility and earthly authority. Other triple goddesses included Brighid, the goddess of poetry, fire, and industry, and the ancient Matronae, or Dea Nutrix, goddesses of motherhood, nurture, and plenty.

Triplicities in Celtic iconography are associated with the three domains of nature, the lunar phases, and the three solar cycles of pregnancy. This association with repeating cycles also links them to concepts of resurrection, renewal, and rebirth. Both the natural and spiritual worlds were divided into the three intertwined, overlapping domains of land, sea, and sky. Each domain had its particular gods and goddesses, sacred animals, and symbols.

Common symbols of triplicity in Celtic iconography are the triskele, or triple spiral, and the triquetra. The simple triskele was a popular motif in Halstatt period art, where it was employed as a solar motif. Swirling, ornate, curvilinear triskeles and triple spirals are the hallmark of the La Tène period. The symbols remained so popular that in Christian times, they were adapted to represent the trinity of Father, Son, and Holy Spirit, adorning many artifacts of the Celtic Church.

Triskele.

Sheela-Na-Gig

Sheela-Na-Gig (Síla na Géige) is a rude name given to some of Ireland's strangest artifacts, ancient stone carvings of grotesquely grinning goddesses squatting and displaying their oversized genitals. The figures are almost invariably emaciated, bald old women, although on occasion they appear as maidens with flowing hair and youthful appearance. The Sheelas were used as protective devices and were considered lucky.

Strangely, the most common appearance of these bizarre fertility images are in church buildings, where they are often tucked into odd corners. The earliest Sheelas date back as far as 3,000 years. They were probably roadside protectors, but they continued to be popular apotropaic devices (symbols designed to turn away evil) in Christian times.

ALERT!

Sheela-Na-Gigs can still be quite controversial in Ireland, especially those located in churches. Despite their ancient age and historical importance, the images are often the target of vandalism by scandalized citizens.

The day after St. Patrick's Day in Ireland is called Sheelas Day, an indication that Sheela represents some form of balance—a bit of grinning, mischievous counterpoise to the pious masculinity of the saint.

There may be a mythological link to the Sheela stones as well, especially in tales of the goddess Etain, who is continually reborn and is often her own mother. A connection can also be made between the name Sheela and *sile*, the old word for "hag" and an epithet of the Cailleach.

The Sun Cross: The Male Power

The eight-spoked wheel is the Celtic emblem of the sun. It is most often associated with the solar/thunder deity Taranis and is often depicted as a wagon or chariot wheel. The eight spokes represent dates of solar significance: the solstices, the equinoxes, and Samhain, Beltaine, Imbolc, and Lughnasadh, the days of the four great festivals of the gods.

When Christianity came to Ireland, it brought with it its own symbolism of trinities, wheels, and fish. For a culture as heavily invested in symbolism as the Celtic people were, the coincidences of the new religion must have seemed striking indeed.

The very best example of the confluence of pagan and Christian symbolism can be seen in the Celtic cross. While other European Christian crosses are usually simple Latin T-shaped crosses, the Celtic cross is altogether different. The Celtic Christian cross typifies the Celts' positive approach to death.

Roman crucifixes are often somber depictions of death. Celtic versions of the crucified Christ, on the other hand, have the

Image of Taranis.

appearance of smiling Celtic deities with mustaches, bald heads, and radiant smiles. Sometimes they feature a youthful Jesus or even a sun or spiral instead of a human figure. Instead of nails and blood, there are spirals, knots, and cavorting animals.

The four posts of the cross are usually equal in length. Although a bottom post is usually added to make it more closely resemble the Latin cross, the upper cross design is usually separated from the lower portion. The four arms of the cross are encircled by a wheel, and the arms are usually cut out with circular notches that can be connected to form a perfect solar wheel with eight spokes. This same wheel is seen to accompany the ancient Gallic sky god Taranis. At the same time, it is strikingly similar to the *chi rho*, a solar emblem associated with the Roman Emperor Constantine that was in widespread use at the time the two cultures began crossing paths.

Another pagan cross symbol that saw continuous use into Christian times was the bride's cross, a solar wheel resembling a swastika, constructed from harvest straw or rushes and hung over doors at Imbolc, in honor of St. Brigid, also known colloquially as "St. Bride." The original cross represents a form of corn dolly, a harvest talisman created annually and kept to ensure prosperity and protect the household. Following ancient tradition, the crosses are woven annually from the straw saved from the last harvest. At the end of the year, they are burned and replaced with new ones.

A typical Celtic-style cross.

The straw cross is still a popular bit of folk custom, created after a story in the mythology of St. Brigid that tells of her creating such an emblem out of rushes to convert an elderly pagan as he lay dying. The most commonly cited power of the talisman is protection from fire, an obvious connection to both the saint and the fire goddess who was her predecessor.

The Cross of St. Brigid.

The Four Tetramorphs

In the Old Testament, a vision of the prophet Ezekiel describes four great beasts associated with the cardinal signs of the zodiac. Christian tradition identifies these beasts with the four chief evangelists, Matthew, Mark, Luke, and John, and their gospels. Thus, it is common for the four to be pictured as

the embodiments of the ancient vision. It is obvious why the concept of saints in the form of animals would be popular amongst the Celts, and so it is very common to see the four apostles pictured as winged creatures—Mark as a lion, John as an eagle, Matthew as a bull, and Luke as an angel.

One of the most famous depictions of the four evangelists in Celtic art are the four portraits placed before the four gospels in the ninth century Book of Kells, an echo of earlier pagan images.

Tetramorph of Matthew.

The Harp

The harp is the national symbol of Ireland, illustrating the extreme importance placed on the island's druid heritage. The image recalls Daurdabla, the great magical harp of the Dagda, the Irish all-father. The harp was the instrument of the Otherworld and the favored music of the gods. It had the power to call forth the seasons and to evoke any emotion. Because of the latter power, the harp symbolizes the joys and sorrows of the Irish people.

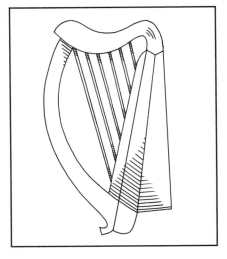

Irish harp.

The harp in the hands of the bards was a magical instrument, capable of eliciting the strongest emotions, inducing sleep, provoking merriment, or bringing great joy or sorrow to the listener. Nobody was immune from the harp's enchantments—neither man, fairies, nor even the gods.

FACT

The instrument we recognize today as a Celtic harp is known as the *clarsach*. Ironically, it made its earliest appearances in Scotland.

The Shamrock

The shamrock is an iconic symbol of the Irish, second only to the harp in importance. The word *shamrock* is derived from *seamróg*, Gaelic for "clover," and most likely refers to the native white clover. According to Irish folk belief, the shamrock is useful as a charm against evil, and the four-leafed variety is still considered a lucky charm today.

A number of plants have emerged over time as contenders to prevail as the "genuine" shamrock. Most of the plants recognized as authentic shamrocks are varieties of clover, but many marketed and sold as houseplants today are in fact varieties of wood sorrel.

It is sometimes speculated that the shamrock was sacred to the druids. Although this is a likely possibility, no evidence supports it. The importance of the shamrock as a symbol is relatively recent, from an early eighteenth-century tradition that St. Patrick used the three-lobed leaf to explain the doctrine of the trinity to Irish pagans. It's an unlikely story, but it stuck. In Victorian times, the emblem was a popular motif for greeting cards and lucky charms, and by the nineteenth century, it became cemented as a symbol of Irish identity and rebellion against English rule.

The Cup and the Cauldron

One of the four great treasures of Ireland was the Cauldron of Plenty, usually owned by the Dagda, and connected with the poet's cauldron of *imbas*, or inspiration. The cauldron was a centrally important ritual item in Celtic religious life, used for divination and in sacrificial rituals. Carefully worked decorative cauldrons were a common sacrifice to gods of lakes and rivers.

FACT

The cauldron was also linked to the Gallic god Taranis, and some early descriptions of Gallic religion described the druid's sacrifices of human victims to the god by drowning in a cauldron.

Symbolically, the cauldron represented the Otherworld in it most mystical form, a realm of inspiration, and the source of life, inspiration, sustenance, and enlightenment. It is the emblem of the domain of water, from the abundance of the ocean to the life-giving waters of the womb. The ocean was to the Celts a great womb of life, and the cauldron was its symbol.

The cauldron of the Otherworld makes frequent appearances in mythological tales, where it is either a source of never-ending sustenance, as in the tale of Dagda's Cauldron of Plenty, or as the catalyst of rebirth by which fallen warriors are resurrected. A cauldron belonging to the underworld is at the center of the earliest Arthurian quest, one that gives an endless supply of food but that will serve no cowardly man.

A Gaulish cauldron.

The Ardagh Chalice

The cauldron of the Celts remained a powerful symbol even in Christian times, although its powers were often ascribed to a more appropriate symbol, the Cup of Christ. Celtic artisans turned their attentions to the creation of many eucharistic chalices, some so fine that they were often ascribed Otherworldly attributes themselves.

One of the finest examples of Celtic Christian art is the Ardagh chalice, created in the eighth century by monks at Ardagh, in Limerick County, who buried it hastily underground—presumably to conceal it from the Viking raiders who had little respect for art. Discovered by two boys digging for potatoes in the nineteenth century, it now resides in the National Museum of Ireland and is

The Ardagh chalice.

regarded as one of Ireland's foremost artistic treasures. The chalice is a veritable catalog of Celtic artisanship, containing examples of casting, engraving, enamelwork, and cloisonné, in addition to decorative fretwork, filigree, and numerous gemstones. Today, in virtually all cases where a real cup is choosen to represent the Grail Chalice in illustration, what you see is actually the Ardagh chalice.

ALERT!

According to some sources, the Ardagh chalice was buried not by priests but by a Danish thief who was hanged around the time a chalice went missing from a monastery in Clonmacnois. In any case, nobody is really certain of the chalice's origin or the real circumstance of its concealment.

The chalice, with its large, broad bowl, is itself reminiscent of a cauldron, a perfect marriage of Christian and Celtic iconography, just as the Celtic cross combines the emblem of the ancient solar lord with the symbolism of the Christian cross. When lifted during the eucharistic ceremony, light would have filtered through the bottom of the chalice, which was fitted with a clear gem.

The beauty of the chalice has led many to associate it with the mythical Holy Grail, providing yet another connection between the grail of Christian legend and the cauldron of pagan fame. In one of the most telling chapters of Arthurian legend, the grail appears to Arthur and his company at the Round Table. It is held aloft by angels and passed from person to person, each of whom finds the cup overflowing with his or her favorite foods and drink—a clear allusion to the Dagda's Cauldron of Plenty.

The Great Horned God

One of the most universal and common Celtic deity images is also the most mysterious. The unknown god or god-type appears throughout ancient Europe and Ireland, and the oldest examples are found in cave drawings and inscribed on Neolithic pottery. The closest thing to a name for the god is Cernunnos, "Horned One," from a small handful of Gallo-Roman inscriptions. This is a bit of a cheat, as the epithet is taken from Roman period inscriptions and may be as much of a guess as the modern appellation, "Horned God."

Image of Cernunnos.

FACT

Cernunnos is not mentioned in any extant mythological texts, although there is some speculation that he may be related to the Irish god Fionn, through the heavy deer symbolism attached to both gods. Fionn is also a master of animals, as recounted in tales where he has the special power to hypnotize a variety of creatures.

The most famous depiction of Cernunnos is taken from the Gundestrup cauldron, whereupon the god, in the form of a stag-antlered man, sits cross-legged and adorned with several torques, the Celtic emblem of divine authority and kingship. He is surrounded by animals of the forest, a typical feature of horned god images. For this reason, the god is sometimes called "Master of Animals."

The Light of Three Rays

The awen, or "light of three rays," is not a proper Celtic symbol per se but is included here as a major emblem of modern druidry, employed by many druid organizations. The name *awen* is drawn from the Welsh, with spiritual connotations of "inspiration" or "essence," and refers to a traditional ideal of poetic inspiration or divine illumination. The awen emblem consists of three lines, one vertical and two diagonal, arranged so as to have the appearance of a road converging on the horizon.

The Awen and the Barddas

The awen symbol was conceived in the eighteenth century by the Welsh bard Iolo Morganwg, who printed the emblem in the *Barddas*, his book of purported druidic philosophy. The emblem was taken from an image he found in The Mabinogion, Lady Charlotte Guest's collection of traditional Welsh mythological stories, where it is cited as emblematic of the Celtic Ogham alphabet. Despite some claims to the contrary, the symbol appears in no authentic ancient Celtic context. Nevertheless, Iolo's lyrical philo-

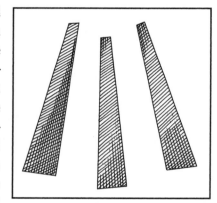

The awen emblem.

sophical exposition of the meaning of awen has been highly influential.

According to a general consensus among modern druid groups, the three parts of the awen symbol represent the three domains of earth, sea, and sky, as well as opposites in harmony. The left and right rays represent, according to the *Barddas*, a harmonious balance of male and female energy, darkness and light, and so on. Altogether, the symbol represents the divine illumination sought by seekers on the path of the druid.

The Tree of Life

The Celtic regard for trees is legendary. The Celts viewed the tree as the center of the universe and the source of all life. The tree represented the marriage of the three domains, with its branches in the sky, its roots in the earth, and the sacred spring erupting from its base.

Religious worship took place in sacred groves. Each Celtic tribe had its own sacred tree, which represented the life of the community. To the Celts, the tree was a source of sustenance, providing food, shelter, and fuel.

Wood from the sacred trees had various magical properties, and trees make many appearances in mythological stories connected to a variety of gods. Some trees were providers of food, some were the proper wood for making spears or house poles, and some were sacred to the gods, useful for divination and prophecy. For more on the tree of life, see Chapter 12.

A representation of the tree of life.

CHAPTER 10

Singers and Storytellers

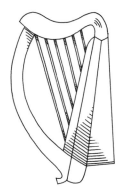

Of all the classes of druidry, singers and poets had the greatest longevity. While by most accounts the earlier continental druids divided themselves into priests, musician-poets, and seers, the latter two became somewhat interchangeable to the Brythonic Celts. The bard and the filidh took on overlapping functions and in later times were almost interchangeable. As Christianity came to prominence, the bards even absorbed many of the remaining functions of the druids. Ironically, the last refuge of the Celtic bards was in the monasteries of Britain and Ireland.

Music and Magic

By the time Christianity was firmly established in the British Isles, the druid priesthood had been largely forced out. Many of the duties they had previously fulfilled were absorbed by the fili (or filidh, plural), a high-ranking bard who functioned as singer, poet, satirist, and diviner. In a time when entertainments were few, the fili was in high demand, despite his pagan origins.

The name *fili* comes from a root meaning "to see," an apt description of the function of the fili, whose "sight" ranged from divinatory seership to the sharp insights he relied on to write effective poetry and satires.

The fili was not a poet or singer in the sense of a modern day entertainer. While filidh of lesser rank and reputation may have been relegated to such pursuits, the compositions of the higher ranks of the filidh were infused with magical potency. A patron for whom a song of praise was written was magnified in reputation and fortune. On the other hand, one who had been satirized faced more than embarrassment; in fact, the satire of a fili could be dangerous to one's fortunes. Needless to say, it was not considered prudent to anger or insult a poet, and the filidh enjoyed the best hospitality and accommodations wherever they went.

FACT

The filidh were highly trained poets and musicians, learned in literature, writing, meter, and composition. Poets of lower rank were referred to simply as "bard," but they received no training. These lesser poets were expected to rely on their inborn talents alone.

Celtic law divided the filidh into a hierarchy of seven ranks, each with its own honor price and allotted retinue. The highest rank among the filidh was ollam dana, or "highest of art," whose honor price was equal to that of a king.

The lowest ranking fili was the fochloc, with a retinue of two. Many of the filidh were eventually absorbed into the ranks of ecclesiastical scholars, and in later times, some of the best-regarded bards were Christian monks. The remainder continued in much the same vein as before, only now as secular poets and petty magicians who functioned outside any religious context.

These later "secular" filidh are sometimes derided as spin doctors of a sort. Without the ancient traditions and highly specialized training of the druids and their support systems, the filidh became reliant on the favor of the kings and nobles who patronized them, with the implication that the once independent poets were beholden to the whims of the patrons who supported them.

Radiant Brow: Taliesin

Of all of the bards of the Celts, none was as celebrated as Taliesin. Taliesin was by most accounts a genuine historical person about whom many myths and legends have sprung up. He is counted variously among the bards of King Arthur's court, in the company of the hero Bran, or in the court of Urien.

The historical Taliesin lived around the sixth century and was most likely a member of the court of Urien of Rheged. Little else is known of the true details of his life, except that he was of such reputation that he came to eventually be regarded as a semi-divine character of almost unlimited talent. By the twelfth century, he was a romantic figure of legend rivaling Merlin and even Arthur.

The name Taliesin means "shining brow," meaning *beautiful*. The common story of his birth explains that he received the name from his foster father, the prince Elphin, who discovered the child sealed in a leather bag in the bottom of a fish weir.

Taliesin was of such reputation that poets often ascribed their best works to his authorship, rather than taking the credit for themselves. The majority of works attributed to Taliesin, therefore, were written by other hands.

An older tale of the events leading up to this discovery tells that the young man, the son of a bard named Henwg, was kidnapped and later abandoned by Irish pirates. The later, more romantic legend recounts Taliesin's birth as divine.

The Birth of Taliesin

The mythological account of Taliesin's birth begins with a young farm boy named Gwion Bach, who was chosen by the goddess Cerridwen to tend to her cauldron of knowledge, in which she is preparing a draught of wisdom for her son, a hapless ugly boy called Avagddi. The potion was complex and had to be stirred for a year and a day. Its first three drops would confer priceless wisdom and insight, while the rest would be deadly poison.

Gwion was to stir the pot, while Cerridwen's blind servant Morda was to tend the fire beneath it. At first, Gwion tended to his business without incident, but one day, as Morda added wood to the fire, the cauldron bubbled up and burst, sending three precious drops flying out to land on Gwion's hand. Gwion (like Fionn before him) unwittingly stuck his burned hand in his mouth and received wisdom and foresight, instantly becoming the wisest man in the world.

When Cerridwen returned and found that her precious gift of prophecy had been usurped by her young servant, she was furious and vowed to kill him. Gwion fled, with the goddess in pursuit. Gwion called on his newfound wisdom and transformed himself into a rabbit, but the goddess became a hound and stayed hot on his heels. Gwion then became a salmon and leapt into the river. Cerridwen became an otter and followed. Gwion became a wren, and the goddess pursued him in the form of a hawk. Finally, Gwion spied a farmstead, and concealed himself as a kernel of corn amongst many others. Undaunted, Cerridwen became a hen and gobbled up all of the corn, including Gwion.

Gwion had the last laugh, however, as the goddess soon found herself pregnant. She vowed to kill the child, but as she gave birth, she saw the child's great beauty and found herself unable to do the deed. Instead, she tied him up in a leather sack and disposed of him in the ocean, where he was eventually discovered by the son of Urien, lord of Reghed.

The Song of Taliesin

In a portion of the famous Welsh poem attributed to Taliesin, the bard recounts his magical transformations in a manner very similar to Amergin's invocation of Ireland:

A second time was I formed.
I have been a blue salmon.
I have been a dog; I have been a stag;
I have been a roebuck on the mountain.
I have been a stock, I have been a spade;
I have been an axe in the hand;
I have been a pin in a forceps,
A year and a half;
I have been a speckled white cock
Upon hens in Eiddyn.
I have been a stallion over a stud.
I have been a violent bull,
I have been a buck of yellow hue,
As it is feeding.
I have been a grain discovered,
Which grew on a hill.
He that reaped me placed me,
Into a smoke-hole driving me.
Exerting of the hand,
In afflicting me,
A hen received me,
With ruddy claws, (and) parting comb.
I rested nine nights.
In her womb a child,
I have been matured,
I have been an offering before the Guledig (Prince),
I have been dead, I have been alive.

The earliest mention of Taliesin is in the poem "Spoils of Annwn," which refers to an (assumed) older legend, in which Taliesin is one of the few to survive an Otherworld quest for the cauldron of immortality. In the second tale (or branch) of The Mabinogion, Taliesin is among one of seven survivors of a host who battled Mathowlch, and it is he who returns the head of Bran to England.

Mystical Threes

In Celtic mystical lore, no number was more sacred or magical than three. When Christianity arrived on Celtic shores, the Celts recognized the doctrine of the trinity to be their own, and so they embraced the new religion and made it their own. Even long after the triad gods of the pagan Celts had lapsed into myth/obscurity, the sacredness of threes remained.

FACT

Triplicities were a persistent theme in the lore of the bards. Their songs were most often composed in three parts of poems or verses grouped by theme. These groups are referred to as triads.

Likewise, there were Three Illuminations, mysterious skills that were required to reach the highest ranks of the filidh: the imbas forosnai, or illuminating wisdom; the tenm laida, "cracking open the nuts of wisdom," and the dichetal do chennaib, "illumination by song." Both the imbas forosnai and tenm laida rituals were reportedly banned by St. Patrick as expressions of dark magic, although the dichetal do chennaib was tolerated as a scholarly exercise. Other important instances of the number three in bardic lore include these:

- The three cauldrons that give inspiration to the poet: warmth, wisdom, and knowledge
- The three enchanting powers of music: joy, sleep, and sorrow
- The three faces of the triple goddess Brighid, the patroness of poetry, fire, and water

The Celtic Harp

The clarsach, or Celtic harp, is the most beloved emblem of Ireland, chosen to represent the country as its national symbol. The iconic Irish harp, however, only dates to around the ninth century, when its image began to appear in Scottish stone carvings. Earlier Irish examples depict a squarish-shaped stringed instrument, probably a lyre adapted from the Greeks. Although the Celtic harp has become almost synonymous with the Irish bards, the harp itself did not become a common instrument in Ireland until around the fifteenth century.

The Dagda's Harp

The Irish father god Dagda, a patron of the Irish bards, possessed the magical harp Daurdabla, "oak of two greens." With the harp, the Dagda could play music that could move men to deep sorrow, profound joy, or to prophecy. It was this magical ability to control emotion through music that the Irish bards attributed to their patron.

The harp is magically bound to the Dagda. One tale tells that it was stolen in the heat of battle by the Fomorians; he is able to retrieve it by singing to it its own name.

The Dagda's harp was also called Coir Cethair Chuir, which means "four angled music," a name that reflects the belief that the Dagda used the harp to invoke the seasons. It has been theorized that the four angles may refer to the solar cross that is the basis for the Celtic calendar.

The harp's songs are referred to as the Three Noble Strains of Ireland, songs of enchantment from which none were immune. These are Goltrai, or the "Strain of Lament," which would invoke the deepest sorrow; Geantrai, the "Strain of Joy," which provoked merriment and foolishness; and Suantri, the "Strain of Sleep," which caused the hearer to fall into a deep, prophetic sleep. These songs are said to originate with the wife of the Dagda's harpist, Uaithne, the sister of Aenghus, who gave birth to three sons:

- Goltraiges, whose birth caused the goddess great pain
- Gentraiges, whose birth was joyful
- Suantres, whose birth consumed her with fatigue

Some combination of the three strains were believed to comprise the whole range of bardic music.

Amergin and Amergin

The archetypal bard of the Irish, who was called Amergin Glungel, "White Knee," was also Amergin of the Milesians, the first Celtic tribe of Ireland. Amergin was the chief of eight sons of the Spanish ruler Míl Espáine (literally, "Soldier of Spain"), by legend, the conquerors of the Tuatha Dé Danann. Amergin was a druid poet of supernatural ability and talent.

According to mythological accounts of the founding of Ireland, it was with the supernatural aid of Amergin and his power of song that the Milesians won Ireland from its divine inhabitants.

As the legend goes, an uncle of Míl, named Ith, sets out on a journey of exploration which brings him to Ireland. He is welcomed there by the three kings of Ireland, Mac Cuill, Mac Cecht, and Mac Greine, who offer him hospitality and think him wise. After Ith has been in their company a time, they ask him to settle a dispute between them, about which nothing is related. Ith responds with a paean to Ireland's beauty and bounty, which for some reason infuriates his hosts. Ith is attacked and mortally wounded, but he manages to reach his ship and relate his misfortunes before he expires. His countrymen return to Spain with stories of the treachery of the Dé Danann kings and also of the bounty of their kingdom.

The eight sons of Míl gather their arms and, along with forty chieftains, set sail for Ireland. The Tuatha Dé Danann call up a magical mist with which to shroud the island, but after three days, the Milesians discover a patch of land. They meet with the wives of the three Irish kings, Banba, Eiru, and Fodhla, and battle them in succession. Each time they are victorious, and each queen in turn demands of Amergin that her name be given to the island after her. Amergin agrees and demands battle with the Dé Danann kings who have been concealing the island. The queens agree, and they nominate the wise Amergin as judge, to set the terms of battle between the two races.

The Dé Danann, of course, are supernatural beings, and they attempt to defeat the Milesians through trickery. They request that the Milesians retreat "beyond the ninth wave" while they prepare their defenses for battle, to which the sporting Amergin agrees. The Milesians return to their ships and sail away from the island. However, when they attempt to return, they are confounded by a magical storm raised up by the Tuatha Dé Danann's powerful druids. They are no match for Amergin, however, who calls upon the island itself:

I invoke the land of Ireland.
Much-coursed be the fertile sea,
Fertile be the fruit-strewn mountain,
Fruit-strewn be the showery wood,
Showery be the river of water-falls,
Of water-falls be the lake of deep pools,
Deep pooled be the hill-top well,
A well of the tribes be the assembly,
An assembly of the kings be Tara,
Tara be the hill of the tribes,
The tribes of the sons of Míl,
Of Míl be the ships the barks,
Let the lofty bark be Ireland,
Lofty Ireland darkly sung,
An incantation of great cunning;
The great cunning of the wives of Bres,
The wives of Bres of Buaigne;
The great lady Ireland,
Eremon hath conquered her,
Ir, Eber have invoked for her.
I invoke the land of Ireland.

At the conclusion of Amergin's song, the sea becomes as smooth as glass, and the Milesians are able to easily land their ships. Numerous battles follow, during which each of the Danann kings is bested in single combat by the three surviving sons of Míl. Amergin then divides the isle among his brothers, and each portion is named for one of the queens of the vanquished kings, as promised. Afterward, the remnant of the Tuatha Dé

Danann was led underground by the Dagda, destined to become the fairy rulers of the Sidhe. They remained in Ireland, inhabiting the ancient tombs, and making occasional appearances to help or hinder the descendants of Míl as they saw fit.

Amergin's most famous song has become Ireland's most famous poem and invocation. The "Song of Amergin" is sung when his ships have landed and he first sets foot upon Ireland's shores:

I am a wind on the sea,
I am a wave of the ocean,
I am the roar of the sea,
I am a powerful ox,
I am a hawk on a cliff,
I am a dewdrop in the sunshine,
I am a boar for valor,
I am a salmon in pools,
I am a lake in a plain,
I am the strength of art,
I am a spear with spoils that wages battle,
I am a man that shapes fire for a head.
Who clears the stone-place of the mountain?
What the place in which the setting of the sun lies?
Who has sought peace without fear seven times?
Who names the waterfalls?
Who brings his cattle from the house of Tethra?
What person, what god
Forms weapons in a fort?
In a fort that nourishes satirists,
Chants a petition, divides the Ogham letters,
Separates a fleet, has sung praises?
A wise satirist.
He sang afterwards to increase fish in the creeks:
Fishful sea—
Fertile land—
Burst of fish—
Fish under wave—

With courses of birds—
Rough Sea—
A white wall—
With hundreds of salmon—
Broad Whale—
A port song—
A burst of fish.

With his song, Amergin proves the Milesians worthy of occupying the land, and the magic of the Tuatha Dé Danann is lifted.

Supernatural Child: Amergin mac Eccit

Amergin of the Milesians was one of two poets who went by that name. The story of Amergin mac Eccit's childhood, as told in the Book of Lienster, is a typical Irish tale of the wise child. It tells that Amergin, the son of a smith, is born ugly and mute, never speaking even into puberty. He sits in rags and filth, eating table scraps and amusing himself with empty nutshells until one day a servant of the poet Athirne startles him, and he utters a spontaneous verse.

That Amergin mac Eccit is the son of a smith is telling. Both bardcraft and smithcraft were considered by the Irish to be magical arts, and both fell under the patronage of the fire goddess Brighid. Under her tutelage, the smith fashioned with metal and earthly fire, and the bard worked with words and Otherworld fire.

Word quickly spreads of the boy's gilded tongue, until the tale reaches the ears of Athirne. Athirne, fearing for his position as king Conchobar's bard, conspires to kill his young competitor. He is, however, tricked into assaulting an earthen copy of the boy instead, and afterward he is forced to compensate the smith. This he does by adopting the boy as his foster son and teaching him the poet's craft. Amergin mac Eccit goes on to become the chief bard of Ulster in Athirne's place.

The poems of the semi-legendary Welsh poet Taliesin have similarities to those attributed to Amergin.

The Filidh

At the decline of druidry, the filidh gradually began to take over from the druids, and absorbed many of their ritual functions, serving as poets, judges, magicians, and seers. With the coming of Christianity, many of the filidh were associated with monasteries, even though the poems they wrote often betrayed their druid roots. Although the relationship between the druids and the Christians was often antagonistic, the scholarly refuge of the monastery proved popular with the druid remnant. Likewise, the monasteries could scarce refuse learned lawmakers, historians, and composers. While many of the religious trappings of the filidh were dispensed with, their orders of rank and social status remained strong until the Protestant Reformation, when many of their associated monasteries were destroyed. Ironically, association with pagan institutions added fuel to Protestant attacks on Catholicism.

The Well of Inspiration

Welsh bards were called Cerddorion, "Sons of Cerridwen," after their patron Taliesin, and those who were especially wise or gifted were said to have drunk from the cauldron of wisdom as he did.

To the ancient tribes of Europe, the cauldron, representing a microcosm of the sea and the sacred well, has long been a symbol of wisdom, inspiration, and immortality. The source of the bards' poetic inspiration was said to be a figurative well or cauldron, from which the gods dispensed poetry and insight to the deserving.

A seventh-century poem, called the "Cauldron of Poesy" attributed to Amergin Glungel, describes the creation of poetry as the product of three figurative cauldrons, which dwelled inside a man and dispensed warmth, wisdom, and knowledge. The poem describes the three qualities required to create poetry and alludes to the supernatural abilities of the accomplished poet:

My perfect cauldron of warming
has been taken by the gods from the mysterious abyss of the elements;
a perfect truth that ennobles from the center of being,
that pours forth a terrifying stream of speech.
I am Amergin White-knee,
with pale substance and grey hair,
accomplishing my poetic incubation in proper forms,
in diverse colors.
The gods do not give the same wisdom to everyone,
tipped, inverted, right-side-up;
no knowledge, half-knowledge, full knowledge—
for Eber Donn, the making of fearful poetry,
of vast, mighty draughts death-spells, of great chanting;
in active voice, in passive silence, in the neutral balance between,
in rhythm and form and rhyme,
in this way is spoken the path and function of my cauldrons.

The poem describes the three cauldrons as gifts of the gods, given to every man in varying measure. It goes on in subsequent verses to explain that for some, the cauldrons may only flow if stirred by "great sorrow or great joy." In other words, some are born with wisdom, but it only blossoms to greatness in the few whose experiences unleash the flow of inspiration:

The Cauldron of Incubation is born upright in a person
from the beginning.
It distributes wisdom to people in their youth.
The Cauldron of Motion, however, after turning increases.
That is to say it is born tipped on its side in a person.
The Cauldron of Wisdom is born on its lips and it distributes wisdom
in every art besides poetry.

Wisdom of the Palms

Access to the well of inspiration was closely linked with seership; in fact, both prophecy and poetry were said to be derived from the same source. The chief method for obtaining magical sight for Irish filidh was a practice called *imbas forosnai*, "wisdom that illuminates," or more literally, "wisdom of the palms." The technique, one of three magical skills of the poet, was described somewhat scornfully in the tenth century by glossarist Cormac mac Cuilennan:

> *Thus then is that done. The poet chews a piece of the red flesh of a pig, or a dog, or a cat, and puts it then on a flagstone behind the door valve, and chants an incantation over it, and offers it to idol gods, and calls them to him, and leaves them not on the morrow, and then chants over his two palms, and calls again idol gods to him, that his sleep may not be disturbed. Then he puts his two palms on his two cheeks and sleeps. And men are watching him that he may not turn over and that no one may disturb him. And then it is revealed to him that for which he was engaged till the end of a nómad (three days and nights), or two or three for the long or the short that he may judge himself (to be) at the offering. And therefore it is called Imm-bas, to wit, a palm on this side and a palm on that around his head.*

The symbolism Cormac describes gives every indication that the imbas ritual is descended from earlier druid rites of seership. Early accounts of druid divinations recall the use of trance sleep in combination with sacrifice —for instance, when a new high king was to be decided, a complex divination ceremony would be enacted. This involved the sacrificial slaughter of a horse, sacred to the goddess Sovereignty, after which the chief seer would be sealed inside the skin of the sacrificed animal. In the darkness, he would fall into a trance, and in that trance sleep, he would receive word of the goddess's choice of spouse—the new high king.

CHAPTER 11

The Fairy-folk: Perils of the Otherworld

The mysteries of the Otherworld remained active in the Celtic imagination. In accord with the new Christian view, however, the Otherworld was no longer viewed as a place of happiness and eternal youth and health but a sort of hell where fairies and devils were sometimes indistinguishable. The fair folk still dropped by to come to human aid now and again, but mainly they were viewed with superstition, as capricious characters who were usually up to no good. Fairies were blamed for just about anything that went wrong, from sour milk to infant death, poor weather, or failed crops.

Fairy Avoidance

Although nowadays one might see many methods promoted to encourage fairy sightings, in ancient times it was considered seriously bad luck—even potentially fatal—to spot a fairy. Even if a sighting wasn't an omen of death, one always risked pranks or disfigurement, or one might even be spirited away to the fairies' underground lair.

One way of avoiding fairies and their magic was to wear ones' clothing inside out, which would confound them. Fairies were also reputed to be terrified of iron or steel, so even a single pin could prove effective against them.

FACT

Fairies in Celtic lore include not only the dignified Dé Dananns, but also phantoms and strange elemental creatures of air, water, and earth, including all manner of goblins, mermaids, leprechauns, and the like. In Christian times, fairies were divided into two classes: the "Seelie court," or the more noble fairies, which included the ancient Dé Dananns, and the "Unseelie court," made up of goblins, spooks, and phantoms.

Fire and embers were also effective at repelling fairies, although these were impractical in general because with fire, the cure could be more damaging than the fairy mischief it was intended to prevent. Other common charms against fairies included holy amulets, knots and pentacles inscribed on doorposts, or even urine sprinkled about one's property.

Changelings

Changelings were fairy children, substituted in the cradle for human children spirited away by fairies. A changeling was often distinguished by its wizened looks, by precocious behaviors or talents, or because the child was sickly or disfigured or of poor temperament. Sometimes, all it took was an unusually hungry baby to prompt suspicion of a swap. Fairy abductions were often blamed on parents or other relatives. Too much attention or praise paid a baby would attract unwanted attention from the fairies, who coveted beautiful or congenial babies.

As a result, "changeling" was a common explanation for anything from crib death to behavioral problems, and medieval chroniclers made much mention of the phenomenon.

Charms against fairy abduction were the same as those against other fairy mischief. Parents might put the child's clothes on inside out, or they might dangle needles or scissors from the child's cradle to dissuade the fairies from entry.

Fear of fairy abductions was persistent in Christian times, and all sorts of extreme measures were taken to prevent substitutions. If a child was believed to be a changeling, he or she might be subjected to all sorts of bizarre treatment, sometimes even cruelty or abuse. One common method of identifying a changeling was to place the child on a shovel held over the hearth fire. Reports of parents' cruel treatment of supposed changeling children continued well into the Victorian era.

Spirits of the Earth

The ancient Celts were animists, finding all of nature to be inhabited by the divine. In Irish folklore, fairies and supernatural creatures inhabit nearly every corner of the natural world, and then some. There are the true fairies, the Sidhe, the fair immortals of the Tuatha Dé Danann who live in large tribes under the earth. There are all manner of household spirits, as well as spirits who inhabit lakes and streams, trees and flowers, mountains and mines. Some were helpful, or at least benevolent with regard to mortals, but some were quite malevolent. Fairies were never referred to by name, but were called instead the "good people."

Leprechauns

One of the best-known characters of Irish folklore is the leprechaun, a fairy creature of short stature and shorter temper. Eternally, the leprechaun evades the treasure seekers who covet his horde of gold, which tradition states he keeps at the "end of the rainbow."

The leprechaun is often depicted as a miniature cobbler, a tricky elf who can be made to divulge where his treasures are buried if he is caught. However, if his captor can be fooled into taking his eyes off the leprechaun for even an instant, he can vanish without a trace. In most tales, the leprechaun is victorious, outwitting his erstwhile human captors.

ALERT!

While the stereotypical leprechaun in the Americas is a coarse mischief maker, the Irish have traditionally viewed the leprechaun as a well-spoken, intelligent, and hard-working creature who likes nothing better than to be left to his work in solitude.

The legend of the leprechaun probably sprang up to explain the hoards of treasure and grave goods buried and dropped into lakes and streams by the pagan Celts. A thieving fairy probably seemed the best explanation for the mysterious caches.

There is some linguistic evidence that a possible root of the word, *luchchromain*, means something like "little stooping Lugh," referring to the clever god of the Tuatha Dé Danann. Another possibility is *leath brogan*, or "little shoemaker." The latter seems less likely, as shoemaking is a later addition to the leprechaun's mythology.

The Lurikeen

The lurikeen of Kildare is nearly identical to the modern concept of the leprechaun. He is a tiny goblin shoemaker, as most tales recount, who is so industrious that he is caught unaware and forced to reveal the location of his hoarded treasure. In order to do so, however, one must keep an eye on him every moment, lest he escape, a feat that is notoriously difficult, as the lurikeen is an exceedingly clever creature.

The Clurichaun

A creature who is closely related to the leprechaun is the clurichaun. Unlike the industrious leprechaun, the clurichaun is a surly, sneering drunk who ruins livestock by riding on them in the night. Clurichauns are also known to torment habitual drunks and raid wine cellars.

The clurichauns aren't completely useless, however. Being a possessive lot, they will protect their favorite wine cellars from thieves and dishonest servants.

The Brownie

The brownie was a creature particular to Scotland, a tiny, wizened brown goblin with large eyes and oversized, pointed ears. A usually benevolent household elf, the brownie was a nocturnal spirit who would venture out at night to tidy up and do household chores. The brownies did, however, expect payment for their services, usually in the form of milk or food left for them. If they weren't rewarded, they would retaliate by souring milk, breaking things, or letting the livestock loose to roam. A particularly unhappy brownie might desert the household altogether. A gift of clothes would rid a house of a brownie forever, being perceived as a great insult.

A version of this legend may be seen in the Brothers Grimm fairy tale about the elves and the shoemaker. An impoverished shoemaker gains himself a pair of tiny helpers, who spend their nights laboring without compensation. When the shoemaker attempts to reward his small benefactors by creating shoes and clothes for them, they promptly vanish.

FACT

The character of Dobby the House Elf in the *Harry Potter* series is undoubtedly based on the Scottish brownie, one of a number of supernatural creatures from the books based on Celtic mythology. Curiously, although both are freed by gifts of clothing, J. K. Rowling portrays this as a positive event in her books.

Pixies

Pixies are a creature particular to the area near Devon and Cornwall, in England. They are usually described as small, wizened creatures, with wrinkled brown skin, bald heads, and pointed ears. They are sometimes described as ancient druids who refused to convert to Christianity and were doomed to roam the earth, rejected by both heaven and hell.

Pixies are largely viewed as harmless pranksters who like to play jokes on unsuspecting mortals, but sometimes they are more malevolent. It is often said that if a curious traveler follows a pixie, he will be lured into the fairy realm, never to be seen again.

Trows and Sea Trows

Trows are creatures peculiar to the areas around the Orkney and Shetland isles. The name *trow* is most likely a corruption of the imported Norse word *troll*, although trows were most often described as rather small in size, albeit grotesque looking. The trows were called "good folk," calling to mind the fairy epithet "fair folk." Like trolls, trows cannot be exposed to sunlight, as they will turn to stone. Trows come in several varieties, from tiny creatures who live under toadstools in the forest, to humanlike fairies who take human wives.

JRR Tolkien's fearsome barrow-wights, the tomb-dwelling phantoms from the *Lord of the Rings* trilogy, were most likely modeled after the trow.

Like the fairies, the trows were rumored to live in barrows and tombs under the earth, where they created treasures of gold and silver and threw merry, boisterous parties to which human fiddlers were occasionally invited—and from which they sometimes never returned. Trows were nocturnal, venturing forth only by night, usually to cause mischief of one form or another.

Sea trows, resembling the Irish selkies, are nocturnal creatures that take the form of fish or seals but venture on land at night, shedding their animal skins to appear in human form. Unlike most trows, the sea trow is attractive in appearance; folklore is filled with tales of lucky fishermen who are able to capture beautiful sea trow brides for themselves by taking their discarded skins.

Spirits of Water

In druid times, water gods and spirits were often benevolent. Lakes and springs were ruled over by gods of warmth and healing. Rivers, wells, and streams were often ruled by goddesses, often the local goddesses of sovereignty. Over time, the darker aspects of those deities became prominent, while their divine features receded. Many water spirits slowly evolved into bogles, terrifying beasts whose specialty was lying in wait for unsuspecting passersby.

Not all of the water spirits were bad. Some, such as the selkie, were tragic, waterbound creatures that could be redeemed through their interactions with humanity. Most waterbound creatures, good or evil, could be captured and pressed into service and/or marriage to humans.

Kelpie: Malevolent Sea Horse

The kelpie was a malevolent creature, a shapeshifter that could take on the appearance of a man but most often appeared in the form of a fine horse with a silken coat and gleaming eyes. The telltale difference between this supernatural creature and its earthly lookalike was the kelp or rushes clinging to its mane. To see a kelpie was an omen of death by drowning; to meet one might mean instant death.

The kelpie's malevolent behavior took a number of forms. Most commonly, it would lurk near docks or ferries, in the form of a lovely horse. A passerby foolish enough to attempt a ride on the horse would find himself stuck tight as the kelpie returned to the water, drowning the unfortunate victim and devouring him. This wasn't the kelpie's only trick, however. If a potential victim chanced by on horseback, it might take the form of a hideous old man, leaping onto the saddle. The kelpie also liked to appear as a handsome young man and seduce young women to their deaths.

One could capture a kelpie and put him to work. If one was clever enough and quick enough, a harness could be tossed over a kelpie's neck, rendering it docile, after which it was reputed to make an exceptionally strong workhorse.

The water horse is a very ancient motif in Celtic territories that may have originated in the ancient horse cults of Celtic Europe. Early images of water horses appear to have been benign in aspect and are related to water deities such as Manannan mac Lir.

A Scottish variation of the Kelpie was the shellycoat, so called for the shells and seaweed that dangled from his mane. The shellycoat was of malevolent character but not as evil as the kelpie. The shellycoat's favorite prank was to mimic the cries of a drowning person, distracting travelers who would frantically search for a crying victim but, after finally reaching the source of the cries, would discover only a hysterically laughing phantom.

The Pooka

The pooka (or sometimes phooka) is an obvious relation to the kelpie. Like the kelpie, he appears as a horse, usually a colt, but can also be spotted in the form of a goat, dog, or rabbit. Sometimes he appears as a wizened goblin. He typically has heavy chains hung round the neck and hangs about on the edges of marshes and lakes. Like the kelpie, the pooka enjoys luring mortals and leaping astride riders' horses, but unlike the kelpie, the pooka is in it for fun, and usually the victim of his pranks comes to no harm.

FACT

In the classic Jimmy Stewart movie *Harvey*, the titular character is a pooka, a great rabbit only Stewart's character is able to see.

That is not to say the pooka is a harmless creature. He has been known to roam the countryside at night, destroying crops, scattering livestock, and souring milk. It is traditional for Irish farmers to leave a portion of their crops behind after harvest for the pooka, in order to be spared his mischief. The pooka's special night is at Samhain, when special precautions must be taken to prevent mischief from befalling one's household.

Many a human reported being ridden by the capricious pooka, but only one man was ever known to have returned the insult. This was the legendary Brian Boru, the greatest of the high kings of Ireland. Brian accomplished this feat by stealing three hairs from the pooka's tail, with which he wove a bridle that he was able to use to control the magical creature. The king rode the horse to exhaustion, after which the pooka agreed not to destroy the property of good Christians or to attack Irishmen unless they were intoxicated. The pooka, being what he was, of course ignored his promise, but he does seem to have a preference for drunks.

Headless Horseman: The Dullachan

The notion of capricious rides doesn't end with magical horses. The Irish dullachan is the original headless horseman, a wild spectral rider that haunts the countryside, carrying his severed head under one arm as he rides. The head is not useless but is gifted instead with supernatural sight, allowing the phantom to see for miles. Woe to anyone who happens to be near, because when the dullachan reins his horse, it is certain that someone nearby will die. The dullachan's visit is unpleasant for anyone who attempts to thwart his mission as well, for they often find themselves doused with a bucket of blood.

Selkies: the Seal People

Selkies ("seals") are the mysterious sea people who inhabit the waters around the Orkney and Shetland isles. The selkies are a type of trow who take the form of seals and live in caverns underwater. Selkies, like most trows, can leave their animal forms on land and have even been known to take human spouses.

Irish and Scottish folklore is filled with stories of humans who take selkie spouses. In most, it is a sort of involuntary enslavement, wherein the would-be husband gains a selkie bride by stealing her sealskin and conceal-ing it so that she may not return to sea. On other occasions, a selkie may fall in love with a human of its own accord, but such love matches are said to be doomed to tragedy. Eventually, selkies must succumb to the lure of their former home, after which they can never return.

A common legend regarding the selkies claims they are fallen angels; specifically, they are angels unwelcome in heaven but too pure for hell, thus doomed to haunt the coastline in their tragic animal skins. They are also sometimes said to be the transformed souls of the drowned.

Selkie men are another matter. Unlike selkie females, who often must be tricked or captured, male selkies have been known to conceal their own skins in order to seek out human lovers. A woman who wished to attract a selkie would do so by shedding seven tears into the ocean. Women who drowned or disappeared were often said to have been spirited away by sel-kie lovers.

Causing harm to one of the selkie folk was to be assiduously avoided, as the death of a selkie is believed to cause furious storms at sea. The selkies are also known as *roane*, or seals.

Merrows: The Irish Mermaid

The merrow is the Gaelic variety of the mermaid: human from the waist up, with the torso and lower body of a fish. Celtic mermaids were quite lovely and are usually depicted preening with a mirror and comb. The Celtic merman, on the other hand, fares nowhere near as well, being hideously gnarled, with razor-sharp teeth and green-hued skin.

Merrows, like other supernatural sea creatures, can become espoused to humans, either by love or by trickery. To take a mermaid spouse, one must steal his or her magical feathered cap, or *cohuleen druith*, without which the merrow is unable to travel under the waves. The trapped creature would then be forced to agree to remain, in hopes of retrieving this magical possession.

Wraiths and Seductresses

An unfortunate consequence of the Christianization of the Celts was that the spirits of the earth, especially female ones, began to take on a sinister cast, becoming evil seductresses, wraiths, and monstrous hags. The tests of the goddess became mere bloodsport for monsters who inhabited the forests, lakes, and streams.

The Banshee

Originally, the banshee, or *ban Sidhe*, was at one time simply a female of the Sidhe, or fairy-folk. Over time, however, the name came to signify a very specific type of unlucky spirit. Because an encounter with a fairy meant that one was literally "walking between worlds," she came to be viewed as an omen of death.

In later folklore, the banshee evolved into a sort of wraith or ghost, often attached to a particular house of family, whose bloodcurdling wail meant the impending death of a member of the household.

The Washer Woman

A related spirit to the banshee was the ban nighe, or "washer woman," a character encountered in Irish and Welsh mythology who also came to be viewed as a shade. The ban nighe was originally a particular aspect of the goddess of sovereignty, who symbolically washed the garments of a warrior and warned him of his impending death. In Christian times, she lost her divine aspect and became an apparition who would appear beside the river, washing the grave clothes of those about to die.

FACT

An early version of the washer woman myth concerns the Welsh sovereignty goddess Mabon, who is inexplicably cursed to wash at the riverside until she bears a son by a Christian. That son is the hero Owain, and the tale was probably symbolic of the passing of dominance over the land from pagan to Christian.

Romanticized tales of the washer woman give a more benevolent aspect to the water goddess. In many cases, she is a mysterious lady who guards a well, stream, or fountain, and whose function is to test the hero or provide him with a task, quest, or geas.

The Korrigan

While the banshee and the ban nighe were not viewed as malevolent, there were creatures who could cause the death of any unfortunate enough to cross their paths. The most malevolent of these was the korrigan, originally thought to be the spirits of female druids who opposed the conversion of Celtic lands to Christianity. She is especially associated with water, and may be another aspect of the Morrigan. There are generally said to be nine korrigans in all.

The korrigan was a wicked spirit, with a number of vile habits. She was fond of sitting by the lakes or wells, combing her long, beautiful hair, and she would attempt to seduce any man who chanced by. Those who spurned her advances would be cursed with death.

Men weren't the only victims of the korrigan. It was she who was largely credited with the kidnap of human infants, replacing them with change-lings, and raising the human children as her own.

Singular Phantoms

Some members of the fairy-folk were so infamous they had no peers. Most of these solitary fairies belonged to a particular locale, although some appear to have had no boundaries to their haunts. To one, these creatures are mis-chievous or malevolent.

One such creature was the fearsome Amadan Dubh, the "Black Fool," also known as the "Stroking Lad." The Amadan lived in a ruined castle and ventured out at random looking for prey, which he enchanted with his pipes before touching them—a touch that rendered his chosen victim crip-pled, disfigured, or paralyzed. The Amadan's choice of victims was capri-cious although occasionally he served to dispense a sort of divine justice, serving his touch on men and women who blasphemed or broke social etiquette.

CHAPTER 12

The Tree of Life

The Celts held the natural world as the giver and keeper of life, and no emblem better represents the intertwined destinies of man and nature than the spreading branches of the tree of life. The tree was regarded as an ancient ancestor of mankind, and is a universal emblem of the macrocosm. The tree was a natural symbol of the three domains, with branches that reach into the sky, its body in the earth, and roots reaching deep into the sacred streams below the earth.

The World Tree

In the Celtic world, the tree was the original denizen of the natural world. Trees provided everything needed to sustain life—fruit and acorns for eating, wood for shelter and weapons, fuel for warmth and cooking, and bark for medicines and tanning of leather. Without trees, life would have been very difficult, if not impossible.

Trees were not viewed as only being good for utilitarian purposes or even simply as sacred. The trees were literally gods, the venerated ancient ancestors of mankind. Each tree had its own sacred purpose. Some provided wood for making strong, flexible weapons; some provided life-saving medicines and healing salves. Many were shelter to sacred animals or birds, and some were regarded literally as doors to the Otherworld.

Communities had their own sacred trees, called *bile*, which usually stood on a plain or in the center of a clearing, where they represented the axis mundi, or center of the earth. The tree chosen as the *bile* was usually older and well established, and was preferably located near a well or stream. Assemblies would be held under this tree, and harming or cutting it was restricted under the strictest of taboos. The sacred tree represented the soul of the tuath, and its harm or destruction could mean fires, illness, or other disasters.

Tree Worship

Druid worship took place in forest sanctuaries and around sacred lakes and pools. There can be no doubt that trees were especially important in the Celtic religion, and they were a central feature in druid worship. The druids' sanctuary was called the *nemeton*, or grove, wherein rituals and sacrifices would be performed. The Greek chronicler Strabo describes the assembly-place of the druids in Galatia as Drunemeton, the sacred oak grove.

FACT

The word *nemeton*, meaning "sacred or holy grove," was the generic name given to the forest sanctuaries of the druids. The root *neme* is connected with many ancient European place names. Some connect the name of Nemed, a Celtic ancestral deity, to the naming of the sacred groves.

Nine Sacred Woods

Druid tradition held nine trees as particularly sacred. Wood from the nine was required to light the annual Beltaine fires to usher in the summer season. An old song preserves the names of eight of the nine:

Choose the willow of the streams, choose the hazel of the rocks
Choose the alder of the marshes, choose the birch of the waterfalls
Choose the ash of the shade, choose the yew of resilience
Choose the elm of the brae, choose the oak of the sun

The ninth is not mentioned but is presumed to be the thorn, or hawthorn, tree. The smoke from the sacred fire, called the need fire, would be used to purify croplands and cattle, and embers from the fire would be used to relight the hearth fires of every home. Each tree described in this chapter was prized for a different reason. All were sacred to one or more gods, providing an invaluable resource both for practical and magical purposes.

The Oak

The druids were especially connected with the oak and the mistletoe that grew on its branches. The word *druid* is derived from the same root as the word for oak, *daur*, and it is often suggested that druid means "oak wise" or "oak dweller." The ancient Celts viewed the oak as the axis mundi, the tree of life at the center of the world. From ancient times, the fruit of the oak provided sustenance for human and animal alike; the acorn was the food of the sacred deer and the boar.

The notion that the oak was a doorway to the land of fairies was a persistent one. An oft-repeated old Irish proverb reflects this belief: "Fairy-folks are in old oaks."

The oak was viewed as a doorway to the Otherworld and was associated with death and rebirth. Both oak branches and mistletoe were commonly placed in graves, and the wood was used in mortuary houses and in the construction of tombs.

Trees were often assigned to one of the gods according to their uses and attributes, and in groves, likenesses of the gods were carved from the trees they embodied. Lugh, the sun god, who was also associated with the underworld and death, was especially connected to the oak, where he dwelled in his eagle form. The god is frequently depicted in art wearing a crown of mistletoe, in which case he can be viewed as a personification of the oak itself.

Sacred oaks were held in such esteem that many Irish saints were attached to sacred oaks or groves. In fact, the names of many ancient monastic communities belie their origins as sacred oak groves, including Derry ("oak," a common place name in Ireland) and Durrow ("oak grove"). The church of St. Brigid was not coincidentally founded at Kildare (Cill-Dara), whose name literally means "church of the oak." The druid-turned-saint St. Columcille founded his monasteries in oak groves. Columcille was so fond of the grove at Kells that he refused to fell any of its trees to build his church and was even said to have spoken an invocation to save it from a threatening wildfire.

FACT

A further tale linking Columcille with the sacred oak tells of a man who took bark from the tree under which the saint lived to tan leather for a pair of shoes and was stricken with leprosy for his folly.

The Ash

The ash tree was very highly regarded as sacred, often serving as the prototypical world tree. To the continental druids, it was second in importance only to the sacred oak, and to the Irish druids, it was the world tree. The name of the ash tree comes from the ancient Saxon root *aesc*, meaning "spear"—and indeed, saplings of ash were preferred by the Celts for the construction of spears. Druids' wands were also constructed of ash, which was prized for its powers over fire and water. Because it was regarded as a solar tree, it was a suitable wood for healing purposes.

The ash was regarded as the world tree by both the Norse and the Irish. The ash grows in open spaces and only thrives in full sunlight. It prefers to be near a source of water so is common near lakes and streams. The ash is sacred to the gods of lightning, and its mere presence was believed to invite lightning and fire. In medieval times, the ash was considered effective as a charm against black magic.

The Thorn (Hawthorn)

The thorn tree in particular is sacred to the fairies, especially when accompanied by the oak and ash. The thorn tree is a low-growing, prickly tree most commonly used as a protective fence to repel invaders or to keep livestock in check.

The thorn tree was closely associated in bardcraft with the art of satire; the never-ending barbs and pricks of the thorn were an apt analogy for the effects of a good satire. Hawthorn was also a favorite of the birds, giving it a reputation as an otherworldly tree. In later times, the thorn tree was thought to be inhabited by fairies and generally avoided.

The Yew

Yew trees are relatively short, broad evergreens, bearing dark green needles and bright red berries. Almost every part of the yew is highly poisonous. The yew is one of the longest living trees in existence, with some specimens living as long as 4,000 years.

The yew was also prized as a magical wood, the material of choice for rune-spells, and it was probably used for divination. The wands of the Irish druids were reportedly made of yew wood, and credited with transformative powers. The yew has traditionally provided wood for weapons, especially bows for archers.

The ancient connection between the yew and seership is echoed in Shakespeare's *Romeo and Juliet*, wherein Romeo's servant Balthasar has a vision of death after slumbering under a yew:

As I did sleep under this yew-tree here,
I dreamt my master and another fought,
And that my master slew him.

The yew is another tree closely associated with death and rebirth, another guardian of the path between the Otherworld and the waking world. Yew boughs were placed in pagan graves and were planted atop ancient burial mounds. Even centuries after the coming of Christianity, the tree remained sacred, and even churchyard burials took place under the branches of ancient yew trees.

A tale from the Book of Invasions tells of the Queen Etain, who loves a Sidhe lord named Midir and runs away with him. Her enraged husband enlists the aid of the druid Codal, who finds her using four yew wands engraved with ogham letters. Curiously, Etain is linked mythologically with the Caer, the lover of Aenghus, whose name means, literally, "yew berry."

Yews remained sacred even into Christian times, and in certain parts of tenth century Wales, one faced a very steep fine for harming or cutting one down.

The Hazel of Wisdom

To the Irish druids, hazel was regarded as a source of wisdom and was connected with sacred springs and wells. In the story of the divine hero Fionn mac Cumhaill (Finn mac Cool), the salmon of wisdom becomes imbued with strong magic after eating the nuts of the nine sacred hazel trees that surround his well. Fionn, whose surname not so coincidentally means "son of hazel," receives the power of prophecy when he accidentally consumes a morsel of the fish. Chewing hazelnuts was a folk charm to attain knowledge or inspiration.

According to legend, the hazel was once a poisonous tree because it was in the fork of a hazel that Lugh hung the head of the giant Balor after defeating him in battle. The tree remained poisonous until felled by the sea god Manannan fifty years later, and the felled tree was made into a shield for Fionn, who called his magical weapon "dripping ancient hazel."

The hazel is especially connected to the sacred number nine. Many tales relating to the hazel figure the tree as appearing in groves of nine. The hazel grows for nine years before it flowers, and in the druid ogham alphabet, it is the ninth letter.

A hazel wand was the mark of authority of the messenger and the judge, an emblem of balance and wisdom. Later, the hazel became associated with witches and the dowser's art, and so came to be called "witch hazel."

The Willow

The Latin botanical name for willow, *Salix*, is derived from the Celtic *sallis*, meaning "near water." The willow, by virtue of its nearness to water, is associated with aquatic and healing gods.

The god most closely connected to the willow is Esus, whose iconic image is depicted in the act of cutting down a willow tree. The smoke of the willow was used in rites of seership.

The Birch

The birch provides bark for making boats and flexible coverings. The birch in particular is considered an effective charm against evil. Its wood, particularly when burned, was believed to drive out evil spirits, especially those that plagued the livestock.

The Elm

The bark of the elm was used to make cord and other flexible products, and was prized for its ability to withstand moisture and splitting. Like the yew, the elm was associated with death and passages, and it often grew atop burial mounds. In the earliest stories of Arthur, the king is felled by a spear of elm wood.

The Alder

Alder was a popular wood among the Celts, and its wood was used for making charcoal for blacksmiths. The alder also produced colored dyes, in particular a red hue associated with warriors, blood, and battle.

The alder was associated with the hero Bran, and it is sometimes personified as a mythological king, referred to in poetry as having the branches of an alder. One ancient Celtic tribe was even named for the tree—the Averni, or "alder people." Because of its associations with fire, alder wood was used as a charm against flooding. The hollow twigs of alder were tied together to make charms for calling the wind.

Apples of Avalon

Apples, or *quert,* were sacred to the Morrigan, and the apples of Annwn (Avalon) healed all wounds. Many Celtic mythological tales feature apples from the Otherworld that confer upon their owner immortality and endless satiety. Welsh legends of Arthur relate that the king seeks out Avalon to heal from grievous battle wounds, and it is there he returns when near death.

The connection between apples and the Otherworld is a deep one: the root of the name Avalon is *Ynys Affalon*, meaning "Isle of Apples."

Apples also figure in the story of Lugh and in the source of Lugh's appellation "Long Arms." Lugh's father Cian is a supernaturally skilled gardener whose apple trees bear fruit as soon as they are planted. Cian offered his gardener's skills to Lugh's grandfather, the Fomorian Balor, in a bargain for the return of a cow he has stolen from Goibnu, the Dé Danann smith. Cian brings the young Lugh along to help with the harvest. The giant observes the young god reaching for spilled apples, and mistaking him for a gardener's assistant, dubs him "little long arms."

In many legends of visits to the Otherworld, an outsider requires a special token to ensure safe passage to and from the land of fairies. This token is most often a branch of the Otherworld apple tree, a silver bough bearing blossoms and fruit that make music when shaken, often luring humans into enchanted sleep. This idea seems to come from older druidical practices, as early descriptions of the bards often mention the ritual use of silver branches hung with bells.

Mistletoe and Ivy

Anyone who has spent any time at all studying the ancient druids has learned that the druids held the mistletoe plant in very high esteem. Classical writers, especially Pliny, point out that of all the plants of the forest, the druids most revered mistletoe. He describes a mistletoe collection ritual, where, on the "sixth day of the moon," the plant is cut with great ceremony using a sickle-bladed knife:

> For they believe that whatever grows on these trees is sent from heaven, and is a sign that the tree has been chosen by the gods themselves. The mistletoe is very rarely to be met with; but when it is found, they gather it with solemn ceremony. This they do above all on the sixth day of the moon, from whence they date the beginnings of their months, of their years, and of their thirty years cycle, because by the sixth day the moon has plenty of vigor and has not run half its course.

> After due preparations have been made for a sacrifice and a feast under the tree, they hail it as the universal healer and bring to the spot two white bulls, whose horns have never been bound before. A priest clad in a white robe climbs the tree and with a golden sickle cuts the mistletoe, which is caught in a white cloth. Then they sacrifice the victims, praying that the gods will make their gifts propitious to those to whom they have given it.

The mistletoe grows high in the branches of trees, especially the sacred oak, with no visible source of sustenance. For this reason, and due to its golden hue and waxy white fruit, the mistletoe was believed to literally sprout from the sperm of the sun. Because of this solar association, mistletoe was held to be a healing plant and attributed power over numerous ailments. It was so highly regarded as a magical plant that even centuries after the last druid vanished from the earth, the herb was known as "all-heal" and served as a charm against fires and lightning.

After a time, even the church intervened to try and stem the enthusiasm for mistletoe, and it was banned from use in churches. Nevertheless, the plant remained a popular charm and is still part of holiday traditions to this day.

While ivy isn't usually considered to be a tree, it was counted as one among the Celts. Ivy was given the reputation as the strongest of all the trees. Although it appeared unassuming, it was hardy and persistent, and although its growth was slow, it could eventually strangle even the strongest oak. Ivy was also counted among the sacred evergreens and was associated with resurrection and the Otherworld.

Tree Ogham: The Sacred Alphabet

The ogham alphabet is a bit of an anomaly in the Celtic world. Writing was a very late addition to Celtic society. When the Celts first began writing religious inscriptions, they usually used the Roman alphabet. So what, then, to make of this mysterious alphabet, found most often on roadside markers and memorial inscriptions? Incidences of the alphabet might appear to be utilitarian, were it not for a few small but intriguing clues.

The Celts aversion to committing religious learning to writing was noted by several observers. Caesar remarked on this taboo:

They commit to memory immense amounts of poetry . . . they consider it improper to commit their studies to writing . . . lest it should be vulgarized and lest the memory of scholars should become impaired.

This characteristic reticence remained even after years of Roman rule. Although the Gaulish Celts eventually learned to make written correspondence and keep written records of mundane public affairs, this was always done using Roman or Greek characters. These languages were also used to inscribe the names of deities, often Roman-Celt hybrids and, occasionally, to record Roman-style curses or other invocations to the gods.

The druids, however, remained steadfast in their refusal to make religious records. Curiously, however, they do seem to have developed their own sacred alphabet, which was used publicly mainly between the fourth and eighth centuries, almost exclusively for funerary inscriptions.

The alphabet is called ogham and is most thoroughly recorded in the medieval Irish Book of Ballymote, where it is credited as the invention of Ogma, the Irish god of eloquence. The alphabet recorded in the Book of Ballymote has twenty letters, with five vowels and three sets of five consonants, although the book refers to numerous variations, each with its own letters and styles.

FACT

The eleventh century monks who penned the Book of Invasions also refer to the ogham alphabet. However, they record it as the invention of the Scythian King Fenius, who is claimed to have created the script shortly after the fall of the Tower of Babel, by collecting together the best of the world's languages.

Very little is known about the exact origins of ogham or its possible religious or ritual uses, but there are many hints that the alphabet had mystical meaning and may have been used for divinatory and other ritual purpose. The Book of Ballymote describes its use as a secret sign language by druids and other elite members of society, who may have used it to communicate with one another where open speech may have revealed secret knowledge to outsiders.

It is perhaps not coincidental that written ogham appears only as the great colleges of druidry began to decline and the practice of druidry became more open and prone to vulgarity. Written inscriptions in the ogham script are found most often in Ireland, almost invariably in funeral inscriptions.

Although ogham appears only relatively recently in the archaeological record, it appears to be quite ancient. The letters are similar in construction to the Norse rune alphabet, and the two are referred to in older texts somewhat interchangeably. Mythologically, the ogham is associated with the gods of the Tuatha Dé Danann, where it is used for communications, curses, and divination. In the story of Midir and Etain, Etain's druid husband Codal uses ogham letters carved into yew staves to discover the whereabouts of his wife and her lover.

Another indication of the ogham's age is its association with the druids' sacred trees. Each letter of the alphabet is named for a different tree, not all of which are native to Ireland.

Ogham letters are formed using combinations of vertical diagonal strokes placed on a midline, written bottom to top (left to right in written manuscripts), with each letter comprising one to five strokes. The midline was not always inscribed but was often created using an edge of the inscribed object.

The following letters, with their corresponding trees, compose the ogham alphabet:

- Beth (birch)
- Luis (rowan)
- Fearn (alder)
- Saille (willow)
- Nuin (ash)
- Huatha (hawthorn)
- Daur (oak)
- Tinne (holly)
- Coll (hazel)
- Quert (apple)
- Muin (vine)
- Gort (ivy)
- Ngetal (reed)

- Straif (blackthorn)
- Ruis (elder)
- Ailm (silver fir)
- Onn (furze)
- Ur (heather)
- Eadha (poplar)
- Ido (yew)

In the sixth century, the following group (*forfeda*) containing an additional five letters was added to the alphabet, most likely reflecting changes in the language:

- Eabab (aspen)
- Oir (spindle)
- Uillende (honeysuckle)
- Ifhin (gooseberry)
- Emoncholl (double hazel)

The Celtic tree ogham has been and is still used as a tool for divination. How it was used by the ancients is unknown, but the method may have been similar to Norse divination using runes. Later mythological stories mention divinations made by carving ogham letters into staves of yew, but they are silent on the details.

CHAPTER 13

Sacred Animals

A recurring feature of Celtic myth tales is the theme of the god, poet, or hero who can transform seemingly at will, taking on the shape of animals or birds. At the root of these tales are the anthropomorphic animal gods of the ancient Celts, deities of forest, lake, and stream who eventually took on human characteristics. Many of the gods of the Irish pantheon have animal forms or origins. The hero Bran, for instance, takes on the form of a hound and is associated with Fionn, who is almost certainly the same personage as the antlered god Cernunnos.

Magical Metamorphosis

A persistent theme in Celtic myth tales was that of metamorphosis, the ability to change from one form to the next. There is also an element of transmigration in the tales, and one persistent theme is the god or hero who takes the form of one animal after another. For example, the druid Finntan survived for a great stretch of time by taking the form of many animals until he was able to relate the ancient history of Ireland to St. Patrick. This may be an allusion to reincarnation, or simply an implication that Finntan absorbed all of the knowledge of the natural world.

The myth of the shape changer may have very ancient roots. Cave paintings and pictographs left behind by the ancient ancestors of the Celts depict shamanic priests in animal garb, often in the process of transformation into animal forms or perhaps illustrating the assumption of animal characteristics or abilities. The belief that these magician-priests could take on the appearance of animals is echoed in these later stories of transformation.

ALERT!

Technically, *shaman* is a word used by the Siberian Tungus tribe to describe their tribal magician-priests. The word is not Celtic but is commonly used to describe priests of similar functions in tribal societies. What name the earliest Celts or their ancestors may have used is unknown and may never be discovered.

Other Celtic ideas about animal transformation came from observance of nature. Unusual behavior in animals often took on supernatural meaning. For instance, goddesses of war would assume the form of ravens or carrion crows to carry off the souls of the dead, while gods of healing and rebirth might appear as snakes or stags—animals who are continually reborn through the shedding of skin or antlers.

One of the best-known tales of magical transformation is the story of Taliesin, the Welsh poet god. The story is typical of metamorphosis stories, with themes of reincarnation and magic, and has many parallels in the story of Fionn. (Read further about Taliesin's transformations in Chapter 10.)

The Love of Aenghus

A number of tales with themes of supernatural transformation as rebirth concern Aenghus, mac Og, the Irish god of youth and love. In one story, Aenghus dreams of a beautiful girl. After awakening, he becomes ill, falling into a depression so deep that he cannot be roused from his bed. After several days of this behavior, his concerned friends call for his mother, the goddess Boann. She diagnoses Aenghus' illness as love sickness—Aenghus is literally pining for the girl of his dreams.

At his mother's behest, messengers are sent to the corners of Ireland to look for the mystery girl of Aenghus' dream. At the end of a year, she is at last discovered in a neighboring kingdom. She is Caer, the daughter of the chieftain Ethal. Unfortunately, she is not to be easily won, as she is a shape changer and lives as she wills. She tells Aenghus that for one year, she takes on the form of a woman, and for the next, that of a swan—and that he may marry her if he can recognize her among the other swans.

He discovers that she will appear at a particular lake on Samhain Eve, and he awaits her there. When she appears in her swan form, she is accompanied by hundreds of other birds. From his dream, he recognizes the necklet she wears. He calls out to her, but she does not wish to leave the water—so Aenghus himself transforms into a swan, and meets her in the lake. Most versions of the story of Aenghus conclude with the pair remaining swans and singing songs so sweet they could enchant people to sleep for "three days and nights."

Variation on Aenghus's Tale

In another tale, it is the brother of Aenghus, Midir, who falls for the maiden Etain (a goddess herself associated with death and rebirth), and takes her for a wife. Unfortunately, Midir is already married, and his first wife does not take kindly to the usurper. She uses magic that causes the maiden to take on the form of a fly although she is such a magical and beautiful fly that Midir does not mind.

Eventually, Midir's wife catches on that the fly that accompanies her husband is Etain, and again she uses magic, this time to cause a great wind to rise up and blow her away. The hapless fly falls into a wine cup, and is swallowed by Etar, the wife of a chieftain. Etar becomes pregnant, and gives birth to a baby girl, whom she of course names Etain. The girl grows up under her care, ignorant of her origins, until one afternoon she chances to be bathing in a river. Midir, riding by on his horse, recognizes her. The girl instantly remembers her past and her love for Midir.

Creatures of the Woodlands

To the Celts, the deer was the most revered of all creatures. Before the advent of agriculture and the keeping of cattle, venison was a staple food of the Celts. The ancient Neolithic ancestors of the Celts revered the deer, and long after its necessity was reduced by the advent of agriculture, the deer remained an important figure in Celtic mythological tales. Stags were associated with gods of the underworld, and they frequently appear in tales as gods or humans in animal guise. Deer frequent the sacred springs and wells and are associated with wisdom and knowledge.

The Boar

The boar is a universal symbol of fertility, masculine aggression, and warrior spirit. Boars are known for their fearlessness, aggression, and stubbornness, but they are also revered for their cleverness and intelligence. The Celts believed the boar originated in the Otherworld, and boar meat was always on the menu in Otherworld festivities.

FACT

Unlike the deer, the boar is often seen as an agent of mischief or malevolence. The famous division between Northern and Southern Ireland is said to have been caused by the mischievous magical boar.

The boar appears many times over as an agent of mischief and a presage of death—he symbolizes the strength of the hero but is also present at his death. At the beginning of the tale of the Tain bo Cuilange, Friuch and Rucht are the swineherds of the gods, and their names—meaning "bristle" and "grunt"—belie their true nature. These two anthropomorphized boars, through their own mischief, set into motion the sequence of events that leads to great disaster—and the death of the hero Cuchulainn.

In the Welsh Mabinogion tale of Culwhch and Olwen, Twrch Trwyth is a mischievous wild boar who terrorizes the countryside. In order to marry his love Olwen, Culwhch must hunt the great boar and retrieve the magical comb, scissors, and razor he carries in his poisonous bristles. The boar of course is no ordinary animal but a Welsh king who was transformed by a curse.

The boar is frequently associated with royalty, especially the burden of royal hospitality. There is evidence that the boar was once regarded as a deity in its own right—the worship of a boar god of the Gauls, called Moccus, seems to have been associated with the Roman Mercury, and it may be this or a similar god who inspired many of the later mythological boar tales.

The Fate of Diarmait

The life of the Celtic hero Diarmait was magically bound up with that of a boar, as recounted in the Fenian Cycle. Diarmait was the son of Donn, a member of the Fianna. Diarmait's mother had another son, his stepbrother and constant companion, who was the son of Aenghus's steward, Roc. Donn despised the boy, who was evidence of his wife's infidelity.

One evening, while visiting with Fionn and Aenghus, Diarmait and his half-brother played. The younger son ran between Donn's legs, and without hesitating, Donn broke the boy's neck. To hide his crime, Donn blamed the death on Fionn's hounds, which would have put Fionn in a very bad position. Fionn used his magical thumb to expose the truth of the matter and revealed Donn as the killer. The boy's father demanded vengeance, but Fionn prevented him from killing Donn. The anguished father instead produced a magic wand, which he used to transform his dead son into a boar. The boar was a giant, invulnerable to any weapon. The steward declared that the life of Diarmait was now tied with that of the boar, and that they would die together. Fionn, however, drove the boar into the forest, and a protective geas was placed on Diarmait, preventing him from hunting boar.

Ironically, Fionn's act of protection was also Diarmait's undoing. When Diarmait was grown, he became one of Fionn's warriors, but eventually, he fell in love with Fionn's wife, Grainne, and stole her away. An enraged Fionn relentlessly pursued the couple, but when the company of the gods saw that the two were truly in love, they persuaded Fionn to forgive Diarmait—or at least to declare peace between him and his former friend.

Diarmait and Grainne prospered for many years and had many children, and one day, they decided to visit their friends in the company of the Fianna. They were welcomed, but as they slept, Diarmait was continually awakened by the sound of hounds. He realized he was missing a hunt and rushed out to find Fionn and company in pursuit of the magical boar. When he asked Fionn why he had been excluded from the hunt, Fionn told him of his geas and the events behind it, which had occurred when Diarmait was too young to remember. Diarmait shrugged off the danger and set off after the boar, but he could not kill it—each weapon shattered as it struck the boar. Finally, in a fit of frustration, he struck the boar's head with the hilt of his shattered sword, and broke the boar's skull. Unfortunately, the dying animal ran straight for Diarmait, fatally wounding him with its tusks.

Diarmait knew that Fionn could bring him water and so heal him, and Fionn obliged—however, as he neared Diarmait with the water, his anger returned, and he let it run from his fingers. He tried again, and again, and each time, he was overcome with fury as he neared his dying friend. Diarmait died, and Aenghus took his body home.

On a deeper level, the story of Diarmait reflects and illustrates the Celtic conviction that the fate of all things are tied to one another—the hunter and his prey, two ends of the same thread of life.

Birds: Messengers of the Gods

Birds play an enormous role in Celtic mythology, figuring as divine emblems and as messengers of the gods. Chief among the sacred birds of the Celts were the raven, the swan, and the crane, although numerous other birds including geese, ducks, and even owls were held sacred at various times.

Many early images of Celtic deities depict them with birds in the place of hands, emphasizing the importance of the birds as divine servants.

The Raven

Because of their dark color and gruesome dietary habits, ravens were especially connected with gods of war and death. But those same gods were also associated with growth and fertility, so ravens were also symbols of new life. It was the raven that accompanied the souls of the dead to the afterlife, and portraits of the deceased often depicted them with the bird. Ravens were sometimes viewed as reincarnated warriors or heroes—the Welsh hero Owain had an army of invincible ravens, which are sometimes interpreted as an army of reincarnated warriors.

The warrior god Bendigeitvran, better known as "Bran the Blessed," was for a time the Welsh/British father god; his name means "blessed raven." Bran's head is rumored to be buried under the Tower of London, where it protects England against invaders. A persistent superstition regarding the tower is that should the ravens who inhabit it flee, England will be without protection.

The raven was the ruler of the domain of air and therefore of communication; the cry of the raven was often interpreted as the voice of the gods. Images of the gods Lugh and Bran often depict them with birds alighting on their heads and shoulders, symbolizing this divine communication. (The Norse god Odin, who is sometimes compared to Lugh and Bran, has as his companions two ravens called Thought and Memory.) For this reason, ravens were favored by the druids for use in divinatory ritual.

The Swan

The swan was revered by the earliest Celts, as far back as the Urnfield and Halstatt cultures. Although they are creatures of water, swans were, oddly, connected with the sun, sometimes even appearing as bearers of the chariot of the sun god. Swans and other water birds adorned numerous religious artifacts of the period, including many small statues and masks.

FACT

Curiously, virtually every Celtic tale of magical swans share another theme, a chain or chains of precious metal by which a magical swan is identified. In some tales, the chains are of gold and silver; in others, the chain is made of common metals. Many times the birds appear linked together in large groups. The theme is an ancient one, which is reflected by the appearance of chained swans on ancient Celtic and pre-Celtic artifacts.

Many of the later Celtic gods appear in tales as swans or with the ability to change into swans. The ability seems closely connected with women although in some stories male gods have the same power, invariably with a female of the same ability. As seen in the tale of Aenghus, both the god and his magical lover have the ability to transform into swans during the festival of Samhain. Sometimes, it is Deichtine, the lover of Cuchulainn, who takes the form of a swan. Yet another tale of Cuchulainn tells of a young girl who pursues the hero in the form of one of the great birds, but she is badly wounded when the god mistakes her for a potential dinner.

One of the best-known stories involving swans is the legend of Lir, the Irish sea god, whose beautiful wife dies giving birth to his children and leaves him bereft. Lir marries the sister of his deceased wife, but she is jealous of the attention he lavishes on his children and decides to do away with them. She accomplishes this by sending the children to swim and, while they are in the water, using a druid's wand to transform them into swans. The children are thus tragically enchanted for 900 years, yet they retain their intelligence and powers of speech.

Domestic Animals

The horse has a long history with the Celtic people and at times was a deity unto itself. Horses were associated by the Gauls with both gods and goddesses and were emblems of the sun. The horse was a tremendously important animal to the Celtic tribes, and its domestication transformed their culture from a society of hunters to a community of powerful warriors, traders, and farmers. Horses were not only a source of meat and milk but also provided labor for agriculture, transportation for people and goods, and allowed huge improvements in hunting and warmaking capability.

By the time the Romans took notice of the Celts, they were already accomplished riders, and the Romans even borrowed many Celtic techniques from the Celtic cavalries for their own armies. The Romans were likewise impressed with the Celtic horse goddess, Epona, who was the only Celtic deity to have a temple within the boundaries of Rome.

The horse was of such importance to the Celts that it was associated with the sun itself. In some ancient cult statues, the god Taranis appears as a horse with a human face. The horse is also linked to a number of ancient goddesses, particularly those of warfare. The best-known of the horse goddesses is Epona. The god Teutates, "Father of the People," was often portrayed as a bearded horse, and one of the names of the Dagda, "Eochaid," comes from a root meaning "horse."

The Welsh revered a goddess similar to Epona, called Rhiannon. Rhiannon, whose son Pryderi/Peredur is also linked to horses, makes appearances as a riding goddess in many later tales. A curious story of Peredur's birth related in The Mabinogion tells that he is abducted at birth and left alongside a foal in a farmer's barn. His mother is accused of his murder, and she is sentenced to carry visitors to her husband's estate on her back. She continues in this manner until her son comes to the gate and is recognized. In this tale again are echoes of transformation, rebirth, and redemption through recognition of true nature.

The Hound

Hounds were another domesticated animal the Celts found invaluable. The hound was the companion of hunters and even of the gods. Hounds were prized emblems of courage and loyalty and were frequently given as gifts by nobles. When bestowed on a courageous warrior, the appellation "hound" was a badge of honor rather than an insult, and the name was even applied to gods, most notably Cuchulainn, the "Hound of Culann."

Hounds were also protective creatures, and a Celtic home seldom went without. Hounds were so well regarded that they were even believed to accompany the souls of the dead to the Otherworld.

The Bull

The bull was an emblem of fertility, potency, prophecy, and regeneration. The bull was important to the druids, an important element in sacrificial ritual and seership. According to numerous accounts, a druid seeking prophetic or poetic inspiration would slumber under the skin of a sacrificial bull, a ceremony also employed in the elections of kings.

The bull was connected to the sacred crane and was the emblem of the mysterious Gallic god Esus, "Lord." Several mysterious Gallic monuments dedicated to Esus contain images of a bull figure with the inscription *Tarvos Trigaranus*, or "bull with three cranes," an image of a bull or bull's head with three cranes perched atop his head or back. The symbolism has never been adequately explained and defies any attempt to decipher it although some have made very tenuous connections between the iconography and the stories of the divine hero Cuchulainn. The bull is the central symbol of Cuchulainn's story, the Tain bo Cuailnge, or Cattle Raid of Cooley, wherein the countryside is laid to waste and the god killed, all over a prized magical bull.

Dragons and Serpents

The serpent was a symbol of wisdom and fertility. A particular dragon/snake hybrid, referred to as the horned serpent, was connected to the torque, a symbol of sovereignty and status, and to the horned god Cernunnos. It was not until medieval times that dragons were viewed negatively; this was probably due to their associations with pagan gods—which is probably why so many tales pit brave Christian knights against wicked dragons.

The dragon, a creature inherited by the Romans, was featured in early tales of the Arthurian magician Merlin, where it was a symbol from prophetic visions and invariably a sign of bad omen. Dragons were not all bad, however. The Welsh so revered the protective red dragon that it became their national symbol.

The serpent was especially connected with healing waters, and the Roman authority Pliny noted in the first century that the druids revered an item they referred to as the "serpent's egg" for its healing powers. The serpent's egg was not an egg per se but an egg-shaped stone considered to possess certain magical properties.

Animals in Celtic Christianity

Celtic Christians continued the traditional pagan reverence of animals. Seemingly endless varieties of animals are depicted in Celtic scriptures, and these creatures can be seen cavorting about with their hunters even on religious stone carvings and crucifixes. One exception to this rule, however, would be the snake, whose prominence as a villain in Judeo-Christian mythology made it unsuitable as an object of reverence. The serpent was also viewed as a symbol of druidry and eventually seen as evidence that the druids were in fact demon worshippers—or at the very least, that they were deceived by the devil. That devil was found among the ancient gods in the form of the horned Cernunnos, whose visage became the emblem of the dark one for centuries to come.

CHAPTER 14

The Sacred Landscape

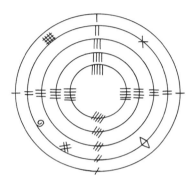

The sacred landscape left by their ancient ancestors had a profound affect on the spiritual and cultural development of the Celtic people. In modern times, people ascribe little if any significance to the landscape; today, the outdoors is rarely considered a necessity of everyday life. The Celts, on the other hand, found themselves intertwined with their surroundings. The land was not simply raw material for exploitation but an intelligent, living presence. The fabric of the land was home not only to man and animal, but also to the spirits of the forest and the crops, the underground dwellings of the ancestors, and the gods themselves.

14

Portals to the Otherworld

While the many ancient stone monuments, passage tombs, and barrows that dot the ancient landscape belonged not to the Celts but to their ancient ancestors, the Celts nonetheless regarded them as highly significant. The real meaning of these ancient sites can only be guessed at because there are no written records, no myths, and few clues of any kind to tell how they were used. Long after the culture that built these monuments had passed out of memory, their descendants attributed their origin to the gods. Although there seems to be some continuity of thought and symbolism between the Celts and their ancient predecessors, definitive evidence remains tantalizingly out of reach.

There are several types of megalithic tombs. These are generally divided among four types:

- Court tombs or cairns are multichambered generational tombs that resemble underground houses covered with earth.
- Passage tombs are complex tombs built to resemble elaborate houses and are covered over with earth and stones, some with elaborate doorways or courtyards. Passage tombs in Ireland often contain cremated remains rather than bodies.
- Portal tombs, cromlechs, or dolmens are doorlike stone structures that resemble passageways. Some of these are simply cairns whose earthen coverings have worn away.
- Barrows or tumuli are earthen mounds containing burial chambers covered with earth; these have the appearance of hills.

Court tombs are some of the oldest Neolithic gravesites. They were most often built on an east/west axis, and might have been used by a single family for several generations. The graves, known as dolmens ("table") or portal tombs (cromlechs, or "crooked stone" to the Irish), appear to be simple stone monuments. However, they are more likely the remains of early barrows from which the earth and contents have long worn away.

Passage Tombs

The underground chambers known as passage tombs were regarded by the Celts as the homes of the gods, entrances used to travel from the Otherworld to the world of mankind. Although they are commonly called tombs, the so-called passage tombs are not simply tombs but also temples.

Passage tombs are named for their long, tunnel-like entrances. Both the symbolism and positioning of the entrances of the chambers of many of these monuments show that the sun played a vital role in the ritual use of the chambers. Most passage tombs are decorated with elaborate carved designs, sometimes with elaborate astronomical calendars, which probably played an important role in the timing of rituals.

FACT

It is quite possible that the solstice rituals conducted in the passage tombs were the origin of the Celtic concepts of solar gates, the idea that the solstices and equinoxes represented passages, or "gates," by which the Otherworld could be accessed.

The famous tomb at Newgrange, for example, is replete with solar symbolism. Like many of its kind, the entrance of Newgrange is a long passage leading to an inner chamber. At the first light of the winter solstice, both the passage and the inner chamber are illuminated. Similar monuments nearby are aligned on the same axis, but they lack the precise alignment of Newgrange. The astronomical alignments, combined with the solar symbolism and presence of cremated remains, have led to speculation that the rituals conducted in the tombs were not simple funerals but ceremonies designed to facilitate the passage of the dead into rebirth—making the moniker "passage tomb" quite appropriate.

The Hollow Hills: Sidhe-Mounds

The earthen mounds known as barrows, long barrows, or tumuli are some of the world's oldest known burial places, dating back to classical antiquity. The barrows of Europe date mostly from the Neolithic era, but often continue into the Bronze Age. The graves themselves generally contain the bodies of the deceased and a variety of grave goods, including food, utensils, and weaponry. These are covered over with stones, and the stones covered with earth. Over time, they take on the appearance of an artificial hill. In some areas, many barrows crowd close together, creating a very unusual landscape.

The elaborate barrow tombs of the ancients were also perceived as homes of the Tuatha Dé Danann. They were referred to as the "hollow hills," and it was believed that one could hear the music and conversations of the fairy courts from within. Superstitious travelers even into modern times were reluctant to venture too close to one for fear they may be kidnapped by its inhabitants. The persistent belief that the hills were the homes of divine ancestors was based on a kernel of truth. Possibly, the Celts had some memory or intuition about the real purpose of the burial mounds—in a sense, they were indeed the dwelling places of their ancient ancestors! The name by which the Tuatha Dé Danann or fairy-folk were commonly known—Aes Sidhe, "barrow people"—is derived from their association with these mounds.

Stone Circles and Alignments

The ancient stone circles of Britain, Ireland, and Scotland represent one of Europe's most enduring enigmas. In their design and function, they are clearly related to the passage tombs that precede them, but they are not tombs. Hundreds of stone circles of varying complexity can be found throughout the British Isles and beyond, first appearing during the Neolithic period and continuing well into the Bronze Age. While some show signs of use as tombs, it is obvious that they served a larger purpose, possibly as temples, calendars, or even astronomical observatories. In many cases, they appear to be all three.

The earliest form these ancient monuments took was the henge, which consisted of a circular or ovoid ridge surrounding an inside ditch or circular pit. These were sometimes surrounded by wooden posts arranged in circles and, later, by stones. Most were relatively small, around 60 feet in diameter, although larger examples could be as large as 1,200 feet. Most consist of a single ring of stones, although as time passed, the circles grew in size and complexity, with some having as many as three concentric rings. Another popular style of stone monument is called an alignment, consisting of rows of menhirs (standing stones).

Literally thousands of stone circles, alignments, and monuments are scattered throughout Europe. Here are some of the best-known:

- Stonehenge, a prehistoric ring of large standing stones, is thought to have been erected around 2200 B.C.E.
- Avebury Henge, a ritual complex located in Southern England, is a monument that rivals Stonehenge in size and importance.
- Uisneach Hill, the "navel" of Ireland, is also called the "Stone of Divisions." Uisneach represented the symbolic center of Ireland and was the legendary location of the first Beltaine fire.
- The Ring of Brodgar is a prehistoric stone circle in Orkney, Scotland.
- The Carnac Stones is an alignment of thousands of stones that stretches nearly two miles in length in Carnac, France.
- The Rollright Stones are long rumored to be the remains of an enchanted king and his men.
- The Callanish Stones of the Isle of Lewis are slender megaliths arrayed in the form of a large Celtic cross.

Stonehenge

The ancient monument of Stonehenge is inarguably the best-known prehistoric monument on earth. Located on the Salisbury Plain in the geographic center of England, the site is more than 3,000 years old and may have been erected on the remains of an even earlier circle constructed from timber. On the plains, there is evidence that a large settlement once surrounded the site.

The origin and purpose of Stonehenge have puzzled historians and archaeologists for centuries. In medieval times, its conception was attributed to the Saxons, the druids, Merlin, and even to the devil himself, who was said to have built it from stones spirited from Ireland. In the centuries following, it was assumed to be a Roman temple and, later, a druid observatory.

Time and patient excavations have shown all of these ideas to be false, although the romantic notion of druids conducting solemn solstice rituals at the monument has been impossible to shake. Beyond a shadow of a doubt, the monument predates the druid orders by thousands of years; nonetheless, Stonehenge is still home to annual rituals conducted by druid revival groups.

Perhaps because people were so accustomed to its presence, Stonehenge wasn't regarded as very remarkable by most people until relatively recently. In fact, in 1915, a lawyer named Cecil Chubb purchased the monument as a gift for his wife for less than $10,000. History records her reaction as less than enthusiastic, and he eventually donated the site to the British government for use as a public park.

When compared to other prehistoric stone circles and monuments, Stonehenge is unique in both structure and layout. Its stone trilithons, the unique groupings of three that make up the remaining ring of the monument, are not found in any other monuments. There is archaeological evidence that Stonehenge may have begun as a ring of timber, which was later replaced with stone. There is also evidence that the monument was rebuilt several times over its long existence.

Despite its name, Stonehenge is not a true henge. A genuine henge consists of a circular or oblong ditch, surrounded by a raised earthen mound or ridge. Stonehenge is technically not a true henge at all because the position of its mound and ditch are reversed.

Standing Stones: Menhirs

The word *menhir* is from the Welsh meaning "long stone." It is a pretty exact description of the monuments, which occur most often as solitary standing stones. Often carefully shaped, they sometimes appear in groups or as part of stone circles. They are often decorated with a variety of symbolism and imagery. Menhirs are primarily an artifact of the Neolithic period.

Though their purpose is unknown, it is assumed they served some religious purpose. Theories about the purpose of menhir range from territorial markers to memorial monuments—at one time, it was even suggested they were sacrificial altars. Roman observers noted that when the stones were erected, sacrifices would be placed in the holes they were set in and that the stones were regularly anointed and hung with garlands of branches and flowers.

There are some hints that they served a religious or magical purpose, as they are tied to various supernatural occurrences in mythological stories. Whatever their purpose, Christians found them loathsome pagan idols and toppled them by the thousands. All the same, literally thousands of the enigmatic stones remain standing. The Carnac site in Brittany, for example, contains more than 3,000 individual stones arranged in clusters. Brittany is also home to the largest standing menhir, which reaches an astonishing height of 30 feet.

The standing stones have many connections with fertility rites, and even in the present day they are believed to promote conception and prevent complications of childbirth.

Echoes of Avalon: Glastonbury

Perhaps the most revered of Britain's sacred sites is Glastonbury, the site of a former great abbey that many believe to be the ancient entrance to Avalon, home of Gwyn ap Nudd, lord of the Otherworld. Among the many legends surrounding Glastonbury, it is rumored to be the location of the entrance to Otherworld, the site of ancient Neolithic chalkworks, the grave of king Arthur and Guinevere, the home of St. Patrick, and even a depository of the Holy Grail! Glastonbury and its towering hill are mysterious, even magical places.

The most recognizable feature of Glastonbury is the Tor, a conical, terraced hill that rises from the surrounding plain. The plains that surround the Tor were once a flood plain, and because of this, the ancient Celtic name for the area was Ynys Witrin, the "Isle of Glass."

There is much speculation about the Tor's seven terraces. Because of their unusual shape and number (seven), there is some debate whether they are natural or man-made and, if the latter, what their purpose might have been. When viewed from above, the terraces create a winding, labyrinthine path, which may have served some ancient ritual purpose.

On visiting the Tor, the visionary poet William Blake was inspired to pen some of his most famous lines:

> *And did those feet in ancient time*
> *walk upon England's mountains green?*
> *And was the holy Lamb of God*
> *on England's pleasant pastures seen?*
> *And did the countenance divine*
> *shine forth upon our clouded hills?*
> *And was Jerusalem builded here*
> *among these dark Satanic Mills?*

Archaeological explorations of the area have found evidence of continuous occupation of the site, from Neolithic settlements to Roman fortifications, until finally it was home to Christian monasteries and a medieval church, which was destroyed in a thirteenth century earthquake. All that remains of the abbey is St. Michael's Tower at the top of the Tor. Ancient groves of apple trees give Glastonbury another connection to the Otherworld, and it features in several mythological tales as the location of the entrance to Avalon.

Avalon and Arthur

Glastonbury is heavily connected with the legend of King Arthur. Early in the Arthurian cycle, Glastonbury was identified as Ynys Affalon, or Annwn, where the mythical Arthur is mentioned for the very first time, in the account of the quest for the Cauldron of Annwn. In the Arthurian romances of the twelfth century, Arthur returns to Avalon mortally wounded, to remain there for eternity.

Besides being connected with Avalon, Arthur's final resting place, Glastonbury is close to the ruins of Cadbury Castle, a hill fort closely associated with the historical Arthur. The fortification dates to the correct period, and nearby place names can be linguistically connected to the name *Camelot*. (*Cadbury* in the Saxon language is "battle fort"; the castle lies near the Cam River.) The connection was first made in writing by antiquarian John Leland in 1532, recording a local legend of some age. Evidence is mostly circumstantial, but it is clear from the archaeological evidence— including quantities of Roman gold and evidence of a great feasting hall— that the fortress belonged to a chieftain of some importance.

FACT

One Glastonbury legend links Arthur with the tradition of the fairy raid or wild hunt. Once every seven years, at sundown on Midsummer's Eve, Arthur and his party would ride out from underneath the Glastonbury hills, making a raucous circuit of the neighborhood before returning underground.

Local legends of Arthur and his court abound, but whether they spring from a germ of historical truth or are simply self-perpetuating is unknown. A number of legends linking Arthur with Glastonbury appeared in written form beginning in the twelfth century, when a Welsh story identified the Tor as the location of the fortress of Melwas, a rival king who kidnapped Arthur's wife Guinevere. Soon afterward, Geoffrey of Monmouth identified Glastonbury as the location of Avalon.

Less than sixty years later, the local monastery claimed to have "discovered" the burial plot of Arthur and his wife, although this was certainly of the genre of "pious fraud," a hoax committed to add income to the monastery's coffers. The discovery was a fortuitous one, coming shortly after a fire had devastated the monastery. During the rebuilding, Abbot Henry de Sully sponsored a search that located a tomb inside a hollowed oak, which contained the skeletal remains of two people. And just in case there was any question of their identity, a leaden cross bearing the convenient Latin inscription *Hic jacet sepultus inclitus rex Arthurus in insula Avalonia* ("Here lies interred the famous King Arthur on the Isle of Avalon") lay above the stone cover. Glastonbury increased greatly in importance afterward, becoming the second most powerful church in England for a time. In 1278, the bodies were reburied with much pomp under the foot of the altar, with King Edward and Queen Eleanor in solemn attendance.

Joseph of Arimathea

Even older than the legend of Arthur is the widespread belief that Glastonbury was where Christianity was first established in the British Isles. The emissary was no less a figure than Joseph of Arimathea, the wealthy apostle of Christ, who was said to have traveled there after the crucifixion. This idea was first put to paper in the ninth century by Archbishop Rabanus Maurus, in his biography of Mary Magdalene. In this work, Maurus claimed that Joseph traveled to Britain along with Mary Magdalene, Lazarus, and other members of Christ's inner circle. In later, more fanciful versions, Joseph arrives accompanied by a youthful Jesus, who receives training from the druids of the island.

The claims about Joseph could be dismissed as so much fantasy, were it not for one curious fact. Church father Tertullian, writing around 200 C.E., marvels at the spread of Christianity in pagan lands, even as it has yet to take hold in Rome:

> . . . *all the limits of the Spains, and the diverse nations of the Gauls, and the haunts of the Britons—inaccessible to the Romans, but subjugated to Christ.*

Why he believes this to be the case is unknown, but his observation probably reflects a widespread belief. The sentiment was echoed about a century later by Church historian Eusebius, who accepted as fact that Jesus' apostles had visited the "Britannic isles."

Through Joseph, the Holy Grail was said to have traveled to England, providing a connection between the chalice and the legendary King Arthur that has excited so many imaginations. The Joseph idea was first put to paper in the twelfth century Arthurian tale "Joseph d'Arimathe," by French poet Robert de Boron. In de Boron's story, Joseph uses the chalice of the Last Supper to catch the blood of Christ as he hangs on the cross. Joseph then carries the cup with him to Avalon, to keep it safe until it comes to be discovered by Arthur and his knights. This is the first story that connects the Grail explicitly with Christianity. The idea proved so popular that by the fourteenth century, the incident was recorded as historical fact by the Benedictine historian John of Glastonbury.

Another legend that connects Joseph with Glastonbury is the sacred thorn, an otherwise ordinary hawthorn tree that grew outside the abbey. It was reportedly remarkable in that unlike other hawthorns, it flowered twice a year—first in the spring, and again at Christmastime. The tree became entwined with Joseph in the sixteenth century, when the legend first began to circulate that the tree originated from the staff of the saint. Supposedly, when Joseph came to the end of his journey, he struck his walking staff into the earth, where it blossomed. It became traditional to make gifts of cuttings from the thorn to monarchs and other VIPs. That tradition continued until the seventeenth century, when the tree was burned as a pagan superstition by Oliver Cromwell's troops. The tree was eventually replanted from one of its own cuttings, but the new tree died in 1991. The original thorn was propagated with many cuttings, however; its offspring, given as gifts, can be seen throughout Britain and as far away as Canada.

FACT

The holy thorn was so well regarded that its opinion was sought after the then-unpopular Gregorian calendar was adopted. It was reported that visitors flocked to the tree on the date of the "new" Christmas, but that the tree preferred the "old" date, refusing to bloom until then.

The Chalice Well

Today, Glastonbury is extremely well trodden by spiritual pilgrims of all stripes. Without a doubt, the biggest draw is not the Tor itself but the sacred well that lies at its foot. The spring that fills the well is believed to have been in continuous flow for nearly 2,000 years, and it has likely been regarded as a holy site for at least that long. The water of the well is heavily pigmented with iron, giving it the appearance of blood. Because of this reddish hue in the water, it is sometimes called the "red spring" or even the "blood spring." The well is tied into the legend of Joseph, where it is suggested as the hiding place of the Grail, which continually refreshed the water with the blood of Christ.

In 1908, archaeologist Frederick Bligh Bond was named director of excavations at Glastonbury Abbey. He made several important discoveries and recreated the original layout of the ancient buildings on the site, which he believed to be of great spiritual significance.

A decade later, still profoundly affected by the site, Bond designed an ornate cover for the sacred well, which he presented to the site as a gift. The wooden and metal cover features an ornate design based on sacred geometry. A *vesica pisces* design of two overlapping circles represents the goddess and the intersection of the Upperworld and the Underworld. A sword symbolizes the divine male and the sword Excalibur, and a foliage design meant to represent Joseph's holy thorn surrounds them.

Tara: Seat of the High Kings of Ireland

The ancient site of Tara (Teamhair na Rí, "Hill of the King"), is one of the most ancient sacred sites in Ireland. Tara is located in Meath, the symbolic center of Ireland. Tara is home to numerous monuments, including the Mound of the Hostages, a Neolithic era passage tomb; various earthworks; and the standing stone Lia Fail, the "Stone of Destiny," which according to legend was one of the four treasures brought to Ireland by the Tuatha Dé Danann.

Tara is the legendary seat of Irish kings. It is where the high kings of Ireland would be chosen and where they would celebrate their coronations. The Hill of Tara is surrounded by an Iron Age-ringed fortification known as the Fort of Kings or the Royal Enclosure. Within this circular boundary are two interior rings, a smaller ring fort and a circular earthwork, which have the appearance of breasts when viewed from above.

It was here that the Feis Teamrach ("mating of Tara") was held, a great assembly of lawmakers, scholars, and priests. This assembly, also known as the Parliament or Feast of Tara, was, according to legend, instituted over 3,000 years ago by King Ollam Fodhla, the namesake of Ulster.

In the manner of ancient tribal assemblies, the Feis Teamrach met every three years (or seven, depending on the account) at the feast of Samhain to discuss matters of history, decide laws, and record history. The ritual owes its name to the ancient king-making rite of sacred marriage, the symbolic mating of the Morrigan and the Dagda before the battle of Mag Tuiread. It is very likely that the ancient assembly evolved from a sexual ritual designed to reinforce the high king's symbolic marriage with the land, represented by the goddess Sovereignty.

Sadly, despite the immense cultural, spiritual, and historical importance of this ancient site, Tara faces serious threats from the encroachments of civilization. In 2006, despite strenuous and continuing protest from activists worldwide, construction began on an extension of the nearby N3 commuter roadway. The extension, dubbed M3, is designed to ease traffic congestion, and its path will cut directly through the Tara-Skryne Valley, where it will pass less than a mile and a half from the Hill of Tara. The proposed path cuts through an area rich with unexplored archaeological sites, including newly discovered monuments and tombs that lie directly in the path of construction.

In 2007, archaeologists discovered the remains of a massive circular henge complex several acres in size, a find of enormous historic significance. Because henges are a rarity in Ireland, this is a significant find. At the time of this writing, however, plans call for a rapid excavation of the site, after which it will be destroyed so as not to delay construction of the new roadway.

Springs and Healing Wells

Water was held especially sacred to the Celts, a symbol of life and nurture and a source of wisdom, intuition, and magic. Water was the vehicle for rebirth and reincarnation and the domain of the gods of healing.

Lakes, streams, rivers, and wells were all considered entrances to the Otherworld, and they were frequently used as depositories of sacrificial offerings to the gods.

Every body of water had its attendant gods and goddesses, nymphs, and spirits. Water was often assigned to a particular deity based on its aspect: bubbling streams and brooks may have belonged to the goddess Coventina or other nymphs. Rivers were often under the provenance of a local goddess. Hot springs were usually associated with solar deities, but they often had attendant goddesses as well, as they were viewed as a marriage of sorts between the solar deity and the goddess of the spring.

Water also figured in the Celtic cult of the head. Severed heads were among the many offerings left at the bottoms of lakes and ponds, and scarcely a well from ancient times does not contain a severed head or three. The heads seem to have been intended to give the waters a healing benefit. In some cases, they may have served an oracular purpose, as attested by the abundance of folk tales involving severed heads that prophesy from magical wells. It is also possible that a healing benefit was sought, as drinking from the skulls of one's ancestors was widely thought to be a curative.

Many of the deities of the Otherworld were originally associated with bodies of water, and water was one of the most popular places to leave offerings for them. Much evidence suggests that natural springs, waterfalls, and even many lakes were the domain of the gods of healing; these were very popular with pilgrims, who left many offerings at these sacred sites. During the period of Roman occupation, these offerings expanded to include "curse tablets," tiny strips of engraved lead containing entreaties to the gods to exact all manner of vengeance on enemies, thieves, straying lovers, or indifferent objects of affection.

ALERT!

Offerings tossed in wells for their attendant "lady" almost certainly derive from these ancient sacrificial practices. When you throw a coin into a fountain for Lady Luck, you are following a very ancient tradition.

Aquae Sulis: The Springs at Bath

The three hot springs of Bath, England, were considered magical by the Celtic Britons, who dedicated the largest to the water goddess Sulis. When the Romans invaded Britain in 43 c.e., they recognized the site as sacred. They identified Sulis with the Roman goddess Minerva, and she was thereafter referred to as Sulis-Minerva. They built a great complex bathhouse around the site, with many elaborate temples and buildings. Both the Celts and the Roman occupiers revered the baths for their healing qualities, and the site became a tourist Mecca.

Dressing the Wells

A possible remnant of the veneration of well goddesses is the practice of well dressing, a tradition of rural England that was first recorded in the fourteenth century and has been continued in one form or another until the present day. The modern ritual begins with the creation of a wooden frame that is covered with a soft clay, into which is incised a design, usually with a religious theme. The design is then filled and colored with flowers, foliage, and berries, after which the frame is erected over the well.

Well dressing is connected to May Day practices and is similar to the Roman festival of the Fontinalia, in which the guardian nymphs of wells were honored with garlands of flowers. The well dressing ritual seems to have similar pagan origins. Curiously, many of the towns associated with the rite are home to hot springs or other water features.

Cloughtie Wells

Cloughtie (or Clootie) wells are named for the strips of rag ("cloots") hung on nearby trees as votive offerings left by petitioners in need of healing. The rags are dipped in the well, often in conjunction with prayers, incantations, and ritual circumambulation. Sometimes, they are touched to an afflicted body part or made from clothing worn by the afflicted. They are then hung from the tree in hopes that as the rag disintegrates, so will the illness.

One such well is the Knockanare Well, whose history betrays its pagan origins. The well, located on the grounds of Blackwater Castle in County

Cork, figures in a story of Fionn mac Cumhaill, wherein the hero was cured after receiving a mortal wound. The site contained a stone Sheela-na-gig until recent times.

Brighid's Well

Numerous wells throughout Ireland are associated with St. Brighid, but the main one is, of course, the well located at Kildare Abbey. Like other sacred wells, Brighid's well features a cloughtie tree and is popular with pilgrims seeking healing or an answer to a prayer. The small chapel adjacent to the well is strikingly similar to descriptions of ancient sacred wells. The narrow chamber is crowded with statuary and literally crammed with offerings—prayers, photos, rosary beads and religious objects, prayers, and other items.

Chalkworks

One of the most mysterious features of the ancient landscape is the enormous hill figures—massive drawings literally carved into the landscape, created by hewing away turf and earth to expose bright chalk below. Only a handful of such figures survive intact, all in the English countryside:

- The Cerne Abbas Giant is also known as the "Rude Man" for his remarkable genitalia. The giant is bald and carries a large club, leading to speculation that he represents the god Ogmios or even the Roman Hercules.
- The "Long Man" of Wilmington may represent a warrior or a god. This enigmatic standing figure appears to hold two spears.
- The Uffington Horse is one of a great number of horse figures, most of which have been lost. The image appears on coins unearthed in local archaeological explorations and may reflect the image of a goddess.

The purpose of the hill figures is unknown, although they have obvious religious import. They may have been intended to promote fertility, mark festivals, or serve as a votive offering.

CHAPTER 15

Celtic Magic and Prayer

Belief in the magical potency of language was an underpinning of Celtic pagan belief and remained pervasive well into the Christianization of Celtic territories. Celtic magic was overwhelmingly language-driven. Celtic spells and prayers are exclusively written to be spoken aloud. They are seldom supplicating; almost invariably, they are commanding invocations. Curiously, even the most pious of prayers take the commanding, authoritative tone of the poet. Also notable is that almost always, be it a prayer or curse, a magical invocation calls upon the powers of nature for effectiveness.

Faeth Fiada: The Cloak of Invisibility

A magical ability of particular renown was the faeth fiada, or "deer's cry," the ability to cloak oneself in mist or to appear invisible. This particular talent of the Tuatha Dé Danann, a gift from the sea god Manannan, was later used to cloak Ireland in a magical mist to prevent the invading Milesians from returning to the isle. It is the faeth fiada that prevents the Sidhe folk from being seen today.

Various other mythological characters possessed the ability, including Diarmuid, the nephew of Fionn. Eventually, this shapeshifting talent passed to St. Patrick, who used an incantation called the "Deer's Cry," which gave him the appearance of a fawn to his enemies.

The incantation, spoken today as a prayer of protection, is called the Lorica, or "Breastplate of Patrick." It reads in part:

> *May Christ shield me today*
> *against poison and fire,*
> *against drowning and wounding,*
> *so that I may fulfill my mission*
> *and bear fruit in abundance.*
> *Christ behind and before me,*
> *Christ behind and above me,*
> *Christ with me and in me,*
> *Christ around and about me,*
> *Christ on my right and on my left,*
> *Christ when I lie down at night,*
> *Christ when I rise in the morning,*
> *Christ in the heart of every man who thinks of me,*
> *Christ in the mouth of everyone that speaks of me,*
> *Christ in every eye that sees me,*
> *Christ in every ear that hears me.*

Protective prayers of the sort became increasingly popular until it was quite common practice to tuck a copy of one onto one's person before traveling. Medieval knights were known to have Patrick's poem inscribed inside their own breastplates.

Although much of the text of the Lorica is explicitly Christian, a portion of the prayer betrays its ancient origin:

> *I arise today through the strength of Heaven*
> *the rays of the sun,*
> *the radiance of the moon,*
> *the splendor of fire,*
> *the speed of lightning,*
> *the swiftness of wind,*
> *the depth of the sea,*
> *the stability of the earth*
> *the firmness of rock.*

The verse is clearly derived from a bardic formula and recalls the ancient invocations of Amergin to the elements. Although ostensibly Christian, the prayer makes no invocation to the heavenly realm, preferring the immediacy of the earthly sphere. There is no way to know whether the prayer was Christianized to disguise its origin or if its popularity necessitated an acceptible alternative.

Blessings and Curses

Almost everyone is familiar with the concept of the Irish blessing, and many people can even recite one or two traditional rhymes, at least around St. Patrick's Day. A great many are also familiar with the so-called Irish curse as well. The evolution of the blessing (and cursing) traditions began with the druids and filidh and the Celt's deeply held belief in the inherent power of the spoken word. The tradition continued in the legends of the saints, who were often renowned for their magical way with words.

The traditional bardic curse was satire, a potent magical skill. The ability to curse with words was the special skill of the bards and the filidh; their scathing satires were greatly feared as they had the power to raise blisters on the face or even cause death through sheer humiliation.

At the coming of Christianity, the ability to magically use words was transferred to the Christian saints, particulary Patrick. Much of Patrick's legend centers upon his many feats of magic, which appears to be a deliberately engineered literary transfer of druidic power to the saint.

Belief in the power of the satire was so strong that every form of satire, including the comic, was officially banned in Britain until well after the advent of Christianity.

Patrick's promotion of Christianity is recorded through legend not as one of humility and example but one of magical force, wherein Patrick's powers are demonstrated to be greater than those of the druids. Ostensibly, this is because he has the power of God on his side, but the stories of Patrick's dominance have a ring of the old bardic contests about them. Patrick's biographers gleefully record Patrick's curses against pagan kings lasting for generations. Patrick's purported autobiography maintains that the conversion of the Irish was accomplished not by prayer but by cursing the fertility of the druids, forcing people to convert simply to avoid starvation and disease.

Sainings

Although its exact origin is unknown, the rite known as a saining is an ancient ritual. The word *saining* is from an old Norse word, meaning "to sign," and refers to an ancient protective gesture not uncoincidentally similar to the Christian sign of the cross. In Scotland in particular, a saining was a ritual of protection and purification, performed at birth and death, and on holy days for the protection of crops, livestock, buildings, and boats. Saining was also performed for the sick or dying. Later saining rituals involved the use of Bibles and prayer, but the underlying symbolism of the rite is clearly pagan. The emphasis on circumambulation, the repetition of the number three, and the use of fire are echoes of the druid purification practices.

For the saining of an infant, a burning branch or lit candle would be carried deasil—in the direction of the sun—around the baby's cradle three times in succession. In later times, this was followed by three circuits with an open Bible, accompanied by prayers. The saining ritual for the dead was more complex. After the body of the deceased was washed, it was dressed and laid on a table. The candle was passed three times around the body as before, after which three measures of salt would be placed on the chest of the corpse. The windows and doors of the house would be opened to speed the egress of the soul, and the candle would remain lit until it had burned away entirely.

The saining of the household, grain stores, livestock, and boats was carried out several times a year, particularly at midsummer and at the New Year, and was carried out using a burning branch of fir.

The Carmina Gaedelica

In the late nineteenth century, a folklorist named Alexander Carmichael began to compile a collection of prayers, charms, spells, and hymns from various places in Gaelic-speaking Scotland. This enormous collection contains a fantastic synthesis of Christian prayer, folk beliefs, and survivals of ancient pagan symbolism. Most of the collected songs and charms invoke the Virgin Mary, or the trinity, but many are so obviously pagan in character that they must be of ancient origin. A favorite saint in the Carmina is Bride, who is also the ancient patron goddess of Ireland.

The *Carmina Gaedelicais* is divided into several categories:

- Invocations
- Seasonal stories and observations
- Blessings
- Incantations

A typical curse from the *Carmina Gadelica* calls upon God to curse an enemy in spectacular fashion:

The wicked who would do me harm
May he take the throat disease,
Globularly, spirally, circularly,
Fluxy, pellety, horny-grim.
Be it harder than the stone,
Be it blacker than the coal,
Be it swifter than the duck,
Be it heavier than the lead.
Be it fiercer, fiercer, sharper, harsher, more malignant,
Than the hard, wound-quivering holly,
Be it sourer than the sained, lustrous, bitter, salt salt,
Seven seven times.
Oscillating thither,
Undulating hither,
Staggering downwards,
Floundering upwards.
Drivelling outwards,
Snivelling inwards,
Oft hurrying out,
Seldom coming in.
A wisp the portion of each hand,
A foot in the base of each pillar,
A leg the prop of each jamb,
A flux driving and dragging him.
A dysentery of blood from heart, from form, from bones,
From the liver, from the lobe, from the lungs,
And a searching of veins, of throat, and of kidneys,
To my contemners and traducers.
In name of the god of might,
Who warded from me every evil,
And who shielded me in strength,
From the net of my breakers
And destroyers.

The verses call down painful physical calamity on the speaker's ene-mies. The ritual also relies on the traditional triple invocation, and it is for-givable to question just which "god of might" is being supplicated here. As is typical of Celtic magic, there is no supplication here; the power is clearly assumed by the speaker.

Ogham Divination and Charms

As discussed in earlier chapters, it is clear that the ogham alphabet was used in a sacred context and that it was likely used in some form for divi-natory purposes. Unfortunately, the circumspect druids never managed to pass their secrets along, and so we are left to guess how ogham divination may have been accomplished.

In the story of Midir and Etain, Etain's husband seeks to recover his lost spouse through the services of a druid, who divines the location of the absconded lovers using staves of wood carved with ogham characters, a practice similar to rune magic used in the north. Reconstructions of ogham divination are largely based on Roman descriptions of the northern prac-tice, using meanings for the characters derived from the druid uses and beliefs about the sacred woods.

Modern ogham divination is carried out by means of a set of twenty or twenty-five staves, or twigs, each carved with one of the ogham letters. The especially ambitious assure that each twig is of the correct tree or plant, but often a simple set of birch twigs will be used. To perform a divination, a set of twigs is scattered onto a specially inscribed diagram or on a mat or can-vas on which a diagram has been drawn. This is usually a series of concen-tric circles marked for the past, present, and future; however, in this practice there are many variations, some of which are quite complex.

The diagram used in most ogham divination is known as the "Shield of Fionn," after the magical shield of the hero. Fionn used his hazel shield to gather the wisdom of the giant Balor while protecting himself from the venom that dripped from Balor's head.

The staves are scattered on the mat and interpreted according to where they fall. The general interpretations are given as follows:

- Beth (birch): New beginnings, purification
- Luis (rowan): Protection against magic
- Fearn (alder): Divine communication, omen
- Saille (willow): Balance, healing, intuition
- Nuin (ash): Healing, protective magic
- Huatha (hawthorn): Fairies, youth
- Daur (oak): Strength, endurance, seership
- Tinne (holly): Protection, survival, unexpected things
- Coll (hazel): Wisdom, illumination
- Quert (apple): Bounty, youth, Otherworld encounters
- Muin (vine): Rebirth, renewal
- Gort (ivy): Marriage, fertility, intoxication
- Ngetal (reed): Disruption
- Straif (blackthorn): Limitations, obstacles, restrictions
- Ruis (elder): Grief, betrayal
- Ailm (Silver fir): Purification, protection
- Onn (furze): Abundance
- Ur (heather): Rest, suspension
- Eadha (poplar): Speech, communication
- Ido (yew): Death, renewal, Otherworld affairs

In moden divination, the letters are notched into twigs or slices of wood or are printed on paper cards. A simplified divination can be performed by simply drawing a three from a bowl in response to a query.

The Magical Tools of the Druid

In addition to their prodigious abilities of speech, the druids employed a number of magical tools, amulets, and charms. The wand or staff, an ever-present instrument of the magician, is recorded in numerous accounts of the druids. The most unusual of these is the *Craebh Ciuil* ("Silver Branch"), which was reportedly a delicate wand in the shape of a branch, hung with musical bells. The silver wand seems to have been an emblem of office for the bards; sometimes branches of bronze or gold are mentioned as well.

In mythological stories, the branch is invariably connected to the Otherworld and has the power to put its hearers in a trance sleep. The branch seems to have been connected with the sea god Manannan originally, but in later tales, it is often granted to heroes by Otherworld goddesses. Silver Branch makes an appearance at the beginning of the account of the Voyage of Bran, who sets out to find the Otherworld after hearing the beautiful music of one of its trees in a dream. In another tale, King Cormac mac Airt returns from the Otherworld with such a branch, which was able to lull the people of his court to sleep with its music.

The druids also employed numerous amulets and talismans, as attested to by archaeological finds and the accounts of observers. These included charms made of various woods and plants, and small metal emblems such as the wheel emblem of Taranis. Stone amulets, called "adder stones," were fossil ammonites that resembled sleeping serpents; these were carried to ward off illness, especially maladies of the eye.

The Greeks and Romans were especially interested in a druid amulet called the serpent's egg, a glass or crystal stone that was believed to have been vomited up by snakes. The serpent's egg was believed to be a powerful talisman, especially efficacious in legal matters. The amulet was so popular that the Romans outlawed it, and one account tells of a Roman soldier who was executed for wearing such a concealed amulet to court.

CHAPTER 16

The Hero's Quest

To say that the hero is a central figure in Celtic mythology and culture is a great understatement. The gods of the Celtic pantheons were warriors, adventurers, and accomplished poets to a one—even the most sensitive poet was also a fearful warrior. It was not simply bravery and fearlessness that was expected of the hero, but also learning, skill, cleverness, and loyalty. A lack of any of these qualities spelled the tragic downfall of many a great Celtic hero.

The Cult of the Hero

Many outside observers remarked admiringly on the fearlessness of the Celts, a reputation that very often kept them safe from invasion. Even though it lacked a central government, Celtic society's cult of the hero provided the glue that held disparate tribes together, offering the Celts a common mythology.

Heroes of particular bravery and importance might become kings, and extraordinary heroes might even become gods. Heroes were very highly regarded as cult figures in Celtic society, praised in song and story, and were laid to rest in lavish tombs when they died. It has long been supposed that many, if not all, of the deities of the Celtic pantheons were heroic ancestors whose great deeds made them immortal in song and story. And even as the ascendancy of Christianity demoted the gods, the hero remained an important fixture in the Celtic imagination.

With the coming of Christianity came Christian heroes, whose deeds of bravery and magic for a time eclipsed in importance even the heroes of the Bible. Celtic warrior kings were eventually eclipsed by the likes of Arthur, Gawain, and Peredur. Irish saints could perform feats of druidic magic, travel to the Otherworld and back, and were even credited with converting many of the ancient divine heroes to Christianity.

Hero Tales

The Celtic tradition of heroic stories is the direct ancestor of the so-called "fairy tale." Although the popular stories have evolved over time to reside in the realm of make-believe, they are firmly rooted in Celtic spiritual traditions. Named for the fairy-folk who inspired them, they contain all of the elements associated with the genre:

- Heroes of fantastic strength, cleverness, and ability
- Quests and magical tests
- Magical and supernatural weapons, musical instruments, and vessels
- Giants, fairies, and elves

Bran the Blessed

Bran Bendigeid, "the Blessed Raven" is a central figure in The Mabinogion, and before Arthur was counted as Britain's greatest champion, he was a hero of unmatched mythical proportion. Bran was by most accounts the son of Lir, a giant who possessed superhuman strength and abilities.

Both Bran's head and his moniker "Raven" associate him with the early Celtic cult of the head, and possibly with the Morrigan. That Bran's severed head was capable of prophecy also connects him with the ancient Celtic practice of augury, divination through bird flight.

The story of Bran as recounted in The Mabinogion begins with the marriage of his sister, Branwen, to Mathowlch, the high king of Ireland. The wedding was held on the shores of Anglesey Isle, and giant tents were erected to accommodate the giant's enormous frame. The marriage feast began with much merriment, but it was soon to be soured by the pique of Bran's half-brother Efnissyen, who was offended that he had never been asked to consent to the marriage.

Efnissyen took out his annoyance on Mathowlch's stables, mutilating his fine horses. The king, outraged and dismayed by this insult from his bride's family, called off the wedding and prepared to return to his ships. Bran, being a man of honor, quickly stepped in and pleaded with Mathowlch to remain. To remedy his losses, he offered the king a new horse for each one injured, plus a great silver staff and a platter of gold. Mathowlch, still smarting, refused.

So great was Bran's desire to do the honorable thing that he offered the Irish king Wales's greatest treasure: the Cauldron of Rebirth, which could be used to restore the bodies of the dead to full health, but for their powers of speech. Mathowlch at last relented and accepted Bran's generosity. He took his new bride home with him, and she bore him a son within the year, whom she named Gwern, "Alder."

Mathowlch, unfortunately, hadn't forgiven his wife's family for the mutilation of his horses. Once he had a son, Branwen was banished to the kitchen, where she was expected to toil as a common servant. Angry as he was, Mathowlch was not foolish enough to let Bran hear of his deeds, so he took great pains to prevent any word of his cruelty from reaching the giant's ears. Ships were prohibited from traveling to Britain, and ships from Britain were seized as they made landing.

This situation obviously could not hold, but Branwen decided not to wait for her brother to investigate his missing ships. No fool herself, she devised a way to contact her brother in secret. She trained a young bird to carry messages and sent it to find Bran. Bran proved easy to locate, and he immediately mustered an invasion force. He left his kingdom under the care of his son Caradoc and sailed for Ireland with his fleet.

FACT

Actually, it was only Bran's armies who set sail to meet Mathowlch's forces. Bran was of such tremendous size that he was forced to wade in the ocean alongside his ships.

Meanwhile, Mathowlch was plagued by visions of a forest that appeared in the midst of the sea, flanked by an enormous mountain. Having no one who could interpret this vision, he summoned Branwen to interpret. She informed the king that the forest upon the ocean was Bran's navy, and the mountain was her brother, coming to rescue her.

Now the king knew that his brother-in-law was coming for him and that he would certainly be defeated in battle. So he devised a plan to trick the giant through flattery. He set about at once constructing a house big enough to accommodate Bran. The house was to be so large that it would hold not only the giant but his army as well. It would be the first house large enough to fit Bran, and the giant's first home, certain to impress him and make him forget his anger at least temporarily.

Mathowlch arranged to have a great feast prepared in the hall of the new home. The king expected the giant and his party would get quite drunk, at which time he planned a surprise attack. From the pillars of the great hall, he hung a great many sacks, each one containing an armed warrior, who would drop down amongst Bran's men and slaughter them.

The Destruction of Ireland

At first, the giant was quite pleased with his new home, and the ruse was successful. When he asked about the sacks hung from the pillars, Mathowlch explained these were provisions of flour and oats. Bran was satisfied with this explanation. His ever-suspicious brother Efnissyen was not so sure, however, and went about squeezing each sack to assure himself. Because Efnissyen was part giant himself, he managed to squeeze each warrior quite to death, and Mathowlch was forced to reckon a new plan.

Before he was able, however, the hot-headed Efnissyen once again made a mess of things. Upon being introduced to Branwen's young son, Efnissyen was reminded of his anger at the wedding, and in a fit of temper he threw the child into the fireplace.

The feast erupted into warfare, and the battle raged for three days and nights before Bran's armies emerged victorious. The battle had such longevity in large part because the magical cauldron that Bran had given Mathowlch enabled him to continually resurrect his forces. Efnissyen concealed himself among the Irish dead and was able to split the cauldron when he was thrown inside it, and the Irish were defeated shortly afterward. Efnissyen achieved some measure of salvation in this act, as the sacrifice killed him.

While Bran was battling in Ireland, a rival chieftain overthrew his son Caradoc and enslaved the British chieftains with dark magic. Caradoc, like his aunt Branwen, expired from grief.

The result of the battle was catastrophic. Every Irish citizen but for five pregnant women lay dead, and the armies of Bran were reduced to seven warriors. Bran himself was wounded with a poison dart and lay dying. Branwen, distraught that her discomfort had brought ruin on all, died of grief on the spot.

The Miraculous Head

The dying giant implored his seven remaining men to cut off his head and return with it to Britain. Upon their return, his men chanced to enter the Otherworld, where they remained for eighty years, having forgotten all of their troubles. The head of Bran remained active and made merry alongside them, until one chanced to open the door leading to the upper world. The men all recalled their mission and the great disaster that had befallen. They returned to Britain and buried Bran's head under the Tower of London, facing the shoreline. The head served as a powerful talisman, protecting Britain from invasion for many generations before it was dug up and turned around by the pious Arthur, who claimed that from that point forward, Britain would be protected by God and by Arthur's armies alone.

Culwhch and Olwen

Culwhch was by most accounts the son of Goleudydd, who was overcome with madness, causing her to wander the countryside over the course of her pregnancy. She recovered her sanity as her labor began in a pigsty, but without sufficient time to remedy the situation. And so the hero was born amongst the pigs, and named Culwhch, "Son of Pig." Culwhch's mother returned home but died shortly afterward.

Culwhch's father remarried a powerful woman who wished Culwhch to marry her own daughter. Culwhch refused, and his stepmother placed him under a curse, requiring that his future wife must be a girl named Olwen, the daughter of Yspaddadden, the dangerous chieftain of the race of giants. As far as love went, this was not a terrible curse, as Olwen's great beauty and demeanor were legendary, but her location was unknown and her father was a terrifying tyrant.

To locate his future spouse, Culwhch gathers together a band of skilled men, including Cei and Beddwyr, heroes who emerge later as transplants into tales of King Arthur. The party wanders in search of Olwen, and they are unsuccessful until they reach the home of a shepherd whose wife admits to being Olwen's hairdresser.

Although terrified of the giant Yspaddadden, the woman reveals that she is related to Culwhch and will arrange for him to meet his future bride. When Olwen arrives for her usual appointment, the woman introduces her to Culwhch. Olwen is immediately charmed, but she warns Culwhch that she cannot marry him without her father's consent. She further warns him that he must accede to any condition whatsoever her father may set and that flinching from any request will be fatal.

Culwhch and his party immediately set out for the giant's property. Unbeknownst to Culwhch, Yspaddadden labors under a curse of his own—that should his daughter marry and beget children, the giant will die. When Culwhch and his party arrive at the giant's castle, the giant attacks them with poisoned stones, which Culwhch and his band are able to catch and return to the giant. After this cycle repeats for three days, the giant relents and admits Culwhch to his court. He agrees to the marriage of the hero and his daughter, but sets strict conditions on the marriage, which cannot succeed unless Culwhch completes three impossible tasks.

The first task laid upon Culwhch is to sow flax for Olwen's bridal veil. Culwhch is led to a barren field, which the giant informs him was sown when he first took Olwen's mother for a bride. The field has so far failed to sprout. Culwhch is ordered to retrieve nine bushels of flaxseed from the field, burn the field, till it, resow it, and harvest nine more bushels of flax— all to be accomplished in one day. The giant is certain that Culwhch cannot accomplish the task, but Culwhch remembers his betrothed's warning, and assures that he can easily accomplish the task.

The Hunt of Twrch Trwyth

The second task laid upon Culwch by Yspaddadden is the accumulation of a great dowry, consisting of thirteen great treasures, including the magical sword by which he is destined to die. Culwhch affirms that these, too, will be easy to gather. The giant's final request is for a shave and a haircut, which can only be accomplished with a special razor, scissors, and comb, which conveniently reside between the ears of the great boar Twrch Trwyth, who, in parallel to the tales of Cuchulainn, can only be hunted with the aid of a magical hound that happens to belong to the long-disappeared Mabon ap Modron.

At this point in the cycle, King Arthur and his men inexplicably make an abrupt appearance to carry on the remainder of the tasks, although many of these tales have either vanished or been left to the imagination.

The flax is recovered by ants grateful to Arthur's companion Kai, who performs heroic deeds on their behalf. Arthur and his party locate and rescue the imprisoned Mabon, and the grateful demigod allows them the use of his magical hound.

The culmination of the story of Culwhch is in the hunt for Twrch Trwyth, the great boar. Like any proper boar in Celtic mythology, Twrch Trwyth is exceedingly large, powerful, and clever. Several attempts to acquire the barber tools through trickery are foiled. The magician Menw takes on the form of a bird and attempts to steal them but is nearly killed by the boar's poisonous barbs.

Although the first written versions of the tales of Culwch date from the early medieval period, there is evidence that the basic elements of the story are drawn from much earlier mythology. In some areas, early stone carvings illustrate elements of the tale, including the great boar with his razor and comb. The recurrence of the sacred numbers three and nine also hint at the deeper meaning of the story.

Twrch Trwyth proves impossible to do away with. All of Culwch and Arthur's forces are unsuccessful in killing even the piglets that accompany him. Arthur himself then battles the great boar for nine days without making any progress. At last, they attempt to negotiate with Twrch Trwyth, who informs them that his annoyance is now so great he intends to venture in Culwhch's lands and destroy them. The warriors follow him from one coast to another, and at last they manage to drive him into the sea, where they recover the scissors and accoutrements with the aid of Mannanan mac Lir.

Quests fulfilled at last, Culwhch returns to Ysbaddadden's castle, but instead of welcome, he is met with hostility. The foolish giant informs him that because his daughter's marriage spells his death, he will never allow her to marry. But Culwhch is now in possession of the sword that can kill the giant, and he promptly cuts off Ysbaddadden's head.

Fantastic Voyages

An important genre of Celtic hero stories is the travel myth, the tale of a heroic voyage. This kind of tale is called an imram ("journey"), and these contain similar elements of Otherworld journeying, usually by sea. According to tradition, there are seven great imrams, but only three tales survive in their entirety. These are the Voyage of Mael Duin, the Voyage of St. Brendan, and the Voyage of Snedgus and mac Ríagla.

Mael Duin

The saga of Mael Duin is the earliest known Celtic travel myth. Many later tales, such as "The Voyage of Brendan," are based on this legend.

Mael Duin was the son of a renowned warrior, Aillill Edge-of-Battle. His father was killed on the battlefield before Mael was born, and his mother became a nun. Mael was fostered with his sister's family, raised never knowing the truth of his origins.

When Mael grows to maturity, he discovers his true background and makes a pact to avenge his father's death. Not knowing where to begin, he consults a druid, who tells him his enemies can be found across the sea. But in order to reach them, Mael must accept a geas and take with him a crew of exactly seventeen men.

Mael prepares his ships and selects his crew of seventeen, yet as he prepares to set sail, his foster brothers beg to come along. When Mael demurs, they attempt to swim after Mael's boat. Fearful they will drown themselves in their stubbornness, Mael at last relents and pulls his brothers on board.

After many days of vigorous rowing, Mael and his party encounter two small islands, their destination. However, when they prepare to disembark, a sudden storm blows up and tosses the boat far out to sea. Mael berates his foster brothers for their sudden misfortune, which must be due to their disregard for the druid's geas.

They continue to sail for days, even weeks, as the storm rages around them. Eventually, the winds recede, and the adventurers find themselves in the sea of the Otherworld, populated with many strange islands. These islands contain many strange and wonderful things, including an island filled with giant ants, another filled with giant horses, another by flaming pigs, and even one populated by phantom horsemen.

On one of the islands, Mael discovers an enchanted apple tree, from which he steals a branch containing three apples. These are the sort of Otherworld apples that can never be fully eaten, and they feed his crew for many days. Eventually, Mael and his crew encounter a walled island. The island contains a fabulous palace at its center, with many treasures on display. Oddly, it is deserted but for a great many cats that wander about. In the kitchen, Mael and his friends find an abundance of food and drink, of which they eat their fill.

As they prepare to return to their ship, Mael's brother suggests they gather some of the treasure that is arrayed about the castle. Mael cautions against it, lest it anger the feline occupants of the palace. Mael's brother cannot resist entirely, however, and snatches a necklace as they depart. At this, the cats begin to glow like embers. They pursue Mael's brother, and when they catch him, they leap on him, and his body is reduced to ashes. Mael grieves, but he returns the stolen treasure and apologizes to the cats before departing once more.

Mael and his companions continue from isle to isle, seeing many more strange, wonderful, and frightening things. One island they encounter is populated with a great number of dark-skinned people, who sit along the beaches weeping terribly. When one of Mael's brothers leaps from the ship to inquire what they sorrow about, he is overcome with sadness and sits among them weeping inconsolably. When he refuses to return to the ship, the others continue without him.

Eventually, the crew encounters the island's counterpart, whose population is filled with immense joy and whose fields ring with laughter. Mael's remaining brother, in his grief, finds the isle irresistible and cannot be prevented from leaving the ship. At last unburdened of his extra passengers, Mael finds himself free to leave the Otherworld. A falcon appears in the sky and leads the sailors back to Ireland, to the small isles where Mael was first blown off course. There, Mael encounters the men responsible for his father's death. When he prepares to confront them, however, they greet him as a great hero on account of his journeys. At this, all of Mael's anger leaves him, and he no longer desires vengeance.

In the course of their island wanderings, it is said that Mael Duin and his companions encounter an island populated with Otherworld women who offer them eternal youth and happiness. Mael marries the island's queen, and he and his men are happy there for the span of a year. Eventually, they become homesick and wish to leave. As they row away from the island, the queen throws Mael a length of string, and when he catches it, she uses it to draw the boat back to shore. This cycle is repeated several times, until Mael's exasperated crew cuts off his hand to prevent a recurrence.

The Voyage of St. Brendan

The legend of St. Brendan of Clonfert, otherwise known as Brendan the Navigator, represents the Christian entry into the imram tradition. Brendan was rumored to have been born in the late fifth century. He was a student of St. Brighid of Munster (an altogether different Brighid from the renowned goddess/saint) and went on to found a number of monasteries. While most historians agree that Brendan probably did conduct some sort of sea expeditions, many of the elements of Brendan's tale are identical to elements of earlier legends, especially the story of Mael Duin and the Voyage of Bran. The story resembles the ancient tales, with much religious allegory and scenes evocative of Dante's *Inferno*.

FACT

Brendan's story did not go unnoticed by the Church. Shortly after he was made a saint, he was adopted as the patron saint of travelers and sailors.

Brendan's legend tells that he began his voyage as penance for burning a religious book containing accounts of many fantastic miracles. An admonishing angel declares that as punishment, Brendan will spend seven years journeying to Tir na Nog, to witness his own miracles and record them in the place of those he had destroyed. Brendan sets sail with an improbable sixty companions in a small Irish boat called a coracle, a primitive leather craft traditionally popular with traveling monks.

Brendan's recorded adventures sound very much like Mael Duin's. He travels to many small islands, each with unique inhabitants, and sees many bizarre and strange sights. Like Mael, he takes on three passengers at the last minute, who all meet fated ends. Also like Mael, he and his men encounter an uninhabited palace filled with food and laden with jewels—although in this version, it is Brendan himself who denounces the thief and prevents any misfortune from befalling the party.

Instead of magical apples, Brendan and his sailors feast on bread and water delivered in answer to the abbot's pious prayers. The party acquires a mysterious "Provider," an old hermit who appears at will and keeps them stocked with food, water, and fish for the best part of their journey.

The most fantastic element of Brendan's story concerns an island that is seemingly unremarkable until the sailors build a campfire to warm themselves and cook their supper. The island suddenly begins to quake and quickly sinks beneath the waves, allowing the party barely enough time to scramble back to their boat. It soon becomes evident that the island is not an island at all but an enormous serpent or dragon, whose name Brendan reveals to be Jasconius. The resemblance of Jasconius to the fabled Jormungandr, the Norse serpent of Midgard, is well recognized.

In another oddly pagan encounter, Brendan encounters an island, called the "Eden of the Birds," inhabited by birds. The cheerful creatures reveal to Brendan that they are an ancient tribe of people whom God has caused to take the shape of birds for eternity, in order to testify to the glories of creation. It is a curious passage. The theme of warriors returning as divine messenger birds is an ancient pagan idea, but Brendan's story is clearly intended for a Christian audience—another sign of the unusual amity Celtic theologians had with the old pagan ideas. The story disappears from later versions, perhaps due to discomfort with this similarity.

The adventures continue in like vein, with more monsters and sea creatures, demonic encounters, and even a visit to Judas, who is stranded on an outcropping of rock, much like Prometheus, suffering eternal, repeating torments. At one stop, Brendan and his crew are forced to flee as they are pelted with flaming rocks and molten metal hurled by a giant from the entrance of a great cave. It seems clear that Brendan and his men, although at sea, are also in hell, and that this version of hell is very much like the ancient Otherworld.

At last, they come to a place of complete darkness, through which they travel for many weeks. When the darkness lifts, they find a beautiful paradise—an island filled with fruit trees and precious stones, where it is eternally daylight. Here, they encounter a monastery, from which appears a mysterious, shining youth, who calls all of them by name and informs the adventurers that they have reached their destination, the Blessed Isle. He exhorts them to fill up their ship with all they can carry and to return home.

When Brendan inquires whether the island should ever be known to mankind, the youth promises that it would one day be known to all. Brendan and his party remain on the island for three days and nights. As they prepare to leave, they seek a blessing from the monastery. Upon exiting, they discover themselves miraculously returned to their own monastery.

Brendan's tale proved incredibly popular and encouraged many to visit his monasteries. Many people attempted to recreate his journeys in order to locate "Brendan's Isle." In modern times, there has been much speculation over the veracity of the story and whether many of the seemingly fanciful details of the story may describe real locations. Some theorize that the giant hurling rocks from his cave may in fact describe volcanoes of Iceland, or that the isle of birds may describe one of the Danish Faeroe islands. Various encounters with sea monsters are said to describe whales and other unfamiliar creatures. There is even an unlikely but persistent belief that the Blessed Isle visited by Brendan was in fact the shore of Newfoundland, which would place Brendan as the first European in America.

Snedgus and Mac Riagla

The Voyage of Snedgus and Mac Riagla was another late addition to the imram tradition, one that is more overtly more Christian than earlier stories. Both heroes are cousins of Columcille, and they begin their journey for reasons which are never revealed. After an encounter with a miraculous spring, they decide to leave the fate of their journey in the hands of God, and they throw away their oars. Their adventures aren't terribly remarkable; in close parallel to the earlier tales, they come upon magical isles filled with birds, creatures, and the like. What is unusual about the story is that among the saints and biblical characters they encounter are ancient kings and mythological figures, including Merlin—who is mentioned as an equal to Patrick, and credited with helping the great saint to intercede with a wrathful God on behalf of Ireland.

CHAPTER 17

The Legends of Arthur

Beyond doubt, the best-known and most enduring of the legendary Celtic heroes is Arthur, the semi-mythological High King of Britain who serves a dual purpose as both a quasi-Christ figure and a pagan god hero. The legends of Arthur constitute a sort of Celtic mystery religion, with symbolism that transcends pagan and Christian mythology.

The Origins of Arthur

The legend of Arthur emerged at a time when Christianity had the most tenuous hold in Celtic lands. During the period in which Arthur's real-life existence was said to have taken place, Britain was a rough place. The Romans had largely given up and left the country at the mercy of squabbling warlords and Saxon invaders. The new religion of Christianity had limited influence outside of its monasteries, and the Church of Rome struggled to keep the local churches in line and away from then-powerful pagan influences. In a very real sense, the character of Arthur perfectly represents this period, a melding of Christian and Celtic spirituality that most beautifully preserves the ancient heroic ideal and merges it with the idealistic hopes of the new faith.

The Name Arthur

There is much speculation about the origin of the Arthurian legend. The name *Arthur* may be Gallic in origin, from *artios viros*, "bear man," or it may be of Roman origin. (In Welsh, the word for *bear* would be "Art" or "Arth.") One theory that seeks to explain Arthurian symbolism claims that Arthur is a personification of the constellation Ursa Major, The Bear, whose Latinized Brythonic name was *Arturus*. Curiously, the folk name for the constellation was "Arthur's Plow." This symbolism may have been understood by later Arthurian chroniclers, and underscored by symbolism such as the Round Table, which may have originally been intended to symbolize the zodiac.

One of the earliest mentions of Arthur is related in the Welsh *The Mabinogion*, in the story of the hero Culwhch. The name Culwhch means "Son of Pig," due to the hero's birth in a pigsty. Culwhch seems to have some relation to an ancient Gallic boar god. This is worth mentioning because there is evidence from this period of another Gallic god, an anthropomorphic bear called Artios. Perhaps the story of Culwhch and Arthur is derived from a long lost Gallic myth.

Historical records of the sixth century mention the heroic battle victories of an unnamed chieftain; these battles were soon afterward attributed to Arthur. In the ninth century, Welsh monasteries recorded a number of battle victories, and the deaths of Arthur and Mordred, and compiled lists of his heroic company, but they give little else in the way of details of his life or identity. In any case, it is generally assumed that Arthur was a chieftain or even a sort of mercenary soldier employed by British kings. Later Welsh legends identified Arthur as a cousin of the hero Culwhch, and it is through these tales that Arthur began to evolve as a mythological hero.

Welsh Origins of Arthur: Culwhch and Olwen

Culwhch is the penultimate Welsh god hero, who is best-known from The Mabinogion romance "Culwhch and Olwen." Culwhch's legends are filled with ancient Celtic religious imagery and certainly date from a much earlier era. Culwhch's story contains many parallels to the tales of Cuchulainn and other divine heroes. Many of the companions of Culwhch, such as the river deity Cei or the one-armed Bedwyr, reappear in the Arthurian corpus as companions of the Round Table.

Culwhch is clearly a prototype of the mythological Arthur, and Arthur makes an appearance in the tales of Culwhch as a cousin or companion, alongside many other characters who later emerge as central figures in the Arthurian tales. Culwhch himself may be related to an ancient Welsh god and is closely associated with boar symbolism; Arthur as the bear seems to round out the woodland gods hypothesis.

FACT

Before Geoffrey of Monmouth, Arthur was perceived as a warrior but not a terribly romantic hero. In many tales he is portrayed as a hothead, even a murderer, and is the victim of trickery on a number of occasions. Arthur is himself placed into the trickster role himself in a number of folk legends and is even sometimes identified as the leader of the raucous and violent Wild Hunt.

Geoffrey of Monmouth

By the twelfth century, a scattering of folk legends had blossomed into a full-fledged mythology, and the familiar legend known today was the work of a twelfth century monk named Geoffrey of Monmouth, who stitched various narratives together into his fanciful history of British kings, *Historia Regnum Britanniae*. Goeffrey's work popularized the myth of Arthur and introduced the character of Merlin. Although Geoffrey always claimed his source was an ancient manuscript, that text was never recovered or mentioned again.

Geoffrey's tale begins with an entirely mythological British king of Roman lineage, a son of the Roman Constantine called Uther Pendragon. Uther takes as his wife Ygraine, the spouse of his enemy, Gorlois of Cornwall, with whom he has become smitten. Uther obtains Ygraine's affections through deceit, with the aid of the wizard Merlin, who agrees to aid Uther's deception on the condition that he be given any resulting child to foster. Uther agrees, and Merlin disguises him as Ygraine's husband, sneaking him into Ygraine's chambers. When Ygraine's true husband is killed in battle that night by Uther's own men, he does not reveal his deception, and she agrees to marry him, not realizing they have already met.

The son produced from their union is Arthur, who is sent for fostering under the watchful eye of the wizard Merlin. Uther dies while Arthur is still young, seemingly without an heir, which plunges the nascent kingdom into chaos. The remaining chieftains squabble for control until the teenaged Arthur emerges as the heir. Later versions of the story introduced the legendary sword in the stone, and either due to fate or Merlin's tinkering, it is only Arthur who can remove the fateful sword. The act convinces the chieftains that Arthur's claim to the throne is genuine, and he is proclaimed king. The holdouts rebel, but they are quickly put in their place on the field of battle.

Arthur's sword clearly relates to the ancient ritual of kingmaking. The name *Excalibur* is linguistically linked (through its Latin name, Caliburn) to Caladcholg, the mythological sword of light possessed by Fergus, the ancient high king of Ulster. The stone is reminiscent of the Stone of Lia Fail, which chose Irish kings by screaming aloud when touched by a worthy candidate.

Knights of the Round Table

Arthur continues in a series of military victories, putting down one rebellion after another until the kingdom is restored. Like any self-respecting hero, Arthur then seeks out the affections of the most beautiful woman in the kingdom and marries her. He builds a fabulous castle in the mythological Camelot and assembles a council for himself out of the wisest, bravest, and cleverest knights of the kingdom, who become the legendary Knights of the Round Table.

As the tale unfolds, however, it returns to its roots in the Celtic myth cycles, becoming a tale of tragedy, betrayal, and ruin. In earlier versions of the legend, Arthur embarks on a series of conquests, and while he is away, his scheming nephew (who is later portrayed as his secret son) takes Guinevere as a mistress and attempts a coup of Arthur's kingdom. In the later, more familiar version of the story, it is Lancelot, Arthur's trusted lieutenant and the most heroic of his knights who becomes his betrayer, after the two return from their fruitless quest for the Holy Grail. The king is forced to face the reality that his best friend and his queen are lovers, and reluctantly agrees to put them both to death. The lovers flee together, but guilt overtakes them, and Guinevere enters a convent. Arthur is mortally wounded in battle with his own son, and the Golden Age comes to a crumbling ruin.

Guinevere

Guinevere, or Gwenhwyfar (anglicized as Jennifer) is the tragic, faithless, sometimes traitorous wife of Arthur. She is renowned as a great beauty, and Arthur loves her upon first glimpse. He marries her despite many warnings from Merlin that she will bring him to ruin. She is unable to conceive him an heir, but despite this, Arthur loves her and refuses to put her aside. In the end, she betrays him in an act that brings Arthur to ruin and death.

Guinevere's origins are mysterious. Her name is undeniably Celtic, most likely meaning "white ghost" or "white fairy." Her fairness and even the root of her name makes her similar to Olwen, the wife of Culwhch, whose name means "white track," or even to Blodeuedd, the faithless wife of Lleu.

The Origin of Merlin

Although the character of Merlin first appears in Geoffrey of Monmouth's fanciful medieval history, he appears to be a composite character based on two separate historical characters: Myrddn, a magician/prophet mentioned in earlier poetic tales, and Ambrosius Aurelianus, a fifth century Romano-British war leader. Myrddn, who might be considered the earliest incarnation of Merlin, was not a wizard but a Welsh warrior bard who received the gift of prophecy as a result of madness caused by the grief of losing his loved ones on the battlefield. Myrddn is described as living among the forest creatures until he obtains the gift of prophecy. (This early origin tale is echoed in later tales of Merlin, where he is said to have lived his final days as a wild madman in the forest.) Myrddn is himself a very curious character, perhaps a druid. One telling story of Myrddn claims that he prophesied his own triple death by beating, drowning, and impalement—a fate not unlike that of certain sacrificial victims. Geoffrey calls his composite creation Merlin Ambrosius.

ALERT!

In later versions of Merlin's biography, it was claimed that his mother was a nun in a convent who was seduced by the devil himself, in order to beget an antichrist. The pious nun repented and foiled the plan by having the child baptized immediately upon his birth.

To further muddy the waters, Ambrosius Aurelianus is one of the leading candidates for the role of the historical Arthur. Little is known of the biography of Aurelianus except that he was Roman by lineage and the survivor of a great onslaught by the Saxons. He organized the remainder of the Britons and achieved a number of victories against the invaders. It is unclear why Geoffrey identifies Merlin and Aurelianus, except that both Myrddn and Aurelianus figure in stories about Vortigern, another early ruler.

Where did the name *Merlin* come from?

Oddly, Merlin is not in itself a proper name but the name of a city—according to Geoffrey, the magician's place of origin. Merlin, according to Welsh tradition, is not one man but a series of three great magicians bearing one title, including the legendary bard Taliesin, with whom he is identified by Geoffrey.

Merlin the Prophet

Merlin, according to Geoffrey, was born the son of a mortal woman and an incubus, to whom his supernatural powers are attributed. Merlin makes his debut as a prophet when, as a young man, he is kidnapped by the warlord Vortigern. Vortigern had been attempting to build a tower fortress, which tumbled down repeatedly until he is advised by his magicians that it will not stand unless the foundations are sprinkled with the blood of a man who has no human father.

The young Merlin is the obvious choice, but he escapes a gruesome fate by revealing the true cause of the tower's collapse. He tells Vortigern that a pair of dragons are doing battle in a lake under its foundations. These dragons are later revealed to be symbolic of the continual battles between the Britons and the Saxons, which only Arthur is able to calm.

Merlin is not simply an accessory to Arthur but a legend unto himself, appearing in numerous tales of his own. Tales of Merlin's parentage are many and varied—some, such as the medieval telling that Merlin was the son of a nun's congress with a demon, are quite ridiculous. Invariably, however, it is understood of Merlin's parentage that he has no human father. It is the wise Merlin who engineers Arthur's birth, bringing Britain a savior.

The Fall of Merlin

Merlin's downfall, like Arthur's, is due to a woman. Unlike Arthur's tale, Merlin's seems more typically medieval, the great man brought down by the scheming wiles of the evil sorceress to whom he has entrusted his deepest secrets. While Morgan and Guinevere appear to be diluted goddesses, Merlin's scheming lover Nimue embodies every medieval superstition about the evil nature of women. Nimue is described as a beautiful but cruel girl who entreats the elder Merlin to teach her his magic; the magician, quite besotted, agrees against his better judgment to do so. Nimue turns out to be quite ungrateful for Merlin's lessons. At the first opportunity, she uses her newfound skills to destroy him, binding him for eternity in a tower of glass or in the interior of an oak. Strangely, these are both clear symbols of the pagan Otherworld.

Other Women in Arthur's Life

One of the strangest additions to the Arthurian legend was Arthur's sister, the fairy woman Morgan. Morgan sleeps with Arthur and bears him an unacknowledged son, who proves to be his undoing. Morgan's name and demeanor recall the ancient goddess of sovereignty and war, the Morrigan —and indeed, the story of Arthur and Morgan echo many of the tales of the encounters of ancient kings with the goddess of sovereignty. Although in the Arthurian stories Morgan is cast as a villain, it is Arthur's dismissive behavior toward Morgan and his son that lead to his downfall. Celtic mythology is filled with tales of heroes who were defeated and killed because they angered or otherwise failed to heed the goddess of the earth.

FACT

Another curious legend dating to around the sixteenth century provides more connections between Arthur and the goddess. It was said that Arthur and his company were transformed into ravens upon their deaths, and that the sight of a raven by a knight or soldier was an omen of his impending death.

It is also telling that the death of Arthur is due to a challenge from his sister's son, a retelling of the archetypal story of the elder king contending with the younger for the affections of the goddess of the land. It is originally Mordred, Morgan's son, who was said to have stolen Guinevere away from

Arthur, and only later is Mordred's parentage associated with Arthur's incestuous affair.

Curiously, although Morgan is portrayed as the greatest villain of the Arthurian stories, there is much that hints at her divine roots. Morgan not only mothers Arthur's son, but it is she who heals him of a symbolic wound to the groin and who provides him with magical protection in the form of an enchanted scabbard that protects him from harm. When Arthur fails her, Morgan removes her protection from Arthur to make way for her son to defeat him. It is also telling that although she is the architect of Arthur's death, she is present at his last journey as she accompanies him to the isle of Avalon, the realm of the dead. It is clear that no matter how muddy the details become, Morgan is intended to represent the goddess Sovereignty.

The Goddess and the Hag

In many Celtic tales, the goddess Sovereignty is represented by an ancient hag who guards the well of wisdom (or dispenses the magical mead that initiates the king). Only the wise or brave man sees through the hag's guise and is given kingship over the land. The hag's guise may represent the difficulties of sacred responsibility, or it may hold an even deeper meaning.

The sovereignty symbolism in the Arthurian cycle is repeated in other aspects of the Arthurian legend. In the story of Gawain and the Loathly Lady, Gawain, Arthur's purest and most chivalrous knight, makes an agreement to marry a hideous hag, a clear representation of the ancient goddess, in return for granting some request or favor. Despite his bride's ugliness, the knight decides to do his duty by her, and she is transformed into a beautiful maiden. It is probably not coincidental that Gawain is the only knight in these tales to achieve the elusive grail, which perhaps owes to its connections the ancient practices of pagan Britain.

Gawain's bride clearly echoes ancient Celtic notions about the goddess. For example, both the Welsh goddess Cerridwen and the Irish Cailleachs have the appearance of withered hags, but each possesses a font of wisdom and riches for those who look beyond appearances.

The Lady of the Lake

Another mysterious character who can be interpreted as fulfilling the role of the goddess Sovereignty is the enigmatic Lady of the Lake, who makes several appearances in key parts of Arthur's life. The Lady is clearly an Otherworld denizen. Although her residence is given as Avalon, she is clearly a water goddess, and most interactions with the Lady take place in her lake, which may be identified with the waters surrounding Glastonbury.

The Lady of the Lake is credited as the foster mother of Lancelot, but she is better known as Arthur's mysterious benefactor. When Arthur's sword of kingship is destroyed in battle, it is the Lady who famously gives him the Otherworld sword Excalibur, which he takes great pains to return to her when he knows he is about to die. The Lady makes a further appearance when Arthur receives his last fatal wound, and she accompanies him to Avalon. Strangely, the Lady of the Lake is later confused with Morgan le Fay, whose name connotes a water fairy.

The Cup of Christ

The best-known tales of Arthur—those of the quest for the Holy Gail—are much later. The origin and meaning of the tales have been debated and speculated upon in countless books. Like Arthur himself, they represent a curious merger of Celtic pagan legends and Christian symbolism. The cup that Arthur and his knights seek out is ostensibly the cup of Christ, present at the last supper, the emblem of the transformative eucharist.

The Quest for the Grail

The grail quest is actually a later addition to Arthurian tales although it is unquestionably drawn from the earliest stories of Arthur and other Celtic heroes and their search for the cauldron of illumination. The exact nature of the grail is also disputed, seen variously as an emblem of conversion, the realization of love, the neglected goddess of the land, or even the marriage bed of Christ. No matter how Christian the tale, however, it is clear the story has its roots in ancient Celtic quests for the cauldron of the gods. Both the cup and the cauldron are symbols of divine grace, emblems of rebirth and spiritual illumination.

Arthur's earliest quest is mentioned only briefly in early Celtic tales. In the enigmatic Welsh poem "The Spoils of Annwn," Arthur is one of the seven heroes who return from the fruitless underworld quest for the cauldron of Annwn. The cauldron reappears in some versions of the story of Culwhch and Olwen, as one of the thirteen treasures collected for Olwen's dowry.

While the tale of the Holy Grail is Christian on the surface, it is deeply pagan underneath. One of the earliest tales of the Holy Grail is the unfinished grail romance of Chretien of Troyes, "Perceval, the Story of the Grail," wherein the grail is the mysterious magical object through which the injury of the mysterious Fisher King can be healed. The injury of the king's groin is an obvious phallic symbol of the vitality of the land, symbolism with clear roots in the ancient connections of the king and the land, the living goddess through which the king's authority was derived. An important symbol of the goddess Sovereignty was a wine goblet, offered to the would-be king on the occasion of his betrothal to the goddess. Curiously, Arthur himself receives a similar wound in many stories.

By the time the grail is associated with Arthur and his knights, its symbolism has been transferred. It is now the cup of the Last Supper of Christ and his apostles, which, according to legend, was filled with Christ's blood at his crucifixion. The transition of the symbol from an emblem of the goddess to an emblem of Christ can be seen as an almost perfect analogy of the uneasy spiritual transition of the Celtic people—Christian on the surface, with a pagan heart and sensibility underneath.

The Goddess and the Grail

Many Arthurian researchers have tackled the multilayered Arthurian symbolism and concluded that in many cases, the story preserves the anxiety of a culture transitioning from a very dual system to a monotheistic outlook. The qualities once borne by the goddess now reside in the mother of

Christ and many female saints, but the deeper symbolism of the goddess is represented by the grail.

Some see a clear parallel between the wounds of the Fisher King (and, later, in Arthur's injuries) and the fate awaiting a Celtic king who did not fulfill his marriage obligation to the goddess. Celtic kingship was wholly tied to the fertility of the land and the prosperity of its people. A king who was not righteous and fair, who did not accept the full responsibility of leadership, would see the land suffer barrenness and drought. Indeed, infertility is a persistent theme in Arthur's story. Although Arthur is a heroic and wise ruler, he is cursed. His wife can bear no heir, and the kingdom he has built is destined to fall to ruin at his death. Even more strangely, it is Arthur's son by his sister, whom he refuses to acknowledge, who becomes the instrument of his ruin.

Mordred and the Death of Arthur

There are a number of versions of the story of Mordred's birth and his role in the death of Arthur. The best-known is that Mordred was the product of an incestuous union between Arthur and his sister Morgause (sometimes, Morgan) and fostered as the true son of Morgause's husband, Lot of Orkney.

His conception is sometimes described as an accidental act, sometimes as the product of a rape brought on by Arthur's lust for his beautiful sister. In any case, Arthur did not recognize Mordred as his son, even when his marriage to Guinevere failed to produce an heir.

FACT

Curiously, Mordred may be one of the only characters of Arthurian legend connected with the historical Arthur. He is the only other person named in the brief sixth century account of Arthur's death at the battle of Camlann, where he is referred to as Mordraut.

Mordred is born at Beltaine, a birthplace he holds in common with Arthur, but also with Culwhch, Lleu, and Mabon. This connection of Arthur and Arthur's son with the divine son archetype, like much Arthurian symbolism, is likely not accidental.

In Geoffrey's tale, Mordred is introduced as a confidant and friend of Arthur, whom Arthur makes regent while he travels abroad to make war on Rome. During Arthur's absence, Mordred betrays Arthur by having him declared dead, then marrying Guinevere and declaring himself king. Arthur returns immediately upon learning the news, and in the ensuing battle, Mordred is killed and Arthur fatally wounded. In Welsh versions of the tale, Guinevere willingly betrays Arthur, a theme repeated in later versions with the character of Lancelot.

In the middle ages, Mordred came to be treated with a bit more sympathy. He is cast as a conflicted character who betrays the father who refuses to acknowledge him as his heir due to the embarrassing circumstances surrounding his birth. As in every tale of the tragic Celtic hero, it is Arthur's own failures that bring about his destruction.

The Green Knight

Another element of the Arthurian tales that has certain pagan origins is the Green Knight, a character who appears in a number of Arthurian romances and poems. He is a bizarre character, almost invariably described as a knight with green skin, eyes, and hair, dressed all in green clothes and armor.

The origins of the enigmatic Green Knight aren't clear, but some see in him an obvious parallel to the Green Man, a medieval archetype of nature, who in turn may be descended from Celtic woodland deities like Cernunnos and Fionn.

Sometimes the Green Knight is a malevolent figure, and sometimes he is a neutral character. The Green Knight, like the hag, appears in a testing context. He is most often matched with Sir Gawain, who is portrayed as Arthur's greatest knight, a paragon of chivalry.

The Green Knight invariably stands between the hero and the object of a quest, and the tale usually involves some sort of test of the hero's character. In most versions of the tale, Arthur's court is in the midst of celebration, and the Green Knight appears as a sudden challenger. He asks that any member of the court step forward and strike a blow against him, and in one year's time he will return the blow. Gawain steps forward, and he slices off the giant's head in one heaving blow. The giant, however, is not killed. He calmly picks up his head, sets it back on his shoulders, and reminds Gawain that he must meet him in the "green chapel" in one year to exact his half of the bargain. Gawain, being utterly honorable, agrees. At the end of the year, he sets off to find the knight at the green chapel.

Gawain's journeys vary, but he almost always undergoes some form of temptation, usually in the form of a seductive maiden. His tests successfully passed, he proceeds to his certain doom—but when he again meets the fearsome knight and lays his head before him, the giant delivers only the most glancing of blows. The Green Knight in these stories seems most likely to represent the hero's lower nature, and the temptations that plague even the most resolute. Having faced his challenges with courage and honor, he now finds the monster much less formidable.

CHAPTER 18

The Exaltation of the Sun: The Celtic Calendar

The ancient Celts reckoned time differently than we do today, and everything from days to seasons were calculated beginning with the end of the previous one. Thus, sunset was the beginning of a day, and the beginning of winter was the end of summer, and so on. The Celtic festival cycle was reckoned on a circular solar calendar, which followed the path of the sun as it moved through the year, and a lunar calendar, based on the cycles beginning with the new moon. The year was divided into two halves, Gam and Sam—literally, light and dark. These two overarching seasons carried other connotations—male and female, working and resting, active and dormant.

Gam and Sam: The Darkness and the Light

The Celts accounted for only two seasons, winter and summer, and both were celebrated at their ends and at their midpoints. The remainder of the Celtic calendar was complex, figured on a lunar cycle aligned to agricultural cycles. The beginning of each season was celebrated at the end of the last, and the solar events ("gates") that opened each season were considered particularly numinous times—fairies roamed the earth, and witches were considered to be especially active.

The notion of the seasons was regarded as a pageant of the gods, an endless cycle of seasonal battles between the god of light and his shadow self. One such pair is the Irish Lugh and Balor. The August 1 feast of Lughnasadh was not just a commemoration of Lugh but a foreshadowing of his symbolic "death," as well as the ascendancy of the harsher solar aspect, personified by Balor, the giant whose baleful glare destroys all it alights on. The cold months see the fertile and youthful sovereignty goddesses take on the aspect of the Cailleach, the hag of winter.

The Celtic Calendar

Chapter 9 discussed the Celtic cross, which symbolizes the sun and the fundamental Celtic calendar. The four cross-arms in the solar circle represent the four stations of the sun—the two solstices and equinoxes. To early astronomers, the sun on these days would behave differently than on other days. During the solstices, the sun would appear to be fixed in place for a time, even appearing to move backward. At the equinoxes, the night and day would be of exactly the same length. The Neolithic ancestors of the Celts held these events to be extremely significant, and their monuments and tombs are positioned to align with the movements of the sun on these days. It is clear that the sacred calendar of the Celts was passed down to them in some form from these ancient astronomers.

These days were not only ritually significant, they were vital markers of the passage of time, used to determine the times for plowing, sowing, and harvesting and to time the birthing of livestock and other tasks necessary for survival. They also determined times for festivals, councils, and other tribal gatherings. The four arms of the Celtic solar festivals were bisected by the cross of the major festival calendar, the so-called "cross-quarter" days.

In 1897, in the forest near Coligny, France, workers uncovered an invaluable artifact—an immense Gaulish engraved bronze calendar dating to the Roman/Gaulish period. The calendar was lunisolar—that is, it reconciled a lunar calendar with a solar calendar. It is assumed that the calendar represents a druid attempt to keep an accurate calendar at a time when the Julian calendar was enforced throughout the Roman territories.

The Coligny calendar includes a series of twelve lunar months, counted from the beginning of the new moon, and a solar year of 354 or 355 days, with a series of intercalary periods to maintain accuracy over time. The following chart shows the correspondence between Latin and Gaulish months of the year:

Latin Month	Gaulish Month
October/November	Samonios
November/December	Dumannios
December/January	Riuros
January/February	Anagantios
February/March	Ogronios
March/April	Cutios
April/May	Giamonios
May/June	Simivisonnos
June/July	Equos
July/August	Elembivios
August/September	Edrinios
September/October	Cantlos
(intercalary month)	Ciallos

The Festival Cycle

The primary days of the Celtic festival calendar were the cross-quarter days, so called because they fall on the quarter-marks of the cross formed by the solstices and equinoxes. The four quarters represented the four major festivals of the Celtic calendar, celebrated at the midpoints between the solstices and equinoxes of the solar cycle. These were determined by an additional lunar reckoning, coinciding with the beginning of the lunar cycle nearest the midpoint between the solstices and equinoxes.

Originally, there were likely only three festivals, each of three days' length, probably hearkening back to the ancient reckoning of time by the three-month cycles of the sun. Later, these became four, possibly when Celtic culture moved to an agricultural calendar or maybe due to the influence of the Roman calendar. The Cath Mag Tuireadh, which appears on the surface to be a collection of simple folk tales, is actually in many ways a calendrical myth. It explains that the Tuatha Dé Danann had four important dates, which correspond to the four stations of the sun:

- Spring (The Equinox), for plowing and sowing
- Summer (The Solstice), for the ripening of the grain
- Autumn (The Equinox) for the harvesting of the grain
- Winter (The Solstice), for rest and consuming the harvest

In the course of the tale, the solar deity Lugh, who also represents the technological endeavors of man, wars against the giant Balor, who represents the unharnessed sun. Lugh emerges victorious, and the spoils of the victory include the secrets of agriculture granted by the ancient agricultural deity Bres, who promises additional harvest times in order that his life be spared. Lugh agrees, and the Tuatha Dé Danann go on to become the masters of agriculture.

FACT

The imagery of the solar wheel is repeated throughout Celtic mythology. In many cases, the name of the goddess is quite literally "Wheel."

The four cross-quarter festivals are today often called fire festivals, from the traditional sacred fires that featured at the center of the celebrations.

They went by various names depending on location, but for the sake of convenience, they are most often referred to today by their Gaelic Irish names. Although they were of obvious significance, little has been recorded about the observations of the solstices and equinoxes.

These are the eight spokes of the reconstructed Celtic calendar:

- Samhain, or "summer's end": Marked a return to cooler weather and the beginning of the winter season. Samhain was the principal festival of the ancient Celts, and most likely the oldest.
- Midwinter, or the winter solstice: Marked the rebirth of the sun.
- Imbolc: Marked the end of the winter season and the renewal of life. Imbolc is the newest of the festivals, possibly added with the adoption of the Latin calendar systems.
- Spring equinox
- Beltaine: Marked the arrival of summer and a commemoration of fertility.
- Midsummer, or the summer solstice
- Lughnasadh: Marked the beginning of the hotter "dog days" of summer and the peak of the agricultural season.
- Vernal equinox

The Liturgical Cycle

In the early days of European Christianity, most individual churches followed their own liturgical calendars, making their own calculations for Easter and celebrating masses and feasts of their own choosing. Over time, however, most calendars began to conform to one another.

It is curious, however, to see which feasts remained important over time and how well they adhered to the ancient festival cycles. When compared to the dates of the pagan Celtic calendar, the following days stand out:

- All Hallows and All Saints, celebrated at the beginning of November
- Christmas, the nativity of Christ, celebrated near the winter solstice

- Candlemas, or the Feast of Brighid, celebrated on February 2, the day of Imbolc
- Easter, of the resurrection of Christ, celebrated near the vernal equinox
- The Feast of John the Baptist, observed at the summer solstice
- Transfiguration, and the "First Fruits of Redemption," celebrated a few days after the traditional date of Lughnasadh, as well as the autumn feast of Lammas

Oddly, many of the solar dates of the Christian calendar were decided by Roman observations. While the Bible gives no particular nativity date for Christ, early Church fathers wrote that the date was chosen deliberately to correspond to "wicked" pagan feast days, to prevent new believers from being tempted by pagan revelry. Whether latter coincidental dates were chosen for similar reasons is a matter of some controversy.

The Solstices: Birth and Death of the Sun

The name *solstice* (literally, "sun standing still") is from the Latin. It refers to the momentary solar event that takes place twice a year, when the sun appears to stand still at the moment the earth's equatorial tilt is most extreme. In the Northern Hemisphere, this occurs twice a year, with the earth's longest day occurring at midsummer, and the shortest at midwinter. The solstices were almost universally observed as times of great significance by the ancients, and to the Celts, they represented the strength of the sun. Thus, the midsummer observances celebrated the virility of the sun god and the promise of bountiful harvest; the waning sun of midwinter signaled the death and subsequent rebirth of the god.

Midsummer

Midsummer, the time of the solstice, was a time for blessings and offerings to ensure the health of the crops and a good harvest. As in other festivals, bonfires would be lit and the livestock driven through the smoke. It was considered particularly fortunate for the smoke to drift over the crops themselves. Burning brands were taken from the fire and carried three times around the household and the cattle enclosures. The ashes from the fire would afterward be sprinkled on the crops. Midsummer was also considered a fortuitous time to gather curative or protective herbs to be used the remainder of the year.

Midsummer was considered a perilous time for sailors and fishermen, who avoided putting out to sea on that day due to a persistent superstition that the sea demanded a sacrifice on that day. It was customary to purify boats in the same manner as homes and cattle, by passing a brand around them. In the seventeenth century, this was considered quite a blasphemous practice and censured by the local priests.

Another popular midsummer ritual was the creation of a wheel of straw or rushes, which would be set afire and rolled from a high place. This mimics a ritual popular in the North, and has obvious solar connections, possibly an echo of a rite dedicated to the god Taranis.

Mythologically, midsummer represented the birth of the sun's shadow side. Although the days grow shorter, the sun from this point forward increases in destructiveness. The scorching heat of the late summer season was often feared, as it could wither fruit, scorch grain, and dry up rivers and wells. In Christian myths, this was the time of year that dragons emerged to lay waste to the countryside until they were defeated by dragon-slaying saints.

FACT

The Celts made notice of the curious solar symbolism as well. A legendary solar-connected druid called Mug Ruith ("Slave of the Wheel"), who may have been an ancient solar deity, was worked into many Irish poems and stories as the executioner of John the Baptist.

At midsummer, the Church observed the feast day of St. John the Baptist. The Feast of John has a very unusual placement in the liturgical calendar. Catholic tradition invariably places the feast days of saints on their death or martyrdom, the day they entered the "Kingdom of Heaven." The Feast of the Baptist, however, is celebrated on his (presumed) nativity. Because biblical narratives place John's birth six months before that of Jesus, the nativity of John is placed at the summer solstice, drawing a curious connection between the figures of Christ and John to the traditional seasonal battle of the Celtic gods.

The birth narratives of Jesus and John now coincided with the birth of the spring sun and the autumn sun. John was easily associated with local mythology, and the midsummer fires were now celebrated in his honor. As the days grew shorter, they represented John's biblical exhortation about Jesus as the Messiah: "He must increase, but I must decrease." The decline of John precedes the birth of the true sun at midwinter. Due to scriptural descriptions of John as a wild hermit, John was also heavily associated with the gods of the woodlands.

Midwinter: The Birth of the Sun

Midwinter marks the shortest day of the year, and marks the darkest, coldest part of winter, when the sun appears to be at its weakest. The decline of the sun is often accompanied by careful vigils and the lighting of fires and candles to encourage the return of the sun's strength.

Christmas, of course, predates European Christianity. Curiously, however, it shares a similar origin to later festivals, as it was quite deliberately instituted to compete with pagan solar nativities celebrated in Rome during the earliest years of Christianity. The first versions of the Christian observance of the birth of Christ were offered as an alternative celebration to the boisterous ruckus of the Saturnalia. Many of the customs we associate with Christmas in fact originated with the Saturnalia celebrations, and European Christians often shunned the holiday as a pagan remnant. The Celtic (and Norse) pagan contributions to the holiday include mistletoe and even Christmas trees.

CHAPTER 19

The Wheel of the Year

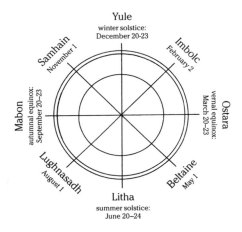

The Celtic calendar is frequently referred to as a wheel, and the ancients likened it to a fiery wheel, a clear allusion to the sun. Sometimes this wheel was linked to the harp of the Dagda, likening the recurring seasons as a repeating story. Whereas spring and summer were the domain of innocence, youth, love and virility, the dark half of the year was given to mysteries, wisdom, aging, and death.

Samhain: The Lowering of the Veil

Samhain, from the more ancient Irish form *Samhuinn*, was the most widely celebrated of the ancient Celtic festivals. It was a celebration of the harvest, of the closing of the year, and the beginning of the new year. Agriculturally, it was the time when the last fruits of the harvest were collected and stored, and the livestock were culled and quartered for the winter ahead.

The dark time of the year had many magical and mythical associations as well. Samhain was also the time when the gates of the Otherworld were thrown open, allowing the spirits of the ancestors and the Sidhe folk to mingle with the living. It was at this time that the fabled Wild Hunt, a procession of animals, fairies, and spirits, was most often said to occur.

The History of Samhain

The Gauls marked the year into just two halves, the dark or winter half being Sam or Samonios, and the light half Gam or its Latinized form, Gamonios. Like other ancient cultures, the Celts marked the beginning of a day at sunset; likewise, the year was counted as beginning in its dark half.

Caesar remarked on the practice in his writings on the Gallic Wars:

> *All the Gauls assert that they are descended from the god Dis, and say that this tradition has been handed down by the druids. For that reason they compute the divisions of every season, not by the number of days, but of nights; they keep birthdays and the beginnings of months and years in such an order that the day follows the night.*

Samonios, the dark half of the year, was reckoned first in the Celtic calendar. The festival marking the beginning of Samonios was Samhuinn (Samhain), a three-day feast celebrated on the new moon closest to the autumnal equinox. As Beltaine marked the beginning of the summer season, Samhain marked its end. In fact, the word *Samhain* most likely means "summer's end" and is the current Gaelic name for the month of November. In the first-century Celtic Coligny calendar, a similar three-day festival ushered in the new year in the late autumn.

FACT

The festival now commonly referred to as Samhain has had numerous names. In Wales, it was known as Calan Gaeaf, "Winter's Eve." In Ireland, it was Oiche Shamra, "Samhain Night," sometimes "Pooka Night." In Manx, it is Sauin.

The Samhain festival marked the transition between two very different seasons. The growth season was at an end, with the majority of crops long harvested. The time for festivals and tribal gatherings was coming to an end, and warfare and trade would be largely suspended until warmer weather returned. This was a last opportunity for merrymaking and celebration before a long winter confinement.

Samhain was celebrated at the cusp of the seasons, marking the end of the light and the beginning of the dark of the year. In mythical terms, the youthful aspect of the goddess Sovereignty gave way to the withered hag of winter, and the fruits and flowers of the warm season were replaced with the barren cold of winter. It was marked at Tara with a great feast, the Feis Teamrach, or "Mating of Tara," at which the high king was symbolically mated with the goddess of sovereignty, a celebration that marked the Samhain night coupling of the Morrigan and the Dagda on the eve of the battle of Mag Tuiread.

Indeed, the Samhain was a favorite time for tribal assemblies, during which all of a tuath would gather together for feasting, games, and amusements but also to settle debts and disputes. In ancient times, great offerings would have been made at lakes, shafts, and at the entrances to the Sidhe mounds, as the denizens of the Otherworld would be particularly receptive. Horse races and other feats of strength were not uncommon at this time, a tradition going back to the earliest days of the Celtic peoples.

ESSENTIAL

In the Ulster Cycle story "The Wooing of Emer," the heroine refers to the festival of Samhain as "when summer goes to its rest."

Samhain was considered a time of great change; it was also a time of great transparency between the world of man and the Otherworld. Samhain was a traditional time for divination and prophecy, an auspicious time for sacrifice. The transformation of the world brought about other transformations, and it was at this time one could enter the Otherworld. Celtic myth tales involving Otherworld magic often take place during Samhain, and it is at this time when Otherworld denizens made benevolent journeys or even warfare against the living. Samhain was the preferred day for beginning an adventure or setting out on a quest, especially a divine one. Many important events in Celtic mythology take place or begin at the time of Samhain. For example, it is at Samhain that Aenghus seeks to recognize his lover Caer in her swan form.

ALERT!

A common urban legend claims that the Samhain celebration was in honor of a ghastly god of death by the same name. Although a few minor Celtic gods have similar names, none has any connection to the Samhain festivals.

Sacred Bonfires

Samhain was celebrated all over Ireland and Great Britain with the lighting of sacred bonfires. As in similar rituals in the north, the Samhain fires were the first fires of the season. In a ritual that would repeat at Beltaine, all other fires would be extinguished and ritually relit from the sacred bonfires. The bonfires themselves were inaugurated by the druids, the first according to some accounts on the hilltop of Tlachtga, where it would be easily visible from Tara.

The bonfires were not the only fire rituals associated with Samhain. A popular ritual called "lating the witches" involved a solemn candlelit procession, the purpose of which was the discovery of dark magic. If a candle flickered or died out during the procession, it meant that the person carrying it was a certain victim of witches, and special precautions would be taken to protect him or her.

Other precautions would be taken as well. As the Tuatha Dé Danann were well known to roam the countryside, it was customary to leave gifts of milk and bread for them, not just on Samhain but on the other festival days as well. This customary offering was sometimes referred to as the fairy tax, honoring the ancient agreement between the Milesian Celts and the denizens of the Otherworld.

Samhain and Hallowe'en (All Hallows)

Even after the demise of the pagan Celtic culture, Samhain remained a popular holiday, and in early Ireland, it was the most important of the four great festivals. There is a common theory that floats about that the institution of Halloween by the Catholic Church was intentionally begun as an answer to the reluctance of the people to give up pagan revelries or the remembrance of the dead.

The truth is actually much less clear cut. The various churches in the first centuries instituted celebrations of their saints and martyrs, which varied according to location, but were celebrated mostly in the spring. By the year 800, German and English churches were commemorating the saints on the first of November, and by 835, most of the rest had followed suit at the urging of Pope Gregory IV. Before this time, however, the Celtic observance was held in the springtime, near the Easter feast.

Also, although there was a definite connection with death and passages, there isn't a lot of evidence that Samhain was held to honor the dead. Most such claims come much too late to be of any use, and the idea is never mentioned in the surviving mythological tales. It is a fair assumption, however, that in this traditional time of tribal gathering, some commemoration would have been made on behalf of the ancestors. It is known that it was sometimes customary to light torches at the entrances of the ancient tombs, to make clearer the passage from the Otherworld.

Christian Practices Rise

From the earliest days of the Church, it was customary to observe a day in memorial to the saints; later, this expanded to include all of the dead.

The saints of the church were celebrated on November 1 with a solemn mass and singing.

As it was already customary to honor one's ancestors during the Samhain period, it was only natural that the Church's own observances followed suit. It became customary to visit cemeteries on this day, to sweep and clean the graves, and echoing the older custom, lights were lit outside of homes and in cemeteries. Water and other provisions would be left out, and the doors left unlocked. The ancient tombs were not neglected, either; the old custom of walking in deasil procession three times about the ancient monuments carried well into medieval times.

The November celebrations were eventually worn away as the popularity of the All Saints festival increased. Within a few hundred years, the commemoration of the dead also moved from an earlier date to coincide with the November observation, so that eventually, the two would be held back to back. In any case, the Christian observations were quite unlike their pagan predecessor, and by the medieval period, the feasts became solemn reminders of mortality and the grisly fates awaiting the sinner.

In medieval times, as during other feast days, it became customary to spend Samhain night going door to door collecting food and other offerings for the poor, often in exchange for prayers said for the homeowner.

However, the Samhain ritual often involved a costumed masquerade, some say in imitation of the fairy procession. If a homeowner gave generously to these masked visitors, the visitors would make a solemn procession around the kitchen fire—a tradition that clearly echoes the ancient Samhain rituals. Were the hosts less than generous, they would be cursed in a similar manner.

Samhain Today

Neopagans, especially Wiccans, have embraced Samhain as their most sacred holiday, an adoption based on Samhain's importance as a celebration of endings and beginnings. The modern pagan take on Samhain is more of a composite holiday, often mingling traditions of the ancient Celts with later European practices. Samhain is generally viewed by modern pagans as a time for reflection and meditation and a time to commune with the spirits of dead loved ones, honor one's ancestors, and prepare for prosperity or good fortune in the coming year.

A typical Wiccan or neopagan celebration of Samhain may include memorials for the departed, visits to cemeteries, and rituals to honor ancestors. Traditional harvest goods like pumpkins, apples, and mead are often featured.

Feast for the Ancestors: The Dumb Supper

A later custom that bears mentioning is the medieval practice of the "dumb supper," still celebrated in many rural areas in Europe and popular as well with modern neopagans. In a typical dumb supper (the word *dumb* having its ancient meaning of "silent"), a banquet is prepared, with places set at the table for both the living and the dead. Prayers are recited, and candles or other sources of light are passed around the table and around each participant. The places set for the ancestors and loved ones are filled with their favorite foods, and the meal progresses in silent communion with the dead.

The Corn Spirit

An autumn tradition that almost certainly carries over from ancient pagan practices is the creation of the so-called corn dolly. While today's corn dolly is a simple harvest craft, it was once imbued with deep spiritual significance. In Celtic territories and elsewhere in Europe, it was customary to leave a small portion of grain unharvested, in the belief that removing all of the stalks would leave the spirit of the grain homeless and unable to return. The reserved grain would be shaped into the form of a man or woman or other symbolic shape and was often treated to lavish ceremonial processions and feedings. The bundle was sometimes dressed in clothing, and would be reverently displayed—sometimes on a pole, or kept in a cradle or bed.

FACT

The word *corn* in this case refers to its oldest use, as a generic term for grain. Today *corn* is used almost exclusively to refer to the Native American maize plant, a grain unheard of in Europe until brought back by New World explorers.

The resulting "doll" represented the essence of the grain, the god of vegetation who would be "born" at the beginning of winter, and ritually sacrificed in the spring by burning or plowing under before the sowing of new crops. There is some speculation that the corn dolly tradition replaced an earlier blood sacrifice.

The earliest reference to this tradition can be found in accounts of St. Eligius (or Eloi) of Flanders, who castigates his countrymen for following local druid customs, among them the creation of the *vetula*, or old woman of the corn.

John Barleycorn

Although the corn dolly represented a mother figure as often as a male figure, the best-known incarnation of the grain spirit is John Barleycorn, immortalized in verse by the beloved Scottish poet Robert Burns.

Burns sets out the story of the grain spirit as an homage to the barley harvest, and the brutal sacrifice of the barley, which results in his resurrection as another sort of "spirit":

There were three kings into the east,
Three kings both great and high,
An' they hae sworn solemn oath
John Barleycorn should die.
They took a plough and plough'd him down,
Put clods upon his head,
And they hae sworn a solemn oath
John Barleycorn was dead.
But the cheerfu' spring came kindly on,
And show'rs began to fall;
John Barleycorn got up again,
And sore surprised them all.
The sultry suns of summer came,
And he grew thick and strong,
His head weel arm'd wi' pointed spears,

That no-one should him wrong.
The sober autumn enter'd mild,
When he grew wan and pale;
His bending joints and drooping head
Show'd he began to fail.
His colour sicken'd more and more,
He faded into age;
And then his enemies began
To show their deadly rage.
They've ta'en a weapon long and sharp,
And cut him by the knee;
Then tied him fast upon a cart,
Like a rogue for forgerie.
They laid him down upon his back,
And cudgel'd him full sore;
They hung him up before the storm,
And turn'd him oe'r and o'er.
They filled up a darksome pit
With water to the brim;
They heaved in John Barleycorn,
There let him sink or swim.
They laid him out upon the floor,
To work him farther woe,
And still as signs of life appear'd
they tossed him to and fro.
They wasted, o'er a scorching flame,
The marrow of his bones;
But a miller us'd him worst of all,
For he crushed him between two stones.
And they had tae'n his very heart's blood,
And drunk it round and round;
And still the more and more they drank,
Their joy did more abound.

In Christian times, corn dollies evolved into a rural household practice, featuring elaborate symbolic figures crafted from straw left over from the harvest. These were usually placed over doorways or in barns as good luck charms; they were typically burnt at Christmastime possibly in mimicry of the old mistletoe traditions. Even today, it is not unusual to see elaborately braided corn dollies given pride of place in winter decorations, and there are literally hundreds of specialized designs that vary from region to region.

Guy Fawkes

Vestiges of the sacrificial vegetation god may survive today in the British celebrations of Guy Fawkes Day. Fawkes was a seventeenth century Catholic revolutionary implicated in the infamous November 5 Gunpowder Plot, in which he attempted to blow up the Houses of Parliament and end Protestant rule in England. Fawkes was caught in the act and swiftly executed. Within a hundred years, an effigy of Fawkes had become a proxy for the ancient corn effigy. The harvest deity was replaced with a figure of the infamous traitor, which would be paraded from house to house by children who would beg coins or sweets in return. Afterward, the effigy would be burned in a great bonfire.

Beltaine: The Exaltation of the Sun

The spring festival of Beltaine or Beltane ("bright" or "shining") was probably celebrated in honor of Belenos ("shining"), an ancient Gaulish sun god. Belenos was widely worshipped, from Gaul to Austria and as far as Italy. The Romans identified him with their own solar deity, calling him Belenos Apollo. Belenos was strongly associated with water, especially hot springs, and his shrines and sanctuaries were dedicated to health and healing.

ALERT!

The Christians were somewhat horrified by Beltaine, which they erroneously associated with the demon Baal. This unfortunate association led to all sorts of speculation about human sacrifices and other dark rituals.

Although there is little mention of Belenos in Irish myth, the festival that bore his name remained an important part of the Celtic religious calendar. Beltaine was celebrated by the druids beginning on the eve before. After every household fire was extinguished, gigantic bonfires, called needfires, were built on the hillsides overlooking the community. The fires were kindled ritualistically, using nine sacred woods.

According to the glossarist Cormac, it was during Beltaine that the druids blessed and purified the community's livestock, driving them between the great fires. Afterward, villagers would themselves leap through the flames, and at the end, the embers from the sacred fire were carried home to relight the household fires. It was these bonfires that were reportedly the largest bone of contention between the Christian establishment of Ireland and the remnant druids.

The story of Patrick and Loeghaire, credited as the last pagan king of Ireland, records such a conflict. The dispute comes at Beltaine, with the preparations for the sacred fires at Tara. According to custom, all fires in the vicinity of the sacred hill of Tara were extinguished, until such time as they could be relit from the sacred bonfire. The prohibition against fires within view of the hill carried the force of law and could be punishable by death. Patrick, knowing of the sacred tradition and fully aware of the possible consequences, traveled to Tara and deliberately lit a bonfire on the plain, which was easily visible from the hill.

One version of the tale claims that Loeghaire moved to arrest Patrick, but found his passionate arguments in favor of Christianity to be so eloquent that he was granted the freedom to preach as he wished. A later, somewhat snarkier version of the story has the king's druid advisors dying miserable deaths attempting to harm the saint, ending with the happy conversion of the king.

St. Patrick is implicated in the origin of a curious medieval ritual in the church. Beginning on Maundy Thursday (the Thursday before Easter Sunday) and continuing for two days thereafter, it became customary to extinguish all of the lights of the church. A small fire would be struck from a flint and blessed. This would be used to light a candle held in the end of a special staff. This was the Arundina Serpentina, a staff capped with a bronze serpent or dragon, from which all of the church candles would be relit. There seems to be an obvious relation between this practice and the Beltaine fire ritual.

Imbolc

Imbolc means "in milk," and refers to the lactation of livestock in preparation for the birth of new babies in the spring. Imbolc is celebrated on February 2, in the midst of one of the coldest months of winter. All the same, it is a celebration of the coming of the light and the promise of new life to come. The "darkest part" is over, and the weather will only become brighter and warmer. Although it may not seem so, winter is ended and spring has begun.

FACT

The western tradition of Groundhog Day is an echo of Imbolc rituals past, likely brought to the New World by immigrants from Ireland and England.

Imbolc was sacred to the goddess Brighid, mother goddess of the Celts. Brighid was goddess of fire, thresholds, and transformation, and so mother and protector of crops, pregnancy, and sexuality. Brighid was the patron of the arts, especially poetry and metalworking. The festival of Imbolc was a festival of lights, celebrated as an encouragement of the sun to ensure fertility in the coming season. Brighid was the daughter of In Dagda, the "Good God." She was wife to the giant Bres, and mother of Ruadan ("Red-Haired").

As with the other great festivals, Imbolc was a time to rekindle sacred fires, especially those of the hearth and the forge. The Church was as eager to embrace this as it was the other ancient festivals, and the day was christened "Candelmas," where it was literally a mass in honor of the lights of the church. The old wax and partially burned candles would be removed from the church, and new candles would be blessed and set in place. Overall, it was definitely a good time of year to be a candle maker.

Brighid

As discussed, the great goddess Brighid, through her absorption into the Irish church, became St. Brigid of Kildare, by legend a powerful abbess whose miracles not so coincidentally coincide with the powers of the goddess whose name she bears. St. Brigid was extraordinarily important to the Irish; she was counted in Irish legend as the foster mother of Christ and is seldom left out of any Irish prayer. She has a special affinity for fire, and is often invoked in prayer as a charm against house fires. The saint's miracles likewise correspond with the powers of the goddess—she is the patron saint of poets, blacksmiths, newborns, and herdsmen. St. Brigid's feast day is celebrated, not surprisingly, on February 1, the feast of Candlemas, where the bride's doll and the fire wheels are still constructed in her honor.

Brighid fulfils a special role among the Celts, being the only goddess who was a mother, a daughter, and a spouse to the gods, fulfilling all of the roles of the divine female. Both the goddess and the saint were said to have two sisters also named Brighid, making them both triple goddesses of sorts.

A traditional custom of Imbolc was the creation of corn dollies, effigies created with leftover grain saved from the previous year's harvest. The dolls would be dressed in finery and often paraded in procession about the village. The dolls represented the resurrection of the crops, as well as the return of the goddess from winter sleep. After her procession, she would be placed in a representative marriage bed to encourage the return of her mate, the sun god. This custom continued well after the mantle had been passed from pagan goddess to saint.

Other customs of the feast of Brighid included the fashioning of sun wheels, or bride's crosses of straw, which were hung over thresholds. These were considered especially protective against fire and lightning. Grains from the sheaves used to fashion Brighid's dolls and crosses were blessed and saved; these would be added to next year's seed, with an invocation to Brighid to protect the crops.

Because Brighid was believed to roam the countryside on her night, it was also customary to leave cakes and a bit of ale outside the gates for her. A linen cloth might also be left draped over a hedge, in imitation of the saint's cloak; this she would bless as she passed by, and the cloth would be protection against all manner of disease, especially in livestock.

Lughnasadh: The Feast of Lugh

The Feast of Lughnasadh falls on the cross-quarter day between the summer solstice and the autumn equinox. The festival was, according to legend, instituted by the god Lugh on the occasion of his foster-mother Tailtiu's death as a funeral feast. It is clear, however, that the feast originated as a commemoration of Lugh's slaying of the giant Balor, and the prizing of agricultural secrets from the dark god Bres. This victory over the Fomorians marked the beginning of the rule of the Tuatha Dé Danann.

In the calendrical pageant of the gods, Lughnasadh commemorates this victory over darkness and celebrates the fruit of that victory, the first fruits of the harvest. It can be looked at as the victory of Lugh, the gentler solar aspect, over Balor, his harsher aspect. The feast of Lugh is held at the hottest time of the year, when the battle against the harshness of the sun was often very real.

Tailtiu seems to have been an ancient agricultural goddess, about whom little is known except for the harvest festival held in her honor. In Lugh's story, she is the Fir Bolg princess who fosters him. During the period of starvation that marked the captivity of the Tuatha Dé Danann by the Fomorians, she performs heroically, clearing a massive plain for planting so that the people will not starve. She dies as a result of her exertions, and the grieving god institutes a funeral feast in her honor. The month of August in Ireland has long been associated with sorrow and mourning—this may reflect a tradition of mourning for the "sacrifice" of the grain.

FACT

Tailtiu is connected with a number of ancient agricultural goddesses, in particular Macha, who dies in childbirth. These goddesses may have been symbolic of the crop, which "dies" while giving up its yield.

Lugh was called "many skilled," and his feast was a pageant of skill as well, from feats of athleticism and competitive games to displays of handicrafts and metalwork. Lughnasadh represented the last period of rest before the major work of the agricultural year began. It was a time for trade between tribes, for sport and friendly competition, and for reciting songs of praise for the heroic deeds of the heroes and the fallen warriors of the tribes. The crops were ripened, and there were trades and goods to be purchased with the new bounty. Lughnasadh was also a popular time for new couples to enact temporary partnerships called "Tailtian marriages." These trial marriages were solemnized at the festival and typically lasted until the next year.

These traditions in particular remained strong through Christian times. Predictably, the church discovered yet another festival to commemorate, which just happened to fall at this time—the Lammas festival. Lammas also celebrated the harvest, and it was celebrated in much the same way, with games and contests and open-air markets. The name Lammas is believed to be derived from "loaf-mass," but this explanation is not universally accepted.

CHAPTER 20

Celtic Traditions in the Modern Age

Today, the term "Celtic spirituality" is an umbrella term, an ambiguous magical term embraced by adherents of a variety of spiritual traditions. There are Celtic Reconstructionists, who attempt to re-enact as closely as possible the ancient religious practices of the Celts, neodruid orders who embrace the romantic ideal of the druid as learned scholar and wise religious teacher. There are the Celtic Christians, both Catholic and Protestant, who look to the gentle traditions of Ireland and embrace the natural world and the inner landscape. Finally, there are the myriad numbers of neopagans and Wiccans, who take inspiration from Celtic traditions and symbolism in their rites.

Modern Druidry

After the near complete domination of the Celtic realm by Christianity, the druids faded into obscurity. They remained nearly forgotten, mere historic curiosities, until sixteenth century authors began to speculate about the nature of druidry. Because of the lack of concrete information in the historical records, these would-be historians found themselves free to speculate, and they eventually wove an enchanting, romantic fantasy of their druid ancestors as noble savages, impossibly educated, virtuous, and lacking nothing in spiritual depth. These romantics touched off a furious interest in druidry which eventually led to attempts to resurrect druidry as a living religion.

The Romantic Druid

The seeds of modern druidry were planted in the sixteenth century, when several authors began to speculate on the nature of the druid religion. This sentiment flowered in the following century, when an English antiquarian by the name of John Aubrey made detailed notes on the measurements, position, and placement of the Avebury stones and other monuments, which he theorized were druid ancient temples.

A somewhat later scholar, another antiquarian, Dr. William Stukeley, picked up Aubrey's notions of noble druid builders and created a history of Britain's druids. Stukeley theorized a massive layout of temples, all part of a larger pattern of earthworks centering on the stone circles at Stonehenge and Avebury, which he supposed were arrayed in a pattern of large serpents or dragons. He painted a romantic picture of druids as romantic and wise, and it is from his work that we get the popular image of the bearded, white robed druid.

William Stukeley reconciled his Christianity and his interest in druidry by constructing an elaborate theory of origin for the ancient druids. He hypothesized that the ancient druids were in fact the ancient Hebrew descendants of Abraham, who, after journeying to Europe, began to practice a form of "natural religion" not unlike Christianity which showed particular reverence for the trinity. It was of course a complete fantasy.

Stukeley visited one Neolithic burial site after another, and declared them all to be druidic. Stukeley's interest in druidry went beyond curiosity into outright enthusiasm; although he was a vicar of the church, he began to fancy he was a druid himself. He christened himself "Chyndonax," after a Greek inscription taken from a druid's tomb, and constructed his own interpretation of a druid grove in his own backyard, where he even conducted his own versions of ancient rituals.

Neodruid Orders

Stukeley's enthusiasm proved contagious, and all this romanticism about druidry inevitably led to the formation of several neodruid orders. In 1781, an Englishman named Henry Hurle founded the first neodruid order, which he called the Ancient Order of Druids (AOD). The order was based largely on a Masonic style infrastructure, and admitted only men. The AOD had members with distinctly different motivations. One group was composed of mystics who encouraged spiritual exploration, while the other preferred a nonreligious, "benevolent society" not unlike today's Rotarians. The group splintered, with one becoming the United Ancient Order of Druids and the other the Albion Lodge of United Ancient Order of Druids of Oxford. The latter group claimed descent from a mythical ancient druid order, Mount Haemus Grove, and its initiates included Prime Minister Winston Churchill. The former group continued much unchanged and still operates today.

FACT

The Mount Haemus Grove, according to the Albion Lodge, was supposedly formed by the last remnant of the ancient druids in 1245. In reality, the reference comes from a brief mention of the area by Stukeley, and it is heavily embroidered upon by later groups looking to add a gloss of historical legitimacy.

This neodruidry continued to be popular, and even influenced the founding fathers of the United States. Revolutionary Thomas Paine was one of several Freemasons who assumed (wrongly, of course) that Freemasonry had originated in the druid grove.

Iolo Morganwg and the Barddas

While English and American Masons and their friends were fancying themselves druids, the Welsh were busily resurrecting another branch of druidry. Two years before Henry Hurle founded his druid order, a Welshman named Thomas Jones convinced a group of exiled Welsh poets to sponsor a national poetry competition, or Eisteddfod (Welsh meaning "chairing" or "sitting"), patterned after an even earlier bardic contest in the twelfth century. The Welsh Eisteddfod was an open competition for poetry, prose, drama, and singing, and became overwhelmingly popular—so much so that it is the most popular cultural event in Wales to this day.

FACT

Thomas Jones's Eisteddfod was not the first reconstruction of the medieval institution. The Eisteddfod was briefly revived in 1176, when the Lord Rhys convened a "sitting" for rather political purposes: to cement his position and to set up regulations for bards, including rules for licensing apprentices, the metering of songs, and other bureaucratic minutiae.

The success of the Eisteddfod inspired other would-be bards. In 1792, a stonemason named Edward Williams, who fancied himself a bard, gathered together some friends and held his own homegrown bardic initiation ceremony, which he called the Gorsedd (Welsh, meaning "throne"). Unlike the other Welsh bards, Williams's group claimed an unbroken lineage from an ancient order of druids. Williams rechristened himself Iolo Morganwg (Ned of Glamorgan), and embarked on a long career of scholarship and creativity punctuated by fraud, alternately translating ancient Welsh poetry and creating forged documents of his own. Morganwg championed Welsh poetic traditions and even rediscovered a number of important works, including that of Dafydd ap Gwilym, who is now acknowledged as Wales's greatest poet.

Eventually, the public took notice of Iolo's efforts, and the modern-day bard became a popular, even revered figure. His Gorsedd became involved in the Welsh Eisteddfod and is still active. Of course, Iolo's Gorsedd ceremonies were about as authentic as his bardic texts, and even today they are carried out by rather silly looking druids arrayed in white robes,

Egyptian style headdresses, and Masonic style regalia, often sporting long white beards and imposing staffs and banners.

The Barddas

While Morganwg contributed a great deal to Welsh scholarship, he also did some of the worst damage. His best-known and most beloved work was a collation of poetry, purported Welsh bardic and druidic philosophy, and mystical theology, culled from supposed ancient manuscripts, which he called the *Barddas*. Iolo's *Barddas* were of course almost entirely spurious—convincing, but forgeries all the same. Morganwg's work was so convincing, however, that his fraud was not discovered until generations later. In the meantime, it was accepted by a number of scholars and esotericists, and Iolo's influence can still be seen in many modern works on druidry and bardcraft.

The *Barddas* purported to outline the druidic philosophy of ancient Britain and contained a mixture of Celtic, Arthurian, and gnostic-tinged Christian mysticism. The *Barddas* described a cosmology of metaphysical emanations and opposing forces of creation and chaos, locked in eternal struggle—very gnostic ideas, but certainly not druidic ones. Other insertions that give away Morganwg's personal philosophy are his comparisons of Jesus and the Celtic deity Esus, his unusual retelling of the Old Testament creation story, and his repeated insertions of Jesus in what are supposed to be ancient pagan philosophies.

FACT

One of the primary preoccupations of the *Barddas* was, oddly enough, a pseudo-druidic alphabet, along with a system of numeration and a system of symbols. Both were entirely fabricated, but this was not discovered until long after their publication. In any case, many of the symbols are perceived to have spiritual value all the same and so are still used as emblems by many modern druid groups.

The latter portion of the text of the *Barddas* is made up entirely of verse, mostly triads, after a traditional form of bardic poetry. These are attributed to a variety of famous Welsh bards, some wholly mythical.

The New Druids

Despite being mostly mythical nonsense, the neodruid movement never entirely lost its charm, but by the early twentieth century, interest was dwindling. The decline would not last long. With new scholarship, a better sense of the ancient religion began to take shape. When the 1960s rolled around, bringing increased interest in the environment and alternatives to mainstream spirituality, interest in druidry as a religion began anew.

There are several types of modern druid organizations. A handful of these groups claim lineage from one or more of the eighteenth-century revival orders, and their beliefs and practices are more in keeping with eighteenth century esotericism than druidry as a strict religious pursuit. Still others, sometimes referred to as Celtic Reconstructionists or neopagan druids, try to emulate as closely as possible ancient druid religious practices, gleaned from historical and archaeological reconstructions, but dispensing with the notions of the romantic revivalists.

The modern day neodruid movement sprang up somewhat simultaneously both in the United States and the United Kingdom. The first such group, the Reformed Druids of North America (RDNA), was formed in 1963 as something of a lark. A group of Minnesota college students were upset with a school rule demanding mandatory attendance of religious services. Not liking any of the available choices, they opted to create their own. They chose druidry and dressed up their new religious organization with tongue-in-cheek style. When the absurd rule was finally withdrawn, pretend druids actually found themselves interested in studying druidry, and eventually the group began practicing in earnest.

FACT

The RDNA has been continually active ever since, and it has even spawned two offshoots that are active and influential in the neopagan community today. The Ár nDraíocht Féin ("Our Own Druidism," also known as the Druid Fellowship), founded by RDNA member Isaac Bonewits in 1983, claims to be the largest neopagan druid organization in the world, with nearly 1,200 members.

About a year after the founding of the RDNA in the United States, a British poet named Ross Nichols, a member of the Ancient Druid Order, became offended by the group's election of a new leader. He set out on his own and organized a new group, which he called the Order of Bards, Ovates, and Druids (OBOD), after the classical system of druidical ranking. The OBOD emphasized a more historical, Celtic-centered mythology and ceremonies, and adopted a calendar of festivals based on the ancient Celtic calendar. The OBOD, like its parent order, places more emphasis on personal spiritual growth and inspiration than on faithfully recreating the practices of ancient druids.

What these newer druid groups and their offshoots had in common was an interest in an in-depth real spiritual experience, in contrast to the generalized esoteric spirituality and clubbishness of the fraternal druid orders and the nationalistic cultural emphasis of the Welsh groups. During the 1980s, membership in these groups and many other newly formed druid groups exploded alongside the Wiccan movement. Today, Celtic Reconstruction and druid orders are equally popular with disenchanted Wiccans and others looking for more authentic pagan traditions.

Meso-, Paleo-, and Neo-

There are three popular terms used today to sort and classify pagan belief systems and to separate modern believers from the indigenous religious practices they emulate. The term *paleopagan* refers to the ancient religions in their original state, as well as present-day practitioners of ancient indigenous religions. *Mesopagan* refers to modern-era groups who have syncretized ancient beliefs with influences from other systems, and is sometimes applied to ecumenical groups like Freemasonry. The term *neopagan* refers to those believers who practice admittedly modern-styled faiths such as Wicca.

Druid groups fall into one or more of these categories, depending on their philosophies and religious practices. The oldest druid groups, often described as *mesopagan*, are the romantic-era, Masonically inspired groups, who put little, if any, emphasis on religion or "authentic" druid practices. They are less interested in the druidry of the historical record, and tend to view their philosophy as what it is: a romantic philosophical or spiritual ideal. Many of the groups labeled mesopagan by their peers refer to themselves as "traditional" or "British Traditional," meaning not ancient tradition but the traditions of the druid revival.

Modern Druid Beliefs

Both the neopagan and so-called mesopagan groups emphasize the sacredness of nature and its importance to human health and spiritual growth. Both adhere to the concepts of awen, or inspiration, and imbas, or divine illumination.

The "traditional" British groups and their heirs follow a calendar based on the ancient solar calendar, with four main festivals to mark the solstices and equinoxes. These are often referred to as the "Gates of Alban," and are perceived as times when illuminating energy floods the earth, and the barriers of the Otherworld are dissolved. These are:

- Alban Eiler, "Light of the Earth," the spring equinox
- Alban Heruin, "Light of the Sea," the summer solstice
- Alban Elued, "Light of the Water," the autumn equinox
- Alban Artan, "Light of Arthur," the winter solstice, celebrated as the new year

Many groups add to these the four cross-quarter days, marking the spaces on the calendar in between solar festivals. These include the traditional holidays of Beltaine, Imbolc, Lughnasadh, and Samhain/Samhuinn.

Celtic Reconstructionist Paganism

Celtic Reconstructionism (CR) is a relatively recent brand of Celtic neopaganism. It is similar in many ways to neodruidry, in that both attempt to achieve some semblance of authenticity in their spiritual practices. Unlike druidry, however, the reconstructionists tend to cast a wider net, with a broader interest in Celtic culture as a whole. Reconstructionists also tend to follow a less rigid initiatory system—where druid orders tend to emphasize the classical ideals of druid priesthood with its lengthy training, hierarchical systems, and emphasis on philosophy, Celtic paganism looks to be more accessible, open, and culturally aware.

CRs also tend to appear more noticeably pagan, with emphasis on ritual, altered states, visionary practices, and polytheistic worship. Many Reconstructionist groups focus on a particular culture, be it Irish, Scottish, or Gallic, and some groups restrict membership to applicants who share a particular Celtic ethnic background. Unlike Wicca and related pagan faiths, Celtic Reconstructionists tend to avoid eclecticism, or the borrowing of elements from other religions or cultures.

The Celtic Influence on Wicca

Other religions that owe much to Celtic spirituality are Wicca and its neopagan offshoots. While Wicca is of course not a Celtic religion, the influence of Celtic ideas and romantic druidry can clearly be seen in much of its symbolism, its emphasis on Celtic deities and folklore, and its adoption of the Celtic ritual festival calendar. Gerald Gardner, the founder of the original Wiccan faith, was a member of the Ancient Order of Druids and the Order of Bards, Ovates, and Druids. Gardner obviously had several influences, including writings on European fertility cults, Freemasonry, folklore, and the nineteenth century revival of medieval and Renaissance ritual magic. He incorporated elements of all of these into a new religion he called Wicca (according to Gardner, from a root meaning "wise") and referred to it as a genuine ancient pagan tradition. Many of Gardner's occult flourishes proved unpopular over time, especially the elements of ritual magic, which were rightly perceived to have nothing to do with historical paganism. The Celtic elements, however, have resonated, so much so that many Wiccan splinter groups have embraced far more Celtic symbolism and cosmology into their practice.

Wiccan cosmology in general posits that there are two polar, harmoniously interacting energies in the universe, usually referred to as the god and goddess, who are sometimes said to represent all of the male and female deities of the world, night and day, and the interacting seasons of winter and summer.

In practice, Wiccans are free to choose among the deities they feel personally attracted to. Celtic deities are overwhelmingly popular for this purpose, and they probably make up the majority of deities venerated by Wiccan believers. The central mythology of Wicca is that of a horned god who takes the goddess as bride and continually dies and is reborn—a recasting of Cernunnos as a solar dying god. The goddess is less specific in attribute—not always recognizably Celtic, but nearly always linked with the Celtic horned god. In Wiccan mythology, the two deities represent the seasonal cycles, a continuing cycle of renewal.

The ritual and initiatory structure of Wicca and many of its offshoots in neopaganism are based on ritual magic, but strangely, its holidays and its emphasis on nature are mostly Celtic. The eight "Sabbats" of Wicca are, in fact, the eight festivals of the Celts:

- Mabon, vernal equinox
- Lughnasadh, after the festival of Lugh, the god of light
- Imbolc
- Samhain, from the Celtic fire-festival ("Samhain" in Gaelic means "summer's end")
- Beltaine
- Ostara, which uses the name of a Norse goddess for the vernal equinox
- Yule, the winter solstice—this is one of the odd ones out, being named for the Norse solstice celebration
- The summer solstice, called "Litha" by modern neopagans

Glossary

Alban gates
Literally, "gates of light," a poetic way of referring to the four stations of the sun by practitioners of modern druidry.

Albion
The ancient name of Great Britain, from a root meaning "white" or "world."

Amadan Dubh
Gaelic, "black fool." The Amadan Dubh is also known as the stroking lad, a malevolent phantom whose touch causes paralysis or disfiguration. The Amadan Dubh wanders at night, playing enchanted pipes.

Andraste
The "unfallen" or "invincible one," the war goddess of the Celtic Iceni tribe. Similar in many ways to the Morrigan, she is associated with warfare, death, and sovereignty.

Anam cara
Anam cara is Gaelic for "soul friend," and refers to a deeply connected platonic relationship between two Celtic Christians, usually same-sex pairs of monks, nuns, or priests. In later times, the tradition extended to the laity, and eventually, the anam cara was an officiant who gave prayers for the dead.

Annwn
The Welsh Otherworld, which later came to be known as Avalon. Annwn was ruled by Arawn, and later, by Gwyn ap Nudd.

Apotropaic
Refers to spells, amulets, and charms designed to have a protective affect.

Awen
A Gaelic word meaning "illumination" or "inspiration." Awen refers to the concept of sacred inspiration, the divine impetus behind poetry, art, and music.

Ban sidhe (banshee)
A female fairy, literally, "woman of the Sidhe." Originally viewed as a benign creature, the banshee came to be regarded as a malevolent ghost whose presence signaled impending death.

Bard, baird (plural)
A class of druidry that included poets, composers, and singers whose specialties were the heroic eulogy and genealogy.

Beltaine
An ancient Irish festival, celebrated on the first of May and marking the beginning of the summer

season. It is believed to be named for the solar deity Belenos.

Bile

The sacred tree of a Celtic community. The bile represented the center of a community and was used for meetings and assemblies. It was taboo to harm the bile in any way—the penalty was often death.

Bogle

In British and Irish folklore, the bogle was a malevolent shape changing goblin-like creature, usually associated with swamps and waterways. The bogle could appear variously as a wizened human or as a dark-hued animal, often a horse, goat, hare, or dog. The bogle's specialty was frightening or killing solitary travelers, usually by trickery.

Book of Kells

A fabulously detailed illuminated scripture attributed to the monks of Iona under St. Columba (Columcille).

Book of Invasions

A mythological history of Ireland written in the twelfth century and presented as a succession of foreign invasions of Ireland. Also called the Book of Conquests.

Bendigeitvran

"Blessed Raven," another name for the British god called Bran the Blessed.

Breasil, Hy-Brasil/Brazil

An Irish Otherworld, located on an island in the Western sea. The name means "princely island," and for a time it was believed to be a real island that could magically materialize every seven years. The country of Brazil is named for the mythical island.

Bronze Age

Refers to the period of human development following the Neolithic period, characterized by the use of tools and weapons of bronze.

Brythonic

Refers particularly to the ancient Celts of Britain.

Cailleach

"Veiled One," referring to the dress of an old woman. The Cailleach is an aspect of the goddess Sovereignty who has the appearance of a hideous hag. She typically represents the dark aspect of the goddess, ruling over the season of winter and burdensome obligation.

Cairn

A mound of stones, usually covering a grave or marking a place of importance.

Cauldron

The cauldron was an important artifact of Celtic mythology, and the Cauldron of Plenty was one of the Four Hallows or Treasures of Ireland. The cauldron was an important ritual item in Celtic religious practice and is connected with several gods. In mythological tales, the cauldron is a catalyst of rebirth or resurrection, a source of divine inspiration. It is believed that the Celtic cauldron may be the inspiration for tales of the Holy Grail quest. The cauldron is associated with the goddess Cerridwen in Welsh mythological tales.

Celt

A group of Indo-Europeans spread through Western Europe and into Britain and Ireland.

Cerddorion

"Sons of Cerridwen," refers to Welsh Bards and musicians.

Cloughtie Well

A sacred well/tree combination, where strips of cloth (cloughts or cloots) are hung as prayers or offerings to the patron saint of the well.

Columcille

"Dove of the Church," old Irish name of St. Columba of Iona.

Cross-quarter days

Refers to the pagan solar calendar. If the four principal solar holidays (the equinoxes and solstices) of the Celtic calendar are arrayed in a cross shape according to their position in the circular Celtic calendar, the cross-quarter days mark the spaces in between.

Craebh Ciuil

"Musical branch," referring to the musical wand of the bards, a mimicry of the magical Otherworld apple branch whose music had the power to cause sleep.

Cran

A tree.

Cuchulainn (Cu Culainn)

Literally, the "Hound of Culann." Cuchulainn was a god of the Tuatha Dé Danann, the hero of the Ulster Cycle.

Daurdabla

The magical harp of the Dagda, which knew the Three Noble Strains of Ireland, and had the power to call forth the seasons. The name means "two green oaks," but it is also called Coir cethair chuir, "four-angled music."

Deasil

A Gaelic word referring to a clockwise motion, mimicking the direction of the path of the sun. Deasil was the preferred direction for ritual processions, blessings, and so on.

Drui, druid

Members of the pagan intellectual class, which included priests, seers, poets, and physicians, as well as the priests of the gods.

The Dullachan or Dullahan

The Dullachan is a variety of bogle, a malicious goblin. He is a riding phantom who trolls the roads at night, carrying his head under one arm; his appearance is an omen of death. The Dullachan is the inspiration for Nathaniel Hawthorne's Headless Horseman.

Eire

The Irish name for Ireland; named for the goddess Eiru of the Tuatha Dé Danann.

Emain Macha

The ancient fortress of the goddess Macha, seat of the mythological court of Ulster and the oldest settlement in Ireland. Emain Macha became Armagh and was also the reputed site of St. Patrick's first church.

Eisteddfod, Eisteddfodau (plural)

From the Welsh, meaning "throne," a meeting of bards wherein apprentices would be graduated, disputes would be settled, and rules of the profession would be decided upon. Today's Eisteddfods are cultural events, usually contests of musical, dramatic, and poetic ability.

Eochaid Ollathair
"Great Horse Father," an epithet of the Dagda.

Flaithi
The Celtic social class just below that of king, representing the nobility.

Fenian Cycle (Fionn Cycle)
The Fenian or Fionn Cycle is one of the four major branches of the Celtic Myth Cycle, a collection of stories centered around the hero Fionn mac Cumhaill (Finn MacCool) and his legendary band of warriors, the Fianna.

Fianna
The Fianna were a legendary band of warriors under King Cormac mac Art, renowned for their fantastic strength and fearlessness. They were named for their leader, Fionn mac Cumhaill (Finn MacCool).

Feis Teamrach
The Feast of Tara, or more explicitly, the Mating of Tara, after the fabled coupling of the Dagda and the Morrigan. The Feis was instituted by King Ollamh Fodhla as a parliamentary meeting to decide laws and attend to other matters of importance to the people of Ireland.

Faeth Fiada
"Beast's cry" or "deer's cry," a spell of invisibility, possessed by the Tuatha Dé Danann and various Christian saints, which was believed to cause a concealing mist or give the user the appearance of a deer.

Fili, filidh (plural)
A druidic order of poet seers. The filidh outlasted the remainder of the druid class, and many converted to Christianity. The specialty of the filidh was satire, but they were also known to perform magic and divination. In later times, the ranks of the filidh were the highest attainable, surpassing even that of the bards. A female fili was known as a ban-fili.

Fionn mac Cumhaill (Finn MacCool)
Fionn mac Cumhaill was a god of the Tuatha Dé Danann, a great hero and the leader of the Fianna, a legendary band of semi-divine warriors.

Fir Bolg
"Spear men," or possibly "belly men." The Fir Bolg were early occupants of Ireland, an invading race who pushed out the Fomorians and who were in turn defeated by the Tuatha Dé Danann.

Fir flathemon
The "justice of the king," the moral obligations of the king which, when properly adhered to, ensured the prosperity of his people and the fertility of the land. Some of the more onerous aspects of this obligation are sometimes personified by the goddess Sovereignty as a hag who must be embraced.

Fomorian
One of a mystical race of sea giants, early inhabitants of Ireland who were driven out by the Tuatha Dé Danann.

Gael
A Celtic inhabitant of Ireland, Scotland, or the Isle of Man.

Gallic
Referring to the Gaulish tribes of Europe.

Gaul
Umbrella term for the early European Celts who resided in the geographical area covering Italy, France, Belgium, and much of Switzerland, The Netherlands, and Germany.

Gates of Alban, or Alban Gates
A term modern druids use to refer to the main festival days of the solar calendar, viewed as metaphorical gates through which connections to the Otherworld could be made.

Geas, geasa (sometimes, geis)
A sacred taboo, usually in the form of a prohibition placed upon a person, often a king. Many heroes of Celtic mythology operated under a geas, the breaking of which was their undoing.

Goddess Sovereignty
An archetype of Celtic mythology, Sovereignty encompasses a number of regional and universal goddesses of Celtic mythology who represent the land and its fertility. It is through Sovereignty that the Celtic kings acquired their divine authority through symbolic marriage with the goddess. Well-known sovereignty goddesses include the Welsh Rhiannon and the Morrigan of Ireland.

Gorsedd, Gorseddau (plural)
From the Welsh, meaning "throne," a gorsedd is a community of bards. Today, a gorsedd is usually preoccupied with the organizing of Eisteddfodau.

Hallstatt
The Celtic culture of Central and Western Europe from about 1200 B.C.E. to 500 B.C.E.

Head of Bran
One of the three sacred treasures of Britain, the severed head of the hero king Bran is reputedly buried facing France, where it acts as a magical talisman to protect England from her enemies.

Henge
A prehistoric ritual structure consisting of a circular ditch or excavation surrounded by a raised earthen ridge and having up to four entrances, usually arranged in the form of a solar cross. Contrary to popular belief, a stone circle is not a henge, although many henges feature stone circles.

Historical Cycle
One of the four branches of Celtic mythology, the Historical Cycle (also called the Cycle of the Kings or King's Cycle) recounts the lives of the legendary kings of Ireland.

The Hollow Hills
A poetic way to refer to the Sidhe mounds, the underground passage tombs in which the fairy-folk were believed to reside.

Imbas forosnai
Literally, "knowledge that illuminates"; refers to the gift of foresight possessed by the filidh seers and the method employed in gaining it.

Imram
Imram translates as "voyage"; generally refers to a particular genre of mythological journey tales.

Isle of Women
A mythological paradise common in popular imram tales, inhabited by beautiful Otherworld women

who could lure men to their shores through mournful singing and enchanted dreams.

Keltoi
The Greek word for the European Celts, from which the word Celt is derived.

La Tène
The proto-Celtic Iron Age culture that thrived from the fifth to first centuries B.C.E., from which many of the hallmarks of Celtic culture originated.

Lia Fail
The Stone of Destiny, one of the four legendary talismans of the Tuatha Dé Danann. The stone would cry out when a true king of Ireland walked upon it.

Lughnasadh
A major festival in the ancient Celtic calendar, celebrated on August 1 in honor of the sun god Lugh.

Mabinogi, mabinogion (Plural)
Originally, mabinogi, from an unknown Welsh root, referred to a series of four romantic tales revolving around the Welsh hero Pryderi (Peredur). The form mabinogion is a modern pluralization given to a collection of folklore stories including the four original tales set down by Lady Charlotte Guest in 1877, which she titled The Mabinogion.

Mag Mell
"Plain of Joy," one of the ancient names of the Celtic Otherworld. Mag Mell was located under the ocean, usually to the west, and ruled over by Manannan mac Lir, the Irish sea god.

Mag Tuireadh (Moytura)
Mag Tuireadh means "plain of pillars." It is the semi-mythical location of two epic battles fought by the Tuatha Dé Danann for the domination of Ireland.

Megalith
From the Greek, meaning "big stone," a megalith is a stone monument or tomb, including monuments like dolmens or stone circles such as Stonehenge.

Menhir
From the Welsh, meaning "long stone," a menhir or standing stone is usually a solitary stone monument, although the term is sometimes applied to a larger standing stone in a more complex monument. The use of menhirs is unknown, but theories on their purpose range from territorial markers to ritual altars.

Mythological Cycle
One of the four major branches of Celtic mythology, the Mythological Cycle is a collection of stories purporting to recount the pagan history of Ireland, from the time of the biblical flood to the coming of the Celtic Milesians. The most important work of the mythological cycle is the Lebor Gabála Érenn, the "Book of the Invasions of Ireland."

Naddred
"Adders," an appellation applied to the druids of Ireland.

Needfire
The druid-constructed festival fires from which household fires would be ritually relit.

Nemeton

A Gaulish word meaning "sacred" or "holy." The nemeton was a sacred space, usually a grove of trees or sacred well, the sacred space of the druids. Many places in Europe still carry names that belie their druid roots; for example, Nemetostatio and Vernemetum in Great Britain.

Neolithic Period

The "New Stone Age," refers to the period in human development (between about 8000 B.C.E.—4500 B.C.E.) characterized by the use of stone tools, and preceding the Bronze Age.

Ogham

An alphabet of inscribed grooves used between the fifth and seventh centuries and attributed to Ogma, the god of eloquence. The ogham was used primarily on wooden staves and stone markers.

Ollam dana

Gaelic, meaning "highest of art." Ollam dana is the highest rank of the filidh, a position equal to that of a king of a tuath.

Otherworld

The underground kingdom of the Tuatha Dé Danann also thought to be intertwined with the visible world. The Otherworld was accessible by sea journey or through the underground passage tombs and Sidhe mounds.

Passage tomb

Neolithic underground tombs consisting of a long passageway and one or more burial chambers; Iron Age Celts believed they were the abodes of the gods.

Psychopomp

From the Greek, refers to a deity or spirit charged with guiding the souls of the dead.

Roane

See Selkie.

In Ruad Rofhessa

"The Red One of Great Knowledge," another epithet of the Dagda.

Sabd (sava)

From the Gaelic, "deer." Sabd was the shape-changing wife of Fionn, who was cursed by an evil druid to retain the form of a deer.

Samhuinn (Samhain)

One of the four major Celtic festivals of the druids, celebrated November 1 and marking the onset of winter. Samhain, meaning "summer's end," is celebrated today as a neopagan and neodruid festival.

Seelie or unseelie

In British and Scottish folklore, fairies were divided into two groups—the largely benevolent seelie, or "blessed" court, and the unseelie court, made up of malevolent creatures who lived to harm humankind. The seelie and unseelie courts were sometimes related to angels and demons.

Selkie

Selkies are the seals of Orkney, magically transformed humans (or, sometimes, angels) who live in undersea caverns. Selkies can take the form of humans while on land, shedding their seal skins. They are known as roane in Ireland.

Sheela-na-gig

A grotesque stone carving of a woman opening her own vulva. Sheelas are found throughout the Irish landscape and may represent the goddess in the act of giving birth to herself.

Sidhe

A fairy mound, believed by the Irish Celts to be the homes of the Tuatha Dé Danann. In reality, the Sidhe were tombs built by the Neolithic residents of Ireland. Later, residents of the mounds came to be referred to as Sidhe as well.

Solstice

One of two days of the year, one in spring and one in winter, when the sun is the farthest from the celestial equator.

Stations of the Sun

A poetic way used to refer to the four fixed festivals of the solar year, specifically, the solstices and equinoxes.

Tain Bo Cuailnge

Literally, the "Cattle Raid of Cooley." The Tain is the central epic story of the Ulster Cycle, wherein Queen Medb of Connacht attempts the theft of the most valuable bull in Ireland, the property of a rival chieftain. The central character of the Tain is the hero Cuchulainn.

Tara

A large hill located in the center of Ireland, Tara was the legendary seat of the kings of the Tuatha Dé Danann and home to the Lia Fail.

Taranis

An ancient Gallic god, one of three alluded to in Caesar's writings on the Gallic Wars. Taranis was a god of thunder and lightning, to whom human sacrifices may have been made.

Tarvos Trigaranus

A mysterious bull god of the Gallic Celts, possibly a form of the god Esus. Tarvos Trigaranus means literally "bull with three cranes" and refers to the peculiar iconography found with images of Esus, of a bull with three cranes perched upon his back or atop his head.

Three Noble Strains of Ireland

The three magical songs of enchantment known by the Dagda's harp, which had the power to invoke perfect happiness, perfect sorrow, and perfect sleep.

Tir Na Nog

In Gaelic Irish, literally, "land of the young," a name for the Celtic afterlife, sometimes identical to the Otherworld.

Torque

An ornamental neck ornament shaped like an open ring with decorated ends, worn as a sign of status. The torque is frequently depicted in images of gods and goddesses and probably had religious import.

Trow

A shape-changing supernatural creature particular to the Scottish isles. The trow may be related to or descended from the Scandinavian troll.

Tuath, tuatha (plural)

A tribe or family group, something like a clan; each tuath had its own king.

Tuatha Dé Danann

Literally, "people of (the goddess) Danu," the ancient Irish gods.

Tynged

Welsh, meaning "destiny" or "fate." A tynged is similar to the Irish geas, a sacred prohibition or curse.

Tylwyth Teg

Welsh, "fair folk." The Tylwyth Teg are the Welsh equivalent of the Sidhe.

Uisneach

A sacred hill located in the center of Ireland, on which can be found the "navel of Ireland," a stone whose markings are used to delineate the counties of Ireland. The stone is also known as "Aill na Mireann," the "Stone of Divisions."

Ulster Cycle

The Ulster Cycle, also known as the Red Branch Cycle, is one of the four major branches of Celtic mythology, a collection of stories and poems centered around heroes of Ulster, the centerpiece of which is the Tain Bo Cuailnge.

Underworld

Another way to refer to the Otherworld, especially in earlier Celtic mythology.

Washer at the Ford

A peculiar character of Welsh and Irish legend, the washer or ban nighe is a phantom crone who appears as a presage of death; she is strongly associated with the Morrigan, the ancient goddess of war and death.

Welsh triads

A collection of related medieval manuscripts containing Welsh mythological tales, poems, and history, arranged in groups of three lines, according to the old bardic custom.

Wicca

A modern neopagan religion dating to the mid-twentieth century, which draws some of its ritual symbolism from Celtic spiritual traditions.

Ynys mBeo

The "Isle of the Living," a name of the Otherworld.

Ynys Witrin

The "Isle of Glass," an ancient name for Glastonbury Tor.

Yspaddadden

One of many giants in Celtic mythology, Yspaddadden was the father of Olwen, the bride of the hero Culwhch.

Celtic History Timeline

4000–3500 B.C.E. and earlier . . . The future Celtic territories are first farmed, and megalithic monuments are built

2500–1500 B.C.E. . . . . Period during which most pre-Celtic megaliths were built

1800–1600 B.C.E. . . . . The Bronze Age

1000 B.C.E. . . . . The appearance of the proto-Celtic Urnfield Culture

900–500 B.C.E. . . . . The Halstatt period—emergence of the first true Celtic culture

600 B.C.E. . . . . Iron Age

500–15 B.C.E. . . . . The La Tène Period, exemplified by an explosion of art and culture. Also referred to as the Heroic Age.

450–450 B.C.E. . . . . Expansion of Celtic culture into Spain and Northern Italy

390 B.C.E. . . . . The Celtic invasion of Rome

279 B.C.E. . . . . Celts invade Greece

200 B.C.E. . . . . Gaulish occupy many parts of Western Europe, including the British Isles, France, Germany, Belgium, and Switzerland

100 B.C.E. . . . . Arrival of the Gaels in Ireland

82 B.C.E. . . . . Rome repels the Celts

70 B.C.E. . . . . First known appearance of the druids

55 B.C.E. . . . . The Romans under Julius Caesar invade Celtic Britain

52 B.C.E. . . . . Rome defeats the Celts in Gaul

43 B.C.E.–409 C.E. . . . . Roman control of Celtic territories in Britain and Wales

61 C.E. . . . . Rome destroys remaining druid communities at Anglesey

62 C.E. . . . . Queen Boudicca defeated and the Iceni rebellion ended

432 C.E. . . . . Arrival of St. Patrick brings Christianity to Ireland

445 C.E. . . . . Vortigern and Myrddn

465 C.E. . . . . Probable birth of the historical Arthur

563 C.E. . . . . Arrival of Columcille in Iona

List of Celtic Deities

Gallic/Romano-Celtic Gods

Arvernus: "King of the Averni," considered an equivalent to the Roman Mercury.

Belenos: A solar deity identified with Apollo.

Borvo: "Boiling," a god of hot springs associated with Apollo.

Camulos: A god of war.

Cernunnos: "Horned One," a forest deity.

Dis Pater: An Underworld god, referred to by Caesar as the father god of the Gauls.

Esus: "Lord," deity whose attributes are unknown but who is depicted on numerous rock carvings. He was sometimes erroneously thought to be an ancient appearance of Jesus. Esus was possibly related to the Norse Odin; his sacrifices involved strangulation or drowning.

Genii Cucullati: Hooded dwarves or spirits, usually depicted in threes.

Lugus: A solar deity whose name is lent to many European places. The Welsh Lleu and the Irish Lugh are almost certainly related.

Maponos: A youthful god who is probably a forerunner of Mabon.

Nodens/Noudens/Vindos: A god of healing and the Underworld, probably related to the Welsh Nudd and the Irish Nuada.

Ogmios: God of eloquence and poetry, a forerunner of the Irish Oghma.

Smertrios: A war god.

Sucellos: "The Striker," a god of commerce and war. Sucellos may have been an epithet of Lugos.

Taranis: A god of thunder, fire, and lightning; identified with both Thor and Jupiter. Sacrifices made to Taranis were made via striking or blows.

Toutates: A god closely associated with Taranis and Esus; the three together may have represented the three "faces" of Lugos. Teutates may be related to the Norse Tyr (Tiw). Druidic sacrifices involving water were dedicated to Toutates.

Gaulish/Romano-Celtic Goddesses

Andraste: A war goddess worshipped by the Iceni.

Arduinna: A forest goddess identified with the Roman Diana.

Artio: A minor bear goddess.

Belisama: A goddess of fire, light, and rivers. A possible consort to Belenos.

Brigantia: The goddess of the Brigantes tribe.

Britannia: The sovereignty goddess of Britain, from whom the British Isles receive their name. Britannia was most likely related to Brighid.

Cathubodua: The "Battle Raven," a war goddess possibly related to the Irish Badb and the Morrigan.

Coventina: A nymph or goddess of lakes, streams, and wells.

Damona: "Divine Cow," the consort of Borvo and possible precursor to the Irish Boann.

Dea Matronae: "Divine Mother," triple goddesses of abundance, motherhood, and fertility.

Epona: A goddess of fertility, horses, and horsemen. Epona was the only goddess to be openly worshipped in Rome. The Welsh Rhiannon is probably related.

Nantosuelta: A nature goddess, sometimes consort to Sucellos.

Nemetona: "Grove," the goddess of the sacred groves.

Rosmerta: "Provider," a goddess of abundance often identified as the consort of Mercury.

Sequana: The goddess of the river Seine.

Sirona: A healing goddess associated with hot springs, sometimes a consort of Borvo.

Sulis: Goddess of the hot springs at Bath, identified with the Roman Minerva.

Welsh/British Gods

Arawn: The ruler of Annwn, the Welsh Otherworld.

Beli Mawr: The Welsh father god, consort of Don and father of Arianrhod and Lludd. Beli is related to the Gaulish Belenos and the Irish Bile.

Bran the Blessed: "Blessed Raven," whose head protects Britain from invasion.

Culwhch: "Son of Pig," possibly a boar god, later a hero of The Mabinogion.

Dylan: A sea god, the brother of Lleu.

Gwyn ap Nudd: Son of Nudd, a sometime ruler of the Otherworld realm of Annwn, although Gwyn and Nudd often appear to be the same person. Lleu Llaw Gyffes, "Lugh of Many Skills," Lugh is associated with hills, agriculture, the sun, and the calendar. Lleu is the equivalent of the Irish Lugh and the Gaulish Lugos.

Lludd: See Nudd

Llyr: The father of Bran, equivalent to Lir, the Irish god of the sea.

Mabon ap Modron: "Divine Son of the Mother," Mabon is certainly equivalent to the Gaulish Maponos, and probably the Irish Aenghus mac Og. Mabon is a god of youth and love who appears in tales of Culwhch and Arthur.

Manawydan: A sea god, equivalent to the Irish Manannan.

Math ap Mathonwy: The creator of Blodeuedd.

Nudd: Also known as Lludd Llaw Eraint, "Lludd of the Silver Hand." Nudd is related to the Irish Nuada and the Gaulish Nodens.

Pryderi: Also known as Peredur, Pryderi was Welsh hero of The Mabinogion, Pryderi is related to Mabon and other youthful deities, and was the inspiration for the Arthurian character Perceval. Pryderi is the nephew of Bran and is heavily associated with the origins of the Holy Grail quest.

Welsh/British Goddesses

Arianrhod: "Silver Wheel," the mother of Lleu, and the sea god Dylan.

Blodeuedd: "Flower Face," the wife of Lleu.

Branwen: "White Raven," the sister of Bran, probably a goddess of love and healing.

Cerridwen: A goddess of wisdom and knowledge. Welsh bards referred to themselves as Cerddorion, sons of Cerridwen.

Don: A mother goddess, equivalent to the Irish Danu and the Gaulish goddess of the Danube river.

Modron: A mother goddess, the equivalent of the Gaulish Matronae and the Irish.

Morrigan: The mother of Mabon. Modron may also be a forerunner of the literary Morgan le Fay.

Olwen: "White Track," the wife of Culwhch, possibly related to Guinevere or Blodeuedd.

Rhiannon: A sovereignty/horse goddess, possibly related to the Gaulish Epona and the Irish Macha.

Irish Gods

Aenghus mac Og: The son of Boann and the Dagda, a god of youth, love and healing. Aenghus was said to inhabit the megalithic tomb at Newgrange.

Balor: The fearsome, one-eyed Fomorian giant defeated by Lugh.

Bobd Dearg: "Red Crow," the successor of the Dagda as leader of the Tuatha Dé Danann.

Bres: The half-Fomorian husband of Brighid, an agricultural god who was superseded by Lugh.

Cuchulainn: "Hound of Culann," the son of Lugh.

The Dagda:: "Good God" also known as Eochaid Ollathair, "All-Father Horse." The Dagda was the leader of the Tuatha Dé Danann, and probably descended from an ancient Gaulish horse deity.

Dian Cecht: A god of healing, the physician of the Tuatha Dé Danann.

Fionn mac Cumhaill (Finn MacCool): A warrior-hunter and god of the woodlands, Fionn was the leader of the Fianna, a band of legendary warriors. Fionn may be related to the Gaulish horned deity Cernunnos.

Goibnu: The smith god of the Tuatha Dé Danann and the son of Brighid.

Lugh/Lugh Lamfada: "Lugh of the Long Arms," also called by the epithets "Many Skilled" and "Good Striker." Lugh means "bright" or "flashing," and Lugh was likely a solar deity, associated with agriculture, technology, and law. The Romans thought him the equivalent of Apollo and Mercury due to his associations with the arts and contracts.

Manannan mac Lir: "Manannan, son of Sea," sometimes thought to be a personification of the Isle of Mann.

Nuada of the Silver Arm: The first king of the Tuatha Dé Danann; Nuada is the equivalent of the Gaulish Nodens, and may be related to the Norse Tyr.

Oghma (or Ogma): God of poetry and eloquence, the son of Brighid. Oghma was likely related to the Gaulish Ogmios.

Irish Goddesses

Aine/Enya: A goddess of cattle, possibly related to the mother goddess Danu.

Badb/Badb Catha: "Raven," or "Battle Crow," a goddess of war and sovereignty who could take the form of a raven or wolf. Badb was equivalent to the Gaulish Cathubodua. Her sisters were Macha and the Morrigan, making her a triple goddess.

Boann: The goddess of the river Boyne, which passes Newgrange. Boann was the mother of Aenghus.

Brighid: "Fire Arrow" or "Exalted" goddess of fire, poetry, and smith craft, the daughter of the Dagda. Brighid was one of three sisters, all named Brighid, and was a triple goddess.

Caer: The wife of Aenghus, Caer possessed the ability to transform into a swan.

Danu: The mother goddess and namesake of the Tuatha Dé Danann or "People of Danu."

Eiru, Banba, and Fodhla: Three queens of the Tuatha Dé Danann who aid the Milesians on the condition that their names be given to their home. Eiru is of course Eire, or Ireland, and Banba and Fodhla are often used as poetic titles for the island.

Etain: A shape changing/reincarnating goddess, the wife of Midir. Etain is sometimes related to the Sheela-na-gig icons that dot Ireland.

Macha: Sister of Badb and the Morrigan, Macha was a sovereignty goddess. Her strong associations with horses make her equivalent to Epona and the Welsh Rhiannon.

Morrigan: "Terrible Queen" or "Phantom Queen"; Morrigan is a sovereignty and war goddess, and the lover of Cuchulainn.

Tailtiu: The Fomorian foster mother of Lugh, whose funeral games inspired the festival of Lughnasadh.

Index

THE EVERYTHING SERIES!

BUSINESS & PERSONAL FINANCE

Everything® Accounting Book
Everything® Budgeting Book, 2nd Ed.
Everything® Business Planning Book
Everything® Coaching and Mentoring Book, 2nd Ed.
Everything® Fundraising Book
Everything® Get Out of Debt Book
Everything® Grant Writing Book, 2nd Ed.
Everything® Guide to Buying Foreclosures
Everything® Guide to Fundraising, $15.95
Everything® Guide to Mortgages
Everything® Guide to Personal Finance for Single Mothers
Everything® Home-Based Business Book, 2nd Ed.
Everything® Homebuying Book, 3rd Ed., $15.95
Everything® Homeselling Book, 2nd Ed.
Everything® Human Resource Management Book
Everything® Improve Your Credit Book
Everything® Investing Book, 2nd Ed.
Everything® Landlording Book
Everything® Leadership Book, 2nd Ed.
Everything® Managing People Book, 2nd Ed.
Everything® Negotiating Book
Everything® Online Auctions Book
Everything® Online Business Book
Everything® Personal Finance Book
Everything® Personal Finance in Your 20s & 30s Book, 2nd Ed.
Everything® Personal Finance in Your 40s & 50s Book, $15.95
Everything® Project Management Book, 2nd Ed.
Everything® Real Estate Investing Book
Everything® Retirement Planning Book
Everything® Robert's Rules Book, $7.95
Everything® Selling Book
Everything® Start Your Own Business Book, 2nd Ed.
Everything® Wills & Estate Planning Book

COOKING

Everything® Barbecue Cookbook
Everything® Bartender's Book, 2nd Ed., $9.95
Everything® Calorie Counting Cookbook
Everything® Cheese Book
Everything® Chinese Cookbook
Everything® Classic Recipes Book
Everything® Cocktail Parties & Drinks Book
Everything® College Cookbook
Everything® Cooking for Baby and Toddler Book
Everything® Diabetes Cookbook
Everything® Easy Gourmet Cookbook
Everything® Fondue Cookbook
Everything® Food Allergy Cookbook, $15.95
Everything® Fondue Party Book
Everything® Gluten-Free Cookbook
Everything® Glycemic Index Cookbook
Everything® Grilling Cookbook
Everything® Healthy Cooking for Parties Book, $15.95
Everything® Holiday Cookbook
Everything® Indian Cookbook
Everything® Lactose-Free Cookbook
Everything® Low-Cholesterol Cookbook

Everything® Low-Fat High-Flavor Cookbook, 2nd Ed., $15.95
Everything® Low-Salt Cookbook
Everything® Meals for a Month Cookbook
Everything® Meals on a Budget Cookbook
Everything® Mediterranean Cookbook
Everything® Mexican Cookbook
Everything® No Trans Fat Cookbook
Everything® One-Pot Cookbook, 2nd Ed., $15.95
Everything® Organic Cooking for Baby & Toddler Book, $15.95
Everything® Pizza Cookbook
Everything® Quick Meals Cookbook, 2nd Ed., $15.95
Everything® Slow Cooker Cookbook
Everything® Slow Cooking for a Crowd Cookbook
Everything® Soup Cookbook
Everything® Stir-Fry Cookbook
Everything® Sugar-Free Cookbook
Everything® Tapas and Small Plates Cookbook
Everything® Tex-Mex Cookbook
Everything® Thai Cookbook
Everything® Vegetarian Cookbook
Everything® Whole-Grain, High-Fiber Cookbook
Everything® Wild Game Cookbook
Everything® Wine Book, 2nd Ed.

GAMES

Everything® 15-Minute Sudoku Book, $9.95
Everything® 30-Minute Sudoku Book, $9.95
Everything® Bible Crosswords Book, $9.95
Everything® Blackjack Strategy Book
Everything® Brain Strain Book, $9.95
Everything® Bridge Book
Everything® Card Games Book
Everything® Card Tricks Book, $9.95
Everything® Casino Gambling Book, 2nd Ed.
Everything® Chess Basics Book
Everything® Christmas Crosswords Book, $9.95
Everything® Craps Strategy Book
Everything® Crossword and Puzzle Book
Everything® Crosswords and Puzzles for Quote Lovers Book, $9.95
Everything® Crossword Challenge Book
Everything® Crosswords for the Beach Book, $9.95
Everything® Cryptic Crosswords Book, $9.95
Everything® Cryptograms Book, $9.95
Everything® Easy Crosswords Book
Everything® Easy Kakuro Book, $9.95
Everything® Easy Large-Print Crosswords Book
Everything® Games Book, 2nd Ed.
Everything® Giant Book of Crosswords
Everything® Giant Sudoku Book, $9.95
Everything® Giant Word Search Book
Everything® Kakuro Challenge Book, $9.95
Everything® Large-Print Crossword Challenge Book
Everything® Large-Print Crosswords Book
Everything® Large-Print Travel Crosswords Book
Everything® Lateral Thinking Puzzles Book, $9.95
Everything® Literary Crosswords Book, $9.95
Everything® Mazes Book
Everything® Memory Booster Puzzles Book, $9.95

Everything® Movie Crosswords Book, $9.95
Everything® Music Crosswords Book, $9.95
Everything® Online Poker Book
Everything® Pencil Puzzles Book, $9.95
Everything® Poker Strategy Book
Everything® Pool & Billiards Book
Everything® Puzzles for Commuters Book, $9.95
Everything® Puzzles for Dog Lovers Book, $9.95
Everything® Sports Crosswords Book, $9.95
Everything® Test Your IQ Book, $9.95
Everything® Texas Hold 'Em Book, $9.95
Everything® Travel Crosswords Book, $9.95
Everything® Travel Mazes Book, $9.95
Everything® Travel Word Search Book, $9.95
Everything® TV Crosswords Book, $9.95
Everything® Word Games Challenge Book
Everything® Word Scramble Book
Everything® Word Search Book

HEALTH

Everything® Alzheimer's Book
Everything® Diabetes Book
Everything® First Aid Book, $9.95
Everything® Green Living Book
Everything® Health Guide to Addiction and Recovery
Everything® Health Guide to Adult Bipolar Disorder
Everything® Health Guide to Arthritis
Everything® Health Guide to Controlling Anxiety
Everything® Health Guide to Depression
Everything® Health Guide to Diabetes, 2nd Ed.
Everything® Health Guide to Fibromyalgia
Everything® Health Guide to Menopause, 2nd Ed.
Everything® Health Guide to Migraines
Everything® Health Guide to Multiple Sclerosis
Everything® Health Guide to OCD
Everything® Health Guide to PMS
Everything® Health Guide to Postpartum Care
Everything® Health Guide to Thyroid Disease
Everything® Hypnosis Book
Everything® Low Cholesterol Book
Everything® Menopause Book
Everything® Nutrition Book
Everything® Reflexology Book
Everything® Stress Management Book
Everything® Superfoods Book, $15.95

HISTORY

Everything® American Government Book
Everything® American History Book, 2nd Ed.
Everything® American Revolution Book, $15.95
Everything® Civil War Book
Everything® Freemasons Book
Everything® Irish History & Heritage Book
Everything® World War II Book, 2nd Ed.

HOBBIES

Everything® Candlemaking Book
Everything® Cartooning Book
Everything® Coin Collecting Book
Everything® Digital Photography Book, 2nd Ed.

Everything® Drawing Book
Everything® Family Tree Book, 2nd Ed.
Everything® Guide to Online Genealogy, $15.95
Everything® Knitting Book
Everything® Knots Book
Everything® Photography Book
Everything® Quilting Book
Everything® Sewing Book
Everything® Soapmaking Book, 2nd Ed.
Everything® Woodworking Book

HOME IMPROVEMENT

Everything® Feng Shui Book
Everything® Feng Shui Decluttering Book, $9.95
Everything® Fix-It Book
Everything® Green Living Book
Everything® Home Decorating Book
Everything® Home Storage Solutions Book
Everything® Homebuilding Book
Everything® Organize Your Home Book, 2nd Ed.

KIDS' BOOKS

All titles are $7.95
Everything® Fairy Tales Book, $14.95
Everything® Kids' Animal Puzzle & Activity Book
Everything® Kids' Astronomy Book
Everything® Kids' Baseball Book, 5th Ed.
Everything® Kids' Bible Trivia Book
Everything® Kids' Bugs Book
Everything® Kids' Cars and Trucks Puzzle and Activity Book
Everything® Kids' Christmas Puzzle & Activity Book
Everything® Kids' Connect the Dots
     Puzzle and Activity Book
Everything® Kids' Cookbook, 2nd Ed.
Everything® Kids' Crazy Puzzles Book
Everything® Kids' Dinosaurs Book
Everything® Kids' Dragons Puzzle and Activity Book
Everything® Kids' Environment Book $7.95
Everything® Kids' Fairies Puzzle and Activity Book
Everything® Kids' First Spanish Puzzle and Activity Book
Everything® Kids' Football Book
Everything® Kids' Geography Book
Everything® Kids' Gross Cookbook
Everything® Kids' Gross Hidden Pictures Book
Everything® Kids' Gross Jokes Book
Everything® Kids' Gross Mazes Book
Everything® Kids' Gross Puzzle & Activity Book
Everything® Kids' Halloween Puzzle & Activity Book
Everything® Kids' Hanukkah Puzzle and Activity Book
Everything® Kids' Hidden Pictures Book
Everything® Kids' Horses Book
Everything® Kids' Joke Book
Everything® Kids' Knock Knock Book
Everything® Kids' Learning French Book
Everything® Kids' Learning Spanish Book
Everything® Kids' Magical Science Experiments Book
Everything® Kids' Math Puzzles Book
Everything® Kids' Mazes Book
Everything® Kids' Money Book, 2nd Ed.
Everything® Kids' Mummies, Pharaoh's, and Pyramids
     Puzzle and Activity Book
Everything® Kids' Nature Book
Everything® Kids' Pirates Puzzle and Activity Book
Everything® Kids' Presidents Book
Everything® Kids' Princess Puzzle and Activity Book
Everything® Kids' Puzzle Book

Everything® Kids' Racecars Puzzle and Activity Book
Everything® Kids' Riddles & Brain Teasers Book
Everything® Kids' Science Experiments Book
Everything® Kids' Sharks Book
Everything® Kids' Soccer Book
Everything® Kids' Spelling Book
Everything® Kids' Spies Puzzle and Activity Book
Everything® Kids' States Book
Everything® Kids' Travel Activity Book
Everything® Kids' Word Search Puzzle and Activity Book

LANGUAGE

Everything® Conversational Japanese Book with CD, $19.95
Everything® French Grammar Book
Everything® French Phrase Book, $9.95
Everything® French Verb Book, $9.95
Everything® German Phrase Book, $9.95
Everything® German Practice Book with CD, $19.95
Everything® Inglés Book
Everything® Intermediate Spanish Book with CD, $19.95
Everything® Italian Phrase Book, $9.95
Everything® Italian Practice Book with CD, $19.95
Everything® Learning Brazilian Portuguese Book with CD, $19.95
Everything® Learning French Book with CD, 2nd Ed., $19.95
Everything® Learning German Book
Everything® Learning Italian Book
Everything® Learning Latin Book
Everything® Learning Russian Book with CD, $19.95
Everything® Learning Spanish Book
Everything® Learning Spanish Book with CD, 2nd Ed., $19.95
Everything® Russian Practice Book with CD, $19.95
Everything® Sign Language Book, $15.95
Everything® Spanish Grammar Book
Everything® Spanish Phrase Book, $9.95
Everything® Spanish Practice Book with CD, $19.95
Everything® Spanish Verb Book, $9.95
Everything® Speaking Mandarin Chinese Book with CD, $19.95

MUSIC

Everything® Bass Guitar Book with CD, $19.95
Everything® Drums Book with CD, $19.95
Everything® Guitar Book with CD, 2nd Ed., $19.95
Everything® Guitar Chords Book with CD, $19.95
Everything® Guitar Scales Book with CD, $19.95
Everything® Harmonica Book with CD, $15.95
Everything® Home Recording Book
Everything® Music Theory Book with CD, $19.95
Everything® Reading Music Book with CD, $19.95
Everything® Rock & Blues Guitar Book with CD, $19.95
Everything® Rock & Blues Piano Book with CD, $19.95
Everything® Rock Drums Book with CD, $19.95
Everything® Singing Book with CD, $19.95
Everything® Songwriting Book

NEW AGE

Everything® Astrology Book, 2nd Ed.
Everything® Birthday Personology Book
Everything® Celtic Wisdom Book, $15.95
Everything® Dreams Book, 2nd Ed.
Everything® Law of Attraction Book, $15.95
Everything® Love Signs Book, $9.95
Everything® Love Spells Book, $9.95
Everything® Palmistry Book
Everything® Psychic Book
Everything® Reiki Book

Everything® Sex Signs Book, $9.95
Everything® Spells & Charms Book, 2nd Ed.
Everything® Tarot Book, 2nd Ed.
Everything® Toltec Wisdom Book
Everything® Wicca & Witchcraft Book, 2nd Ed.

PARENTING

Everything® Baby Names Book, 2nd Ed.
Everything® Baby Shower Book, 2nd Ed.
Everything® Baby Sign Language Book with DVD
Everything® Baby's First Year Book
Everything® Birthing Book
Everything® Breastfeeding Book
Everything® Father-to-Be Book
Everything® Father's First Year Book
Everything® Get Ready for Baby Book, 2nd Ed.
Everything® Get Your Baby to Sleep Book, $9.95
Everything® Getting Pregnant Book
Everything® Guide to Pregnancy Over 35
Everything® Guide to Raising a One-Year-Old
Everything® Guide to Raising a Two-Year-Old
Everything® Guide to Raising Adolescent Boys
Everything® Guide to Raising Adolescent Girls
Everything® Mother's First Year Book
Everything® Parent's Guide to Childhood Illnesses
Everything® Parent's Guide to Children and Divorce
Everything® Parent's Guide to Children with ADD/ADHD
Everything® Parent's Guide to Children with Asperger's
     Syndrome
Everything® Parent's Guide to Children with Anxiety
Everything® Parent's Guide to Children with Asthma
Everything® Parent's Guide to Children with Autism
Everything® Parent's Guide to Children with Bipolar Disorder
Everything® Parent's Guide to Children with Depression
Everything® Parent's Guide to Children with Dyslexia
Everything® Parent's Guide to Children with Juvenile Diabetes
Everything® Parent's Guide to Children with OCD
Everything® Parent's Guide to Positive Discipline
Everything® Parent's Guide to Raising Boys
Everything® Parent's Guide to Raising Girls
Everything® Parent's Guide to Raising Siblings
Everything® Parent's Guide to Raising Your
     Adopted Child
Everything® Parent's Guide to Sensory Integration Disorder
Everything® Parent's Guide to Tantrums
Everything® Parent's Guide to the Strong-Willed Child
Everything® Parenting a Teenager Book
Everything® Potty Training Book, $9.95
Everything® Pregnancy Book, 3rd Ed.
Everything® Pregnancy Fitness Book
Everything® Pregnancy Nutrition Book
Everything® Pregnancy Organizer, 2nd Ed., $16.95
Everything® Toddler Activities Book
Everything® Toddler Book
Everything® Tween Book
Everything® Twins, Triplets, and More Book

PETS

Everything® Aquarium Book
Everything® Boxer Book
Everything® Cat Book, 2nd Ed.
Everything® Chihuahua Book
Everything® Cooking for Dogs Book
Everything® Dachshund Book
Everything® Dog Book, 2nd Ed.
Everything® Dog Grooming Book

Everything® Dog Obedience Book
Everything® Dog Owner's Organizer, $16.95
Everything® Dog Training and Tricks Book
Everything® German Shepherd Book
Everything® Golden Retriever Book
Everything® Horse Book, 2nd Ed., $15.95
Everything® Horse Care Book
Everything® Horseback Riding Book
Everything® Labrador Retriever Book
Everything® Poodle Book
Everything® Pug Book
Everything® Puppy Book
Everything® Small Dogs Book
Everything® Tropical Fish Book
Everything® Yorkshire Terrier Book

REFERENCE

Everything® American Presidents Book
Everything® Blogging Book
Everything® Build Your Vocabulary Book, $9.95
Everything® Car Care Book
Everything® Classical Mythology Book
Everything® Da Vinci Book
Everything® Einstein Book
Everything® Enneagram Book
Everything® Etiquette Book, 2nd Ed.
Everything® Family Christmas Book, $15.95
Everything® Guide to C. S. Lewis & Narnia
Everything® Guide to Divorce, 2nd Ed., $15.95
Everything® Guide to Edgar Allan Poe
Everything® Guide to Understanding Philosophy
Everything® Inventions and Patents Book
Everything® Jacqueline Kennedy Onassis Book
Everything® John F. Kennedy Book
Everything® Mafia Book
Everything® Martin Luther King Jr. Book
Everything® Pirates Book
Everything® Private Investigation Book
Everything® Psychology Book
Everything® Public Speaking Book, $9.95
Everything® Shakespeare Book, 2nd Ed.

RELIGION

Everything® Angels Book
Everything® Bible Book
Everything® Bible Study Book with CD, $19.95
Everything® Buddhism Book
Everything® Catholicism Book
Everything® Christianity Book
Everything® Gnostic Gospels Book
Everything® Hinduism Book, $15.95
Everything® History of the Bible Book
Everything® Jesus Book
Everything® Jewish History & Heritage Book
Everything® Judaism Book
Everything® Kabbalah Book
Everything® Koran Book
Everything® Mary Book
Everything® Mary Magdalene Book
Everything® Prayer Book

Everything® Saints Book, 2nd Ed.
Everything® Torah Book
Everything® Understanding Islam Book
Everything® Women of the Bible Book
Everything® World's Religions Book

SCHOOL & CAREERS

Everything® Career Tests Book
Everything® College Major Test Book
Everything® College Survival Book, 2nd Ed.
Everything® Cover Letter Book, 2nd Ed.
Everything® Filmmaking Book
Everything® Get-a-Job Book, 2nd Ed.
Everything® Guide to Being a Paralegal
Everything® Guide to Being a Personal Trainer
Everything® Guide to Being a Real Estate Agent
Everything® Guide to Being a Sales Rep
Everything® Guide to Being an Event Planner
Everything® Guide to Careers in Health Care
Everything® Guide to Careers in Law Enforcement
Everything® Guide to Government Jobs
Everything® Guide to Starting and Running a Catering Business
Everything® Guide to Starting and Running a Restaurant
Everything® Guide to Starting and Running a Retail Store
Everything® Job Interview Book, 2nd Ed.
Everything® New Nurse Book
Everything® New Teacher Book
Everything® Paying for College Book
Everything® Practice Interview Book
Everything® Resume Book, 3rd Ed.
Everything® Study Book

SELF-HELP

Everything® Body Language Book
Everything® Dating Book, 2nd Ed.
Everything® Great Sex Book
Everything® Guide to Caring for Aging Parents, $15.95
Everything® Self-Esteem Book
Everything® Self-Hypnosis Book, $9.95
Everything® Tantric Sex Book

SPORTS & FITNESS

Everything® Easy Fitness Book
Everything® Fishing Book
Everything® Guide to Weight Training, $15.95
Everything® Krav Maga for Fitness Book
Everything® Running Book, 2nd Ed.
Everything® Triathlon Training Book, $15.95

TRAVEL

Everything® Family Guide to Coastal Florida
Everything® Family Guide to Cruise Vacations
Everything® Family Guide to Hawaii
Everything® Family Guide to Las Vegas, 2nd Ed.
Everything® Family Guide to Mexico
Everything® Family Guide to New England, 2nd Ed.

Everything® Family Guide to New York City, 3rd Ed.
Everything® Family Guide to Northern California and Lake Tahoe
Everything® Family Guide to RV Travel & Campgrounds
Everything® Family Guide to the Caribbean
Everything® Family Guide to the Disneyland® Resort, California Adventure®, Universal Studios®, and the Anaheim Area, 2nd Ed.
Everything® Family Guide to the Walt Disney World Resort®, Universal Studios®, and Greater Orlando, 5th Ed.
Everything® Family Guide to Timeshares
Everything® Family Guide to Washington D.C., 2nd Ed.

WEDDINGS

Everything® Bachelorette Party Book, $9.95
Everything® Bridesmaid Book, $9.95
Everything® Destination Wedding Book
Everything® Father of the Bride Book, $9.95
Everything® Green Wedding Book, $15.95
Everything® Groom Book, $9.95
Everything® Jewish Wedding Book, 2nd Ed., $15.95
Everything® Mother of the Bride Book, $9.95
Everything® Outdoor Wedding Book
Everything® Wedding Book, 3rd Ed.
Everything® Wedding Checklist, $9.95
Everything® Wedding Etiquette Book, $9.95
Everything® Wedding Organizer, 2nd Ed., $16.95
Everything® Wedding Shower Book, $9.95
Everything® Wedding Vows Book, 3rd Ed., $9.95
Everything® Wedding Workout Book
Everything® Weddings on a Budget Book, 2nd Ed., $9.95

WRITING

Everything® Creative Writing Book
Everything® Get Published Book, 2nd Ed.
Everything® Grammar and Style Book, 2nd Ed.
Everything® Guide to Magazine Writing
Everything® Guide to Writing a Book Proposal
Everything® Guide to Writing a Novel
Everything® Guide to Writing Children's Books
Everything® Guide to Writing Copy
Everything® Guide to Writing Graphic Novels
Everything® Guide to Writing Research Papers
Everything® Guide to Writing a Romance Novel, $15.95
Everything® Improve Your Writing Book, 2nd Ed.
Everything® Writing Poetry Book